A Caring Society?

Care and the Dilemmas of Human Service in the Twenty-First Century

Michael D. Fine

First published 2007 by
PALGRAVE MACMILLAN
Houndmills, Basingstoke, Hampshire RG21 6XS and
175 Fifth Avenue, New York, N.Y. 10010
Companies and representatives throughout the world

PALGRAVE MACMILLAN is the global academic imprint of the Palgrave Macmillan division of St. Martin's Press, LLC and of Palgrave Macmillan Ltd. Macmillan® is a registered trademark in the United States, United Kingdom and other countries. Palgrave is a registered trademark in the European Union and other countries.

ISBN-13: 978 0 333 9939 2   paperback
ISBN 10: 0 333 99339 X   paperback
ISBN-13: 978 0 333 99338 5   hardback
ISBN-10: 0 333 9938 1   hardback

This book is printed on paper suitable for recycling and made from fully managed and sustained forest sources. Logging, pulping and manufacturing processes are expected to conform to the environmental regulations of the country of origin

A catalogue record for this book is available from the British Library.

Library of Congress Cataloging-in-Publication Data
Fine, Michael D., 1952–
    A caring society?: care and the dilemmas of human service in the twenty-first century/Michael D. Fine.
        p. com.
    Includes bibliographical references and index.
    ISBN 0–333–99338–1 (cloth) – ISBN 0–333–99339–X (pbk.)
        1. Caregivers. 2. Caring. 3. Home care services. 4. Human services.
II. Title.
HV65.F56 2006
362'0425—dc22

                                                                    2006045715

Printed by Biddles Ltd, King's Lynn, Norfolk

Contents

List of Figures and Tables   viii

Acknowledgements   ix

Abbreviations   xii

1   Introduction: The Emergence of Care as Public Concern   1

    Care on Trial   2
    From Private Practice to Public Issue   6
    Care as a Social Ideal   10
    Social Care, Human Services and Social Change   13
    Care in the Social Science Literature   18
    The Argument and Shape of the Book   20

Part 1   Theories and Arguments about Care   23

2   Defining and Claiming Care   26

    The Language of Care   27
    A Labour of Love. Feminism and the Theorizing of Care 31
    Care as Practice and Process   34
    A Profession of Care. Care in Contemporary Nursing
    Theory   39
    The Changing Meanings of Care in Nursing   41
    Patricia Benner and the 'Primacy of Caring'   44
    Nursing Practice   47
    Care in Nursing Theory and Practice   48

3 Promoting an Ethic of Care for an Unjust World 52

Origins of the 'Ethics of Care' Debate 53
Natural Caring 55
Extending the Moral Domain of Care 57
Are Justice and Care Compatible? 60
Care and Social Capital 63
Care, Power and Social Justice 66
Doulia: A Public Ethic of Dependency Work 68

4 Carers and Care Work. Social Policy Analysts on Care 75
An Alternative Vision of Care 76
Care as Women's Work at Home 79
Care Work and the New Social Divisions of Care 81
Care as the Production of Welfare 87
The Disability Critique 92
Care as a Citizenship Issue 95

Part 2 The Politics of Care in the Twenty-First Century 102

5 Demography, Ageing and the Need for Care in the
Twenty-First Century 105

The Demographic Transition 106
The Epidemiological Transition and the Need for Care 118
Predicting Future Needs for Care 126
Apocalyptic Demography and the Limitations of Care
Projections 137

6 Work/Life Conflict and the Politics of Child Care 141

Understanding the Demand for Child-Care Policies 142
Employment and Work/Life Conflict 146
Time for Care 149
Post-Industrial Welfare Regimes 155
Child Care and Employment 159

Part 3   Care and Social Theory   169

7   The Body, Individualization and the Transformation of
    Personal Life   171

    The Rise of the Body in Sociological Theory   172
    Care Work as Body Work   173
    Body Work as Dirty Work   175
    Individualization in Contemporary Social Theory   178
    Individualization, Identity and the Self   179
    Life Politics and the Transformation of Intimacy   182
    Individualization, Women and Family Care   183
    Problems with the Individualization Thesis   186
    Individualization and Care   188
    Formal and Informal Care   190
    Care as a Social Response to Bodily Need   194

8   Risk, Care and the New Logic of Global Capitalism   199

    The Bureaucratic Iron Cage   203
    Informational Capitalism and the New Economy   204
    The Rise of the Service Economy   207
    Care and the Segmented Labour Market   208
    Public Policy, Employment and Human Services   212
    Risk and Modernization   214
    Risk and Welfare   217
    Restructuring Care Provision   219
    Conclusion: Work and the Future of Care   221

References   226

Index   253

List of Figures and Tables

Figures

4.1	Modes of participation in the market for care	88
4.2	A schematic overview of the production of welfare approach	90
8.1	Modes of care provision: A basic schema	200
8.2	Simplified model of hybrid forms of shared care	201

Tables

3.1	Comparing the propositions of an ethics of care and of justice	61
5.1	Fertility rates and life expectancy in OECD countries 1970–2000	108
5.2	Young age ratios in OECD countries, 1980–2050	112
5.3	Old age ratios since 1980 in OECD countries, 1980–2050	114
5.4	Disability-free life expectancy at birth	124
5.5	Projected number of dependent elderly people in private households, England	131
5.6	Estimated and projected numbers of primary carers aged 10 or more years, Australia	134
5.7	Health spending and demographic structure in selected countries 1997	139
6.1	Rationales for public support of child care	144
6.2	Evolution of the female employment/population ratio in OECD countries, 1980–2000	148
6.3	Time devoted to family care of children	151
6.4	Proportion of young children who use day-care facilities up to mandatory schooling age, 1998/1999	160
6.5	Care regimes in Europe: Strategies for care of children and elders	167

Acknowledgements

This book addresses the dilemmas that care and human services now present us with in the twenty-first century, but my interest in the topic has grown from my experience in the past, especially from the research work and activism with I have been involved since I first began researching in the field of aged care more than two decades ago. Over this time, more people than I could possibly thank by name developed my interest in care and the problems of human services – some in their capacity as participants in research projects with which I have been involved, others as supervisors, colleagues and mentors.

I learnt much through research on care for older people in Sydney, Australia, and through my ethnographic study of a nursing home and the welfare state system in the Netherlands, for which I undertook fieldwork while training as a Dutch practical nurse (*ziekverzorgende*) from 1977 to 1979. Later, while I worked on my doctoral thesis, teaching at the University of Sydney and at the Institute of Nursing Studies at Sydney College of Advanced Education, I had the good fortune to meet and work with colleagues, friends and students who challenged me to think deeply about the problems of those who work in health and aged care. I was also inspired by family carers I met, by those I got to know through the Australian Association of Gerontology, and by the Combined Pensioners, community activists and others who fought to get a better deal for those who were dependent on residential and community services. To each of you I owe a great debt.

I became more interested in the link between social policy, economics and care through my work over a number of years at the Social Policy Research Centre at the University of New South Wales. There I had the opportunity to undertake research concerning aged care and health and community care, and to develop my understanding of child care and disability support in a series of empirical and policy studies undertaken over more than a decade. I would like to take this opportunity to thank my mentors and supervisors there, especially Sara

Graham, Sheila Shaver and Peter Saunders, as well as colleagues
including Cathy Thomson, Michael Bittman and Karen Fisher, and
the international visitors with whom I have had the privilege of working. Thanks also to those working in the Commonwealth and New
South Wales public service, and to those who worked with or received
services from projects being studied or evaluated, for sharing your
experience with me.

More immediately, I would like to thank Macquarie University for
supporting the early stages of this study through a New Staff Grant,
for the opportunity to work on the manuscript while on study leave,
and for the assistance I have received from my colleagues and students
in the Department of Sociology and through the recently established
Centre for Research on Social Inclusion. Deborah Griffin provided
invaluable assistance with the research for over a year. Thanks also to
Neena Chappell and the staff of the Centre on Ageing at the
University of Victoria, British Columbia, for their help and interest
while I was there, and to Marge Rietsma-Street and others who made
my time in Canada so stimulating. A number of colleagues from
Sydney and around the world have also helped me find new research
studies and other work to read, read my early drafts and engaged with
me, often critically, as I have been writing. I would like to express my
particular thanks to Angela Voerman, and to Caroline Glendinning,
Ruth McManus and Rolf Rønning for their critical interest and stimulating contributions.

It is hard enough to attempt to thank everyone from whom I have
learned over this time, but as I have been writing I realise that my
interest in care developed well before my research. My experience of
receiving care as a child, from my parents, grandparents, aunts and
uncles, and of having responsibility for giving care, also, has clearly
been germane to my longer-term interest. My children and especially
my wife, Ina, have also helped me understand that care is much more
than just an academic topic. I take this opportunity to record my
thanks to all of you.

Finally, I would like to acknowledge those who have helped me
produce this book and see it published. Thanks to Catherine Gray, of
Palgrave Macmillan, for believing in the work and for your encour-
agement and advice. Thanks too, to Mari Shullaw and Juanita
Bullough for your sound editorial advice, and to Sheree Keep and
Sarah Lodge for your outstanding help.

Permissions

I would like to acknowledge the permission given to me by the publishers of *The Journal of Sociology and Health Sociology Review*, for permission to draw on material that also appears in articles of mine they have recently published. I also acknowledge the kind permission of the University of Toronto Press (www.utpjournals.com) for Table 1 in U. E. Reinhardt, 'Commentary: On the Apocalypse of the Retiring Baby Boom', *Canadian Journal on Aging*, 20 (supplement 1) (2001): 193; Taylor & Francis Ltd (www.tandf.co.uk/journals) to publish a table from F. Bettio and J. Plantenga's article in *Feminist Economics*, 10(1) (2004): 85–113; and Thomson Publishing Services on behalf of Taylor & Francis Books (UK) for figures drawn from M. Bittman, 'Parenting and Employment. What Time Use Surveys Show', in N. Folbre and M. Bittman (eds.), *Family Time. The Social Organization of Care* (London, Routledge, 2004): 152–70.

Permission was also kindly granted by the OECD to publish the figures set out in Tables 5.1, 5.2, 5.3, 5.4, 6.2 and 6.4. In preparing these the following source tables were used: Table HE6.1 Trends in life expectancy at birth, men, 1960–2000; Table HE6.2 Trends in life expectancy at birth, women, 1960–2000; Table SS15.2 Proportion of young children who use day care facilities up to mandatory schooling age, 1998/1999; Table GE4.1 Total fertility rates; Table GE4.2 Mean age of women at first childbirth; Table GE4.3 Completed fertility by year of birth of the mother (1930–1965); Table GE5.1 Divorce indicators, from *Society at a Glance: OECD Social Indicators 2002 Edition*, © OECD 2003 <http://www1.oecd.org/scripts/publications/bookshop/redirect.asp?pub=812003051P1>.

The editors and publishers gratefully acknowledge permission to reproduce copyright material. Every effort has been made to trace copyright holders, but if any have been inadvertently overlooked the publishers will be pleased to make the necessary arrangement at the first opportunity.

Abbreviations

ABS	Australian Bureau of Statistics
ADL	Activities of Daily Living
AIHW	Australian Institute of Health and Welfare
AOC	Association of Carers
CAVA	Care, Values and the Future of Welfare (research programme at the University of Leeds)
DALYS	Disability Adjusted Life Years
DHSS	Department of Health and Social Services
ECEC	Early Childhood Education and Care
ECHP	European Community Household Panel
GHS	General Household Survey
HIV/AIDS	Human Immunodeficiency Virus/Acquired Immune Deficiency
HREOC	Human Rights and Equal Opportunities Commission
IADL	Instrumental Activities of Daily Living
ICIDH	International Classification of Impairment, Disability and Handicap
NCCED	National Council for Carers and their Elderly Dependants
NHPF	National Health Policy Forum (Washington)
OECD	Organisation of Economic Co-operation and Development
OED	Oxford English Dictionary
PSSRU	Personal Social Services Research Unit (University of Kent)
SARS	Severe Acute Respiratory Syndrome

CHAPTER 1

Introduction: The Emergence of Care as a Public Concern

We have to think in a new way about care.
(Betty Friedan, 1993: 376)

Care is an essential feature of social life, yet it no longer fits into the contemporary world in the way that it has in the past. As we search for new ways to achieve the ideals of care in the twenty-first century, debates are increasingly heated and controversial. In a world in which the pursuit of profit and self-interest intrudes into almost every aspect of our being as markets threaten to dominate our personal and social relations, visions of a caring society offer hope of a much-needed alternative. Yet although they draw on a common language of compassion, such visions seem increasingly troubled and discordant. This contested character of care, I argue, reflects the conflicting interests and concerns that drive individuals and groups to promote the cause of care and to define and claim its ideals as their own.

In this book I review contemporary debates and disputes about care and examine the implications of the transformation of care from a private concern to a public issue. Reflecting the fundamental importance of the topic to human affairs and the significance that the concept of care has for different disciplines and professions, the topic is inevitably one that requires a broad interdisciplinary perspective. In the analysis I advance a broadly sociological perspective, in that debates around care are shown to manifest the changing relations between the state, the market, families and individuals in the ageing, post-industrial societies of the developed world. Because care essentially deals with the management of interpersonal relationships involving dependency, power and the use and control of scarce resources, particular attention is also paid to political and economic analyses of the place of care in twenty-first century societies.

As care is reshaped and reimagined in the twenty-first century, the account documents the shift in emphasis away from the rigid dichotomies between 'care', the unpaid responsibility of women, and 'work', men's duty as family breadwinner, that prevailed for much of the twentieth century. It becomes clear from the different perspectives and competing accounts that there is a struggle to define this inspiring yet apparently elusive concept. Care can be understood as a form of meaningful work, as social solidarity, as an expression of interpersonal relationships and as a source of personal meaning. But it can also be reduced again to a set of household duties for women, recast as a form of custodial protection, or fashioned as a product to be packaged and sold for corporate profit, its costs kept low by reliance on unskilled and casualized labour and by competition between providers. A single definition of care remains elusive, I argue, in part because it refers at once to an ideal set of values and a series of concrete practices. The outcomes of the struggle to define and claim care matter, but they are not pre-ordained. The debate, for this reason, is as urgent as it is profound.

Care on Trial

Questions about what care is and who should be responsible are not simply academic. Our response to such questions in our private lives shapes our identity, defining who we are as individuals and as members of social groups. Such questions are also increasingly addressed as questions involving collective responsibility and as issues of public concern. The way they are answered in turn tells us much about the type of society in which we live. The case of one care-giver, recently brought to trial in Sydney, Australia, parallels a number of other such cases in advanced democracies across the globe, illustrating the legal ambiguities in the search for answers to such questions. In attempting to assign criminal responsibility, the case drew attention to the limits of individual liability for care, and to the problems that arise when care is managed as a purely private matter within the family. The case is presented in Box 1 in a way that is intended, respectfully, to maintain the confidentiality of the mother and others concerned.

BOX 1   LEGAL JUDGMENT ON RESPONSIBILITY FOR CARE

Death of a ten-year-old child at the hands of his mother
The case involved the death of a ten-year-old child who, it was alleged, was killed by his mother. In court, the mother was found guilty but not sentenced to prison, instead receiving a five-year bond requiring good behaviour. The judgment sparked wide controversy and the sentence was seen by some, who took what they called a 'pro-life' view, as far too light.

The idea that a mother should love and care for her child is widely and deeply held. The mother had pleaded guilty to killing her son and was seen as having broken a natural law. What sort of mother, after all, would kill her own child? But the fact that the ten-year-old son was autistic and the case involved sole, ongoing responsibility for care that went well beyond what might be considered reasonable, clearly weighed heavily on the judge.

Evidence in the trial revealed that the mother had lived a 'harrowing life' for years before the incident. There was a history of domestic violence in which she suffered cruelly at the hands of her husband. Her husband had also had two nervous breakdowns, which the mother had had to manage. Her own father subsequently died, his death placing her under even greater pressure. Details were also given in court of another serious issue, but the reporting of this was suppressed. These problems led to the mother suffering serious depression, and subsequently to her suffocating her son and attempting suicide.

A key element in the sentence handed down was the judge's recognition of the extent of the social responsibility for the well-being and support of those who are not capable of caring for themselves. The mother accused of murder was found to have accepted responsibility for care of her son and to have fulfilled the duties involved well. In taking responsibility for her autistic son every day for the ten years of his life, managing the ongoing practical responsibilities without help, the judge found that she had met her legal responsibilities for care. The public (in this case the governments of the state of New South

Wales and the Commonwealth of Australia), however, had failed to accept the social responsibility that comes with the power of government.

Just as the protection of life is a universal responsibility, with enforcement delegated to the state, so too is it clear that there is a broad social interest in ensuring that care is available to all those who require it. Responsibility for providing care and support, in other words, is not something confined to a single individual. Wider patterns of social accountability must be acknowledged. Women, more so than men, have assumed duties of care in the home, but this does not mean that they alone are responsible. Nor can care be understood purely as the unpaid work of women in the family home. Neither can the boundaries of care be drawn any more around the unpaid work undertaken within the family or household, or confined to the work undertaken by those who work in what are often referred to as the 'caring professions'.

The case raises a number of very fundamental challenges for anyone attempting to answer the question of what care is and who should be responsible for it. Necessary as the 'labour of love' that care is, it can not be reduced to the practical activity of the work involved in providing support. Neither can it be comprehended solely as an attribute of families or of close personal or professional–client relationships, or as an ideal form of personal commitment that does not have significant costs and dangers for all of the parties involved. Rather, care is a complex, contested, multilayered concept that refers not just to actions and activities, but to relationships and to values and attitudes about our responsibility for others and for our own being in the world. It is at once an activity or form of work, as a system of social relationships that extends from the intimate and personal to a broader set of ties acknowledging our mutual dependency, and an ethical position that involves an approach to the self and a commitment to others. By extension, care can also be understood as an open and supportive orientation to strangers, to the community, to society at large (both national and global) and to the natural world. In viewing care, however, what might be thought of as the negative or dark side of care, the enforced dependency of care-givers and the potential for harm to the recipient, needs to be recognized alongside the more positive attributes.

Providing care is a physically and emotionally demanding activity, in which body work is combined with emotional labour. But, despite its importance, care work is typically treated in policy, research and in popular discourse in what Julia Twigg has called 'a schizophrenic fashion'. This involves a double-sided attitude where care is simultaneously 'denigrated as a low-level job yet also lauded as "special work", involving the supreme virtues of "love" and "care"' (Twigg, 2000: ix).

The tensions in this stance, rooted in the traditionally gendered and private nature of the work of care, are compounded when care work becomes public. In the world of the twenty-first century, in which the right to work and earn is no longer the sole preserve of male breadwinners, the need for care must be reconciled with the rights of women and men to seek work, the real demands that employment and the market make on us all, as well as with the political and economic constraints of public policy. If care work is to go beyond what has been experienced in the past – where typically it has been marginalized and exploited, those undertaking it, unpaid family carers and paid workers alike, effectively penalized for their dedication and commitment and those receiving it too often silenced or made unnecessarily dependent – new approaches are required.

Females have long borne responsibility for providing care and for fashioning the site of that care into a home. But, inspired by feminism in the late twentieth century, women seized new opportunities to gain independence and control through employment and participation in the public world beyond the home. The subsequent growth in employment has limited the time available to individuals to care for themselves and their families. The outcome is that the need for care appears to have been rising at precisely the moment that traditional sources of supply have contracted, creating what Hochschild (2003) and others have called a 'care deficit'.

Questions about care are evident at an intimate and personal level for all of us at different times in our lives. As concerns about work/life balance and about the restructuring of the public services and citizenship rights have revealed, fears and disputes about the viability of existing arrangements for care, and about who, if anyone, will take responsibility for it in the future, have become a leading cause of insecurity and social division. These concerns are increasingly directed at the way that public institutions operate and at the reliability and trustworthiness of the private solutions offered in their place. The aim of this book is to go beyond these anxieties, to clarify the meaning of the term 'care' in different contexts and to identify and explore from a broad sociological perspective the dilemmas that need to be faced about care in the twenty-first century.

From Private Practice to Public Issue

For all its importance, the social phenomenon of care has only recently begun to receive serious attention from social researchers. Bodies of research on specialized professional topics were developed, but these treated each field as unique and requiring particular professional expertise. The result is that there is little if any exchange of ideas between fields such as child care, disability, mental health and ageing. Neglect of the broader phenomenon of care came about, it appears, because the provision of care was regarded as the prime responsibility of the family, with the tasks routinely falling to women, for whom it was seen as natural, even instinctive behaviour (Barrett and McIntosh, 1982). Care was seen as an integral component of social support involving personal devotion and duty which gave expression to the continuing primacy of bonds of kinship and marriage. Under these conditions, informal care was easily confined to the invisible, taken-for-granted, private sphere of the domestic setting and its fundamental importance for social life ignored (Graham, 1983).

Despite the apparent suddenness of the shift, the social changes that have brought care out into the public domain and made it increasingly problematic have developed incrementally over the last two centuries or so, the period of modernity in the West. In the final decades of the twentieth century the extent of these changes reached a point where the availability and provision of care became an ever-more-contentious aspect of modern life. Four major developments stand out in this process.

The first major development, chronologically, was the expansion of occupational specialization and the development of what is now referred to as the field of human services. The nineteenth and early twentieth centuries saw the rise of professional expertise and the propagation of specialized organizations, professions and workforces whose primary concern was to provide particular types of care to individuals who were unable to care for themselves and needed care not available through the family. With it came the production of specialized professional fields of knowledge, in particular nursing, medicine, social work and social policy, that have increasingly come to shape the way that care is conceived and implemented.

The second major development occurred as a result of the emergence of the post-war welfare state, which underwrote a significant expansion of the range of options available and made them more accessible to the broad population. Access to services increasingly came to be seen as a right where need could be established, leading, in turn, to the further growth of services and programmes as well as to problems of financing, distribution and organization.

A third, even more recent and still ongoing force for change has been the impact of feminism. The transformative impact of this singularly powerful force for social change became undeniable in the late twentieth century. The increase in political and social rights won by women did much to remove the legal and social dependency of females on males. This was extended by the subsequent move of women away from confinement in the domestic sphere and into the world of paid employment.

Finally, the capacity of families to provide care has been increasingly put under pressure by globalization, the rise of financial capital and the penetration of market principles into even the most intimate spheres of personal life. This has been accompanied by a decline in the importance of social practices and forms of collaboration, making it ever more difficult to sustain care systems that operate with a distinct rationality based largely on the principles of redistribution, reciprocity and an altruistic concern for the well-being of others. The stresses caused by the conflict between the altruism required of family life and the self-interest needed in the marketplace are evident in the widespread yearning for a more sustainable work–life balance.

These developments intersect in the sphere of care and human services, often in seemingly contradictory ways. As access to formal services was extended in the twentieth century through welfare state programmes and rising levels of affluence, opportunities for the employment of women outside the home expanded. Employment growth was concentrated in the service sector of the economy, including services that supplied care alternatives that further helped release women from the confines of the domestic setting, enabling them to enter the public world and to increase their engagement with the local community (Hernes, 1987). As public responsibility for care grew, fears were expressed by conservatives and others that individuals were being made dependent on the state and that family responsibility was being usurped (Fox Harding, 1991; McPherson, 1999). Combined with the financial and political pressures that accompanied the 'fiscal crisis of the state' from the mid-1970s onwards, subsequent developments saw the restructuring of much social policy. This led to counter-claims that the state was winding back responsibility and a concern for sharing and equity, handing it over to the market and voluntary providers and in some areas, such as community care, attempting to transfer the burden back to the family and on to the shoulders of unpaid women (Finch and Groves, 1983; Ungerson, 1990). The case of child care services to enable mothers to seek employment, whose development varied considerably between countries but whose expanded access inevitably seemed to lag behind need, served to illustrate the problems involved for each side in the debate.

Care has thus moved from being what C. Wright Mills (1959) might have called a private concern to become a public issue. Whether in the home or as formal services and programmes, issues linked to care these days receive almost constant attention in the media, albeit with a strong emphasis on local aspects of the stories. In the process, care became a battlefield for competing ethical value positions, and it has been problematized and opened up to academic as well as more popular and political scrutiny. Demographic developments, in particular the ageing of the population and the reduction in the birth rate, and medico-technical developments that bring moral dilemmas to the fore, serve to accentuate these developments, lending an aura of crisis, uncertainty and foreboding to the debates that continue to be produced around sites of care.

Alongside the concerns expressed by writers and researchers about the viability of existing care arrangements, others have sought to take advantage of the inspirational value of the concept. Drawing on the positive connotations of the word, some feminists and others have sought to promote the ideals of care as a general social ethic, in much the same way that the ethics of work and of justice have served as guiding principles for social life (Noddings, 2002). Care is increasingly also being referred to as a value and practice that runs counter to the ideals of competition, consumption and self-interest which are seen to be at the heart of neo-liberal ideology (Folbre, 2001b; Pocock, 2003; McKnight, 2005).

In turn, care has been invoked as the key to the restructuring of social policy. This, at least, appears to be the reasoning behind the attempts, such as that advanced by the Organisation for Economic Co-operation and Development in '*A Caring World. The New Social Policy Agenda*' (OECD, 1999), to promote the restructuring and repackaging of social policy. As Donald J Johnston, OECD Secretary-General commented, a caring world involves

a new balance in the rights, obligations and opportunities of individuals and all the different institutions involved in social protection, including developments such as 'workfare', 'patients' charters',
a more responsive public sector and the greater involvement of the
private sector and not-for-profits in the delivery of social policy.
This is a novel direction in social and health policy. The new social
policy agenda is how to achieve social solidarity through enabling
individuals and families to support themselves. (OECD, 1999: 4)

The OECD's vision for a caring world is intended to be based on a
new balance between individuals and the different social institutions.
The approach matches reduced public sector provision with calls for
greater involvement of the private and not-for profit sectors. There is
also a call for an increased emphasis on enabling individuals and families to support themselves. Caring is thus used by the OECD as an
adjective to suggest a devolution in the responsibilities of the state,
with increased responsibilities for families and unpaid volunteers.

In other cases, proposals for the achievement of a caring society
point to the need for reordering gender relations and responsibilities
within families, whilst acknowledging the responsibilities of employees,
employers and the state. The Dutch government, for example, established the Commission for the Re-Division of Unpaid Work (*Commissie
voor de Hervedeling van Obetaalde Arbeid*) in the mid-1990s. This led to the
promotion of a 'combination scenario', and subsequently a new Work
and Care Law in mid-2000 that sought to promote the growth of
labour market participation amongst women whilst reinvigorating care
within the family by negotiating the division of work and care between
women and men in individual households (Knijn, 2001). Similar
proposals have been advanced in Australia for 'consultation'
(HREOC, 2005), whilst changes have been introduced to the marriage
contract under Spanish law, with the support of all parties, requiring
men to 'share domestic responsibilities and the care and attention'
given to children and elderly family members (Tremlett, 2005). More
common still are the policies introduced recognizing the contribution
of informal care-givers (Lingsom, 1997; Lloyd, 2000). A wide range of
measures are involved, including information services for carers,
support for advocacy services, access to supportive payments and
funds for the direct purchase of assistance, and the introduction of
respite services to give carers a break from their responsibilities.

Reflecting its increasing importance as a form of public provision,

Mary Daly has argued that care has become a 'policy good' (Daly, 2002), a necessary condition for social life managed by public policies rather than simply being left to the family or the market. Care, she argues, is now 'at the forefront of public–private relations. While it originates in the private world of love, intimacy, families and friendship, much of it is now carried out in the public world of work, organizations, markets and government' (Daly, 2002: 261). The fact that care can not be defined narrowly, or be seen as belonging exclusively to a single identity, occupational group or governmental programme, is one of the features that appears to make it so attractive as topic for social analysis. Chamberlayne and King (2000: 8) point out that it is an activity that can be carried out by a range of different social actors: 'Caring offers a doorway to the study of informal systems of welfare, to the extending of comparative social policy to that level, and to the transcending of the welfare regime approach.'

In contemporary discussions of care, issues of gender and the comparative economic efficiency and effectiveness of different approaches are central concerns. But, as we will see later in this book, these are tempered by the accompanying concerns of the impact of the demography of ageing societies, by the moral concerns for family care-givers and the rights of care recipients and, increasingly, by concerns for the impact of innovations in medicine and (bio-)technology.

Care as a Social Ideal

The concept of care invoked in many contemporary discussions is at once familial, interpersonal, intimate and holistic. Mother/child care is often explicitly identified as the prototypical model and it is often suggested that care by the family is more personal and meaningful than that provided by anonymous public services. The meaning of the term 'care', however, is open to considerable dispute. Arlie Hochschild has captured this sense of openness and ambiguity in relation to the way that particular groups attempt to define and own the term 'care' and to use it in ways that impose their views on others (Hochschild, 2003).

The *traditional* model of care, based on unpaid care by women as wives, mothers and daughters in the home, she argues, is not dead, but lives on as a form of cultural nostalgia in images on gift cards, as the daily practice for a residual but significant proportion of families, and as the default position invoked by conservatives. Promotion of this model continues uninterrupted, as discussed in Chapter 6, in the familial policies of many European countries which seek to sustain the breadwinner model of the family (Mahon, 2002a). In the liberal welfare regimes of English-speaking countries, too, this approach continues through the promotion of various programmes that reward stay-at-home wives in heterosexual marriages while penalizing single mothers, and through care payments of various kinds that encourage women to remain at home and assume the duties of care for family members.

The traditional approach is echoed in, yet stands in contrast to, the *postmodern* ideal of care evoked by the image of the supermum, the woman who can do it all, career, care and the full consumer lifestyle, either alone or with a partner. According to Hochschild, the post-modern solution to the problems posed by the work/life conflict is to seek to ignore the difficulties that care throws up and to manage the time bind that increased hours of work involves by promoting self-sufficiency and the use of a variety of consumer-friendly solutions. To reduce the need for care, each member of the family needs to be inde-pendent. The use of timetables to schedule various tasks, reliance on consumer products such as fast food, and the use of television and computer games as babysitters when the children get home early from school are all techniques that are recommended in the self-help litera-ture cited by Hochschild. Of course for women (and men) who don't have caring responsibilities, the simplest solution is to keep it that way, and avoiding childbirth is perhaps the most common way to achieve this. Post-modern approaches to care are also evident in the postpone-ment of partnering and childbirth, and in the hiring of private nannies, babysitters or other domestic helpers by those able to afford it. The technological solution of electronic surveillance is increasingly utilized, while the issuing of mobile phones to children so that they can call and tell mum where they are has already become widespread. Each of these measures helps to sustain the image of independence, self-sufficiency and style that seem part of the culture of post-modernity. This model of care, in which individuals are left to fend for themselves, with the help of the market, is one typically invoked in neo-liberal welfare programmes. This is especially so as talk of the need to confront the demographic pressures of an ageing society is used to promote programmes based on user payments and other individualized risk management and mitigation strategies.

Modern solutions to the problems posed by care, Hochschild argues, see the importance of developing alternative egalitarian approaches to care that relieve the family of sole responsibility and allow women to assume their place as public citizens alongside men. What she terms *cold modern* ideals of care rely predominantly on formalized institutional care solutions, adapted to manage those who need care at different points in their life course. The approach is perhaps best exemplified in the model of the Israeli kibbutz or Eastern European socialism, where communally based child-care centres were held as the model for modern child-rearing. Specialized homes for the aged, the mentally ill and the disabled are equally recognizable icons of cold modern care in Western capitalist societies. The model is cold, in Hochschild's terms, in that care is seen primarily as a burden, a responsibility that limits citizens from achieving in other areas of their lives. In recognition that responsibility for care at home almost invariably falls to women, this approach has also been advocated by some feminists (Dalley, 1988) as a means of underwriting collective responsibility for care.

What Hochschild calls the *warm modern* ideal of care, in contrast, seeks to sustain the ideals of egalitarianism, promoting shared caring between women and men, with formal services used when necessary to supplement and extend the capacity of the family to support those who need care. The approach calls for changes in both male behaviour and in the organization of the workplace. It is warm, for Hochschild, because we do not seek to relinquish responsibility for personal support but instead share it to enrich our intimate lives. The approach is perhaps best exemplified by the social democratic welfare regimes of the Nordic countries, although it is a set of ideals that is far more widely held at the grass-roots level than policy initiatives might suggest. Perhaps more than any other, this approach sees care as embedded in a complex set of social circumstances, and therefore calls for changes in at least three main areas: male behaviour, the organization of the workplace, and social policy. What is at stake here, as Hochschild points out, is 'the value placed on care' (Hochschild, 2003: 222).

Although care is clearly a key element of social solidarity, not all who provide or depend on it understand it to be so. In so far as there is a contemporary discourse on the topic, it is one that continues to be best summarized by the phrase 'burden of care' and by the ongoing debates about who should bear that burden, how this should be done, at what cost and who should be required to meet that cost. Care can give meaning and identity to the lives of those who provide it. At one level this is acknowledged in the way that care is widely idealized as altruistic and socially desirable behaviour. At the same time, care involves responsibility for repetitive, time-consuming activities. It demands self-sacrifice, hard work, long-term commitment and knowledge, often in combinations that require professional expertise beyond the capacity of any one person, family or even social network to maintain. The effects of social isolation, emotional burnout, long-term personal problems and forms of referred dependency are also an inherent part of the conditions under which care is provided.

These apparently conflicting characteristics of care-giving are matched by similar ones associated with the receipt of care. Receiving care can involve a form of dependence that requires submission and relinquishment of a sense of autonomy by the recipient and the exercise of control by the care-giver, or it can be a process of assistance that recognizes the integrity of the recipient and helps to establish or restore the individual's capacity for personal autonomy. The dilemmas of giving and receiving care are directly concerned with attempts to reconcile or manage these inherent contradictions.

Social Care, Human Services and Social Change

Developments in care and the corresponding expansion and elaboration of human services have not occurred of their own accord. Each change, in turn, reflects the transformation of social organization and support arrangements that has been taking place in the post-industrial societies of the twenty-first century, although the process commenced well before this time. (I refer here in particular to North America, Western Europe, and the Asia Pacific region, in particular Australia, New Zealand and Japan, although these developments are not exclusive to these countries.) Along with the development of industrial capitalism in the nineteenth and twentieth centuries came a search for more effective organizational forms. This was initially satisfied by the expansion of bureaucratic models of service provision and of institutional, 'industrial' forms of care, accompanied by the development of organized professional and semi-professional workforces.

More recently, the pace of social change has increased. With social relations becoming increasingly individualized and fragmented, profound changes have been taking place in the need for care, in its availability from family, and in the provision and use of formal interventions. In-kind services have increasingly become the subject of commercial models of purchase and delivery. Care payments of various sorts have become more widespread, including those intended as support or financial compensation for care-givers, and payments intended as a form of voucher, to promote the purchase of care from commercial or other sources (Glendinning et al., 2000; Daly, 2002). With the restructuring of welfare state arrangements that provided security in the decades after the Second World War and the experience of traditional responses to care proving to be inadequate, calls for a new understanding of what it means to become a caring society have been increasingly common.

The development of effective responses to the challenges and dilemmas facing care and human services arise from two main sources. First, a fundamental social change has been taking place in family formation and behaviour, with potentially profound long-term implications. This is reflected in the shift in both the demographic composition of society, particularly through the reduced rates of birth, and in the capacity of the family to provide unpaid care for all who need it. These developments reflect, above all, the decision by women to pursue personal independence and paid employment through their engagement in the labour market and the pursuit of careers. Marriage, family formation and the raising of children have ceased to be an economic necessity, and have become, instead, a matter of individual choice. While manifesting an increased 'freedom of choice' for women, these developments also heighten 'insecurity and risk' (Esping-Anderson et al., 2002: 2), posing a significant challenge to more traditional, familial models of care. Although it is by no means necessary, or even possible, to confine all such responsibility to women, care has been culturally linked to gender and traditionally assigned as a feminine attribute and duty. The broader process of social and cultural change closely underlies the search for a new gender balance in the way that care is understood and provided.

Second, the massive economic transformation of industrialized societies that commenced in the final decades of the twentieth century is resulting in the decline of industrial patterns of social and economic organization and the emergence of a strengthened form of market capitalism as part of increasingly integrated globalized economic order (Esping-Andersen et al., 2002). The shift to globalized, post-industrial, service-based economies, in which knowledge and other service industries employ more people than manufacturing, brings with it different demands, opportunities and risks (Stehr, 1994). At their heart is the increasing entrenchment of what economists term a dual labour market. Many of the new jobs are professional or semi-professional in character, requiring increased qualifications and skills, offering those in employment considerable rewards in return for hard work and dedication. In contrast to this are the jobs in which there is little recognition of skills or personal circumstances, and where employment is increasingly casualized, with little or no opportunity for career development. Many of the new service industry jobs, especially those in the fields of social care and human service delivery, are confined to this lower tier of the labour market. The security of life-time employment, the hallmark of the social settlement based on the male breadwinner family of post-war industrial societies, is increasingly scarce in both labour markets. Risk is replacing security and predictability for both workers and the self-employed, delivering opportunities and wealth for the lucky ones but increasing insecurity, precariousness and marginalization for others (Esping-Andersen, 1999; Castells, 2000; Esping-Andersen et al., 2002).

These changes are linked to the allocation of welfare functions, including care, between the major institutional sectors, or pillars, of modern welfare societies: the market, the state and the family (Titmuss, 1958, 1979; Esping-Andersen, 1990, 1999; O'Connor, Orloff and Shaver, 1999; Esping-Andersen et al., 2002). In capitalist societies, the market is the primary source of welfare throughout adult life for most citizens, the prime source of income earned through employment as well as the source of much of the welfare that is purchased. The market is also an important source of social inequality and risk, reasons for public intervention in key areas of need, such as social and health care services. The state, the source of legitimate political and legal authority, is also the chief institution through which collective solidarity is expressed. Through the various arms of government and statutory authorities, the state is concerned with both regulation of different actors and the redistribution of resources, as well as being an important direct provider and funder of public welfare and care services. Family represents the third important pillar, through the sharing and redistribution of income between family members and in terms of care provided to its members. Non-profit associations arising from civil society, often called the 'third sector', are also an important source of support services and innovation in many countries. Their operation and the characteristics of civil society reflect the play of the other major pillars, assuming in some instances the character of a market provider, in others that of instruments of public policy or extensions of kinship-based family networks, so that it would be wrong to consider this as analytically autonomous from the three major pillars (Esping-Andersen, 1999: 32–46; Deakin, 2001).

Demographic developments, such as population ageing, and social and economic changes, most importantly the large-scale entry of married women into the paid workforce, have also seen the demand for formal care increase, just as the sources of supply of unpaid care at home have been decreasing. Yet along with other changes there has also been a widespread restructuring of public sector provisions, placing greater responsibility on the provision of support at home that appears to many to be based on the assumption of plentiful domestic support. In the fields of aged care, mental health, disability support and health care, for example, there have been important moves towards deinstitutionalization and the expansion of community care. These developments have been closely paralleled by changes in the relationship between formal programmes and services and the support provided by the family, the household and informal networks. For children, the availability of formal child care has also increasingly been seen as a social necessity, a way of enabling working mothers to enter the paid workforce, and as a form of early intervention and support for children considered 'at risk'.

Changes in the way care is provided have also taken place as a result of improvements in what might be considered the administrative technology of care, with the introduction of innovative organizational approaches such as case management and care packaging emerging along with computerized information systems and new means for controlling the cost of care and matching it more closely to the needs of individuals (Davies, 1994). Detailed transformations in the way that care outcomes are specified and performance-monitored continue to affect the organization and operation of care services, as governments have changed the principles of funding and moved from models of direct public provision to the promotion of market-based competition, the use of contracted, non-government service providers and, in some instances, to increased reliance on the voluntary or community sector. Significant changes have also been taking place in the organization, operation, finance and control of

services and in the emergence and influence of consumer movements. An increased emphasis is now placed on the consumption of
care services (Barnes, 1997), a development marked by a shift in
attention in the process of service production away from regulating
service inputs towards measuring and rewarding outputs and
outcomes.

There has also been considerable movement towards the incorporation of the recipient of care into decision-making and the care
process. The importance of this approach has been spelt out very
strongly by a number of writers concerned with the support of
disabled people (Morris, 1993a; Shakespeare, 2000a and b), but it is
also an issue increasingly raised in all spheres of care provision. Betty
Friedan, best known for her feminist writings in the 1960s, for example, later turned her attention to issues of ageing, arguing that just as
she refused to let women be defined as sex objects when she was 35,
she also rejects older women or men being seen simply as passive
objects of care:

> We have to think in a new way about care. We have to break
> through the mystique of age that defines us only in terms of fearful
> deterioration and the disabilities we become victim to if we let
> ourselves be defined solely as objects of care. If I am right, there
> needs to be a different way of handling sickness, disability and care
> in age. (Friedan, 1993: 375–6)

Care has often been conceptualized as a unidirectional activity, something that the care provider does to the recipient. This approach has
been strongly challenged, and the ideal of care is increasingly understood as an active collaborative activity of relationships (Bowden,
1997; Lloyd, 2000; Fine and Glendinning, 2005).

Through their physical capacity and social position, care-givers
may themselves be in a position of relative power, although this is by
no means absolute (Kittay, 1999; Fine, 2005a). Conflict between care-
givers and recipients is an ever-present possibility, one that in practice
is often only managed by the care-giver surrendering her own life,
providing care at the cost of considerable personal sacrifice. Conflict,
power and dependency also need to be understood as part of the
broader social order in which care is produced, an issue that is readily
apparent in the broader political struggles over care provision in post-
industrial societies. Although less apparent, they are no less important

in affecting the way that individual care-givers are positioned, socially, as dependents in their own right, and in the way that care is perceived in social debates as a social issue that is of marginal or, at best, second order importance. In recognition of this fact, there has been the development of a new awareness of care, as a system of values and consciousness, which many believe has enormous potential to reshape the way that modern societies are organized. The values of care, in this vision, like women, would no longer be seen as something best confined to the domestic sphere, but instead would come to be a value that is central to public and political life (Tronto, 1993). This is a challenge that extends to rethinking the position of care in social theory.

Care in the Social Science Literature

Changes to the way that care is organized and provided have not taken place unnoticed. In some cases, such as the expansion of health or child-care services into areas where there has been a long-standing deficit, change has been generally seen as desirable and welcomed widely. More typically, changing patterns of care and ways of conceptualizing its nature are the cause of controversies and bitter local and national conflicts. Instead, health and social care services are made to adjust, to absorb increasing levels of demand within the constraints of finite resources. They are portrayed as being in almost constant crisis in virtually every advanced society. The result is an ongoing and very unsettling process of political crisis management at the local, regional, state, provincial and national levels.

Despite its importance, there were few if any references to care in the literature of the social sciences until recent years. In the mainstream literature on sociology, for example, care appears to have been taken for granted, either subsumed within alternative rubrics such as social support or family, or simply omitted from the larger picture (Thomas, 1993; Fine, 2005b). Nancy Folbre (2001b) suggests that in the case of mainstream economics, care seems to contradict many of the most basic tenets of the discipline. Unpaid domestic care, for example, is regarded as unproductive and is treated as non-existent in national accounts. Similarly, the altruistic motives of care seem so totally to contradict the assumption of self-interest and competition that is at the heart of neo-classical economics that it has proven convenient to ignore the issue entirely. The way around these problems, in both disciplines, has been to treat care as a specialist field of research. As a result, outside of specialist academic journals and conferences, there is little in the way of literature which sheds light on the practices or transformation of care and its social importance. This position is simply no longer tenable.

As Mary Daly and Jane Lewis (2000) point out, interest in developments in the delivery of various forms of care have fed into the renewed interest in the meaning and importance of care that has derived from feminist scholarship. Where the various forms of child care and care of adults have been regarded as specialist fields, with little exchange possible between experts, there is now an opportunity to develop more analytic and illuminating approaches to the phenomena. Such an analysis must inevitably cross a number of disciplinary boundaries. At one level, it is necessary to examine philosophical and conceptual perspectives on care. At another, more practical level, the analysis should help to bring together the different specialist fields, drawing out commonalities and identifying meaningful differences between types of support, different programmes and national contexts. The approach must also support an exploration of the relationship between vulnerable individuals needing care, their family members and intimate others who provide informal care, service providers and professionals of various kinds. This analysis must also draw attention to the links between the personal negotiation of care arrangements at the micro level and the macro level structures and processes of the market and the state which constrain and direct care arrangements.

Daly and Lewis (2000), like many others before them, have argued that the analysis of care must necessarily be based on an examination of the way in which gender and gender relations shape both the demand for care and the way in which care is provided. As Kittay (1999) demonstrates, an equally important task is to consider how gender has been constructed by the way that care is managed. So too must the analysis encompass the economics and politics of care and human services, which, as Baldock and Evers (1992) have argued for aged care, is at the 'cutting edge' of social change. To do this is to acknowledge how developments in care and human services have become a direct manifestation of the way in which relations between the state, the market, civil society and individuals are transformed and are constantly being reshaped, tested and contested.

The Argument and Shape of the Book

An extensive literature already documents the experience of giving and receiving care and the details of policies and service delivery. I have sought here to complement this detailed descriptive work by mapping out the contemporary terrain of conceptual debates on care. Drawing on recent research and theory, the book critically explores the most influential of the competing arguments prevalent in three quite distinct sets of debates, each of which provides a different perspective from which to consider explanations and accounts of changes in the need for and provision of care.

The first perspective, set out in Part 1 of this book, deals with theories and arguments concerning the phenomenon of care. Care has become a powerful and yet disputed term that different groups seek to define and claim as their own. I therefore consider the meaning of the term and then examine the way it is deployed in the theories of professional nursing in Chapter 2. Chapter 3 examines the ethics of care debate, a profoundly important development that first emerged as a feminist theory in the 1980s. When initially introduced by Carol Gilligan, it posited a radical and controversial finding that identified the principles of care as a system of values closely associated with women, and distinguished it from the abstract principles of justice that were found to be more closely linked to male thought. Other writers, most notably Joan Tronto, later came to propose an ethic of care as a counter to the male work ethic which is seen as based on promoting a sense of competition between individual, rational men. As she explains,

> As a type of activity, care requires a moral disposition and a type of moral conduct. We can express some of these qualities in the form of a universalist moral principle, such as: one should care for those around one or in one's society. Nevertheless, in order for these qualities to become part of moral conduct, people must engage in both private and public practices that teach them, and reinforce their senses of, moral concerns. In order to be created and sustained, then, an ethic of care relies upon a political commitment to value care and to reshape institutions to reflect that changed value. (Tronto, 1993: 177–8)

Tracing the development of the approach, the chapter reviews the corrections that other writers, including Sevenhuijsen, Williams and

Kittay, have sought to make to this formulation and considers the relevance of their prescriptions for linking personal responsibility and public life. The debate continues in Chapter 4 to trace the transformations in the way that care has been approached in British and European social policy analysis. Given the impact that the availability of resources has on decisions concerning the funding of services (both public and private) and the propensity for the demand for care services to outstrip supply, an understanding of economic perspectives and an analysis of care provisions is increasingly essential for anyone wishing to engage in the public debates.

The perspective set out in Part 2 focuses on two of the core social policy debates surrounding care – the contrasting discourses associated with aged care and child care. The demography of ageing societies, it is widely believed, foretells a coming crisis in care, one that some suggest might already be evident, as outlined in Chapter 5. By comparing analyses of the future need for aged and child care, discussed in Chapter 6, it can be seen that changes in the demand for care can not be simply projected directly from raw population figures. Work/life conflict, too, has emerged as a major concern and threat to families and women's lives. To understand the potential for future developments, what is required, it is argued, is a more sophisticated understanding of the political economy of care, as well as its characteristic of substitutability of sources, the so-called 'substitution issue' (Lingsom, 1997). Although the affordability of care has emerged as a major issue for ageing societies, the dilemmas to be faced, I argue, are far greater than simply finding the cheapest alternative form of provision.

As well as the practical significance of these conceptual debates about the nature and meaning of care, care also provides a uniquely significant perspective from which to understand and assess social life in post-industrial societies. In Part 3 of the book, I therefore step away from specialist writings on the topic of care to consider the application of contemporary sociological theory to the topic. Four main themes are identified: the body, individualization, risk and the new organizational logics. Care and the body, individualization and the transformation of personal and domestic life are considered in Chapter 7, while risk, the concept of risk society and political–economic developments and the new organizational logic of network society are examined in Chapter 8. A key argument advanced in this final section of the book is that the central place of care in social life means that it can no longer be regarded as a marginal or special-interest topic in sociological theory. Instead, it is necessary for social theorists to engage more deeply with the phenomena involved, giving far more attention to this neglected but vital element of human solidarity.

Each of the three perspectives from which debates surrounding care and human services are examined provide important and complementary perspectives from which to understand the dilemmas of care and human services. The approach taken in this book is focused on contemporary debates about care in advanced liberal democracies. Comparative analyses examining approaches to care in Asia, Africa and elsewhere in Europe would be likely to produce a very different set of conclusions (Liu and Kendig, 2000; Keith, 1990). The approach is intended not to provide the final word, but to open up discussion in ways which will introduce some new readers to the issues and encourage them and others to contribute.

PART 1

Theories and Arguments about Care

Care is a word that today has what marketing experts call a high recognition factor and a positive image. From the brand names of domestic cleaning and car maintenance companies, to descriptions of parent–child relations and feelings of deep affection between lovers, it seems to be used almost everywhere. The concept appears to describe much that is good and desirable in an indifferent and hostile world; the very idea of care seems capable of inducing a warm feeling of approval in most people. Like apple pie and motherhood (both of which may be considered to be particular expressions of it), who could possibly be opposed to the values of care?

The answer, of course, depends on what the term means. Care is an emotive and value-laden term, equally capable of evoking an inner glow or a degree of hostility that must at times shock those who see care as a personal virtue. People who justify their actions as spreading love and compassion, like those who work to protect or support the vulnerable, are often ridiculed in public debate as 'bleeding hearts'. Those who provide care are also vulnerable to accusations of interference, or of self-interest masquerading as compassion. Care itself has come to be seen as a 'burden', holding back and exploiting care-givers who are required to make significant personal sacrifices in the process of providing the support. Parallel claims are often presented by or on behalf of the recipients of care, for whom relying on others can be a form of enforced personal dependency. Numerous examples from recent history, from the provision of care in orphanages and work houses (Penglase, 2005), to national programmes such the adoption of indigenous children in Australia by white families for much of the twentieth century (Wilson, 1997), have also shown that actions once portrayed to be caring may, in the light of history, be re-evaluated, showing that other, much darker forces were also at play.

Rolf Rønning (2002) cites the following attack, presented at a gerontology conference he attended in Britain, as a further illustration of the arguments used to reject the notion of care as the solution to the needs for support amongst frail older people:

> Empowerment at the individual level is, we would argue, about having the power to exercise choice and exert control over one's life. 'Care' has come to mean its antithesis. Older people needing 'care' are seen as dependent, as unable to exercise choice and control and as needing somebody to be responsible *for* them, rather than responsible *to* them. (Clark and Spafford, 2002 cited in Rønning, 2002: 34–5; emphasis in original)

Here, care is not seen as an ethically superior concept. Rather, the recipients are seen as suffering a socially constructed dependency as a result of their subjugation to care provided by others. Attacks such as this raise important questions. How is care to be conceptualized and understood? If care deserves to be a considered a positive concept, as Rønning argues, why is it so contested? Is it possible to develop a definition, an approach or a theory that could avoid these problems and serve instead to see care recognized as a common value for modern societies? Part 1 of this book addresses these questions, drawing on the rich discussion that has developed in recent years by focusing on the 'arguments about care' that have emerged, the competing normative perspectives from which different analyses, narratives and rationales of care are constructed.

As might be expected of a topic that is at once profound and deeply philosophical, and at the same time experienced as a basic everyday activity and a common attitude concerning all manner of things that people value, vast amounts have been written on various aspects of the subject. The focus in Part 1, as elsewhere in the book, is on published accounts in social science and related literature that have been influential over the past 25 years. First, it is important to consider the broader question of the definition of care. Where does the term come from and what are the meanings currently implied by those who use it? This is the key question addressed in Chapter 2. In Chapters 3 and 4, the discussion moves on to take into account two major perspectives reflecting different political and economic contexts and disciplinary orientations: debates originating within feminism drawing on psychology, philosophy and political theory originating largely in the USA; and writings from the field of British policy studies which, in turn, have been strongly influenced by the link with European, particularly Scandinavian, research in this field. Reviewing contributions from each of these fields uncovers important differences and debates, both between and within perspectives.

CHAPTER 2

Defining and Claiming Care

As the anthropologists McKechnie and Kohn (1999) have argued, care is a concept currently coming to the fore in many contemporary debates, pushed on not just by the increasingly public character of care and the clash of its apparently altruistic values with consumerism and market-based efficiency, but also by medical and ethical debates linked to new technologies for diagnosis and intervention. What is understood by the term, its characteristics and the ideals it embodies is not fixed, but is currently being (re)constructed and refashioned, constantly fought over by various protagonists who seek to claim its mantle for their cause. But as the increasingly common cross-referral between perspectives suggests, there is also evidence of convergence around common themes, as the concept of care is defined and redefined to justify the claims and counter-claims made of it.

Following the work of Raymond Williams and other political cultural theorists, it is clear that the words and concepts used to describe social life actively shape the way the world is understood and experienced, influencing our daily practices as individuals and the policy responses to issues and problems that are recognized or obscured (Williams, 1976; Fraser and Gordon, 1994). Theory, language, definitions and terminology matter because they shape the way the world is understood and frame public debates and policies. Focusing on the development and use of a language of care by care theorists, this chapter therefore examines the emergence of new definitions and conceptions of care that have accompanied the move of care from a private concern to a public issue.

In the first section of the chapter, I review the meaning and semantic background of the term 'care'. The evidence examined suggests that alongside an altruistic, positive and often romanticized interpretation of the meaning of the word, there is another, less positive meaning which can not be ignored. This is followed by an examination of the way that care has been defined and conceptualized in much feminist scholarship. Particular attention is given to the contribution made by Joan Tronto in developing a normative conception of care as a process, linking ideas about care as a disposition to those who see it as work. The final section is in the form of a case study of care in nursing theory, examining the way that care has been claimed and reimagined as an area of professional expertise by nursing theorists. Attempts to define and claim care, I argue in this chapter, are both an important field of theoretical debate in the social sciences and an expression of the political and cultural contest of ideas that is essential if the vital social importance of care is to gain the recognition and social profile required in the twenty-first century.

The Language of Care

The term 'carer' (or 'care-giver' in the USA) refers to 'a person whose occupation is the care of the sick, aged, disabled, etc; [or] one who looks after a disabled or elderly relative at home, especially one who is therefore unable to work', according to the Oxford English Dictionary (OED, 2003). Yet until very recently the words 'carer' and 'care-giver' were unknown. It was only in 1978 that their first modern recorded use appeared (OED Online, 2003). Prior to that, the term 'carer' would have been considered at best archaic and, if used, would have had a very different meaning. Uses of the term 'carer' recorded by the OED in 1691 and 1850 refer simply to 'one who cares', that is a worrier, a person ridden with anxiety.

BOX 2   CHANGING MEANINGS OF THE WORDS 'CARE' AND 'CARING'

It is often wrongly believed that the term 'care' in the English language can be traced to words in Ancient Greek and Latin. In Greek, the root of the term 'charis' was used to signify outward grace or favour. Charitas signified that someone or something was of grace, of goodwill, of kindness. The Latin term 'caritas'

---

derives from the Greek and is usually translated either as love or as charity. Linking the word 'care' to the Latin *caritas* appears to have been an interpretation fostered by the Roman Church, for whom the biblical injunction of the ideals of 'faith, hope and charity' (sometimes translated as 'faith, hope and care') often stand as a sort of summary of the basic principles of Christian virtue.

According to Reich (1995), the Latin word for care is *cura*. The poet Virgil described the entrance to the underworld as being inscribed with the words 'vengeful Cares' (*ultrices Curae*), a reference to the mythical Cura, who in Greco-Roman myth fought with Jupiter over the creation of the first humans. Care in this sense was a dark force of responsibility, dragging one down to earth. For Seneca, a stoic philosopher, the word *cura* instead took on the meaning of solicitude, or concern, and was seen as an uplifting and wholesome potential, that enabled a person to become fully human. The word *cura* was also used in Latin in ways that suggest opposing characteristics: on the one hand, as a burdensome responsibility that drags people down and, on the other, as a power which enables humans to achieve their real potential. These contradictory tendencies are symbolically played out in the Greco-Roman myth of Cura, narrated and analysed by Reich.

In English, lexical authorities, such as the Oxford English Dictionary (OED), attribute the origins of the words 'care' and 'caring' not to Latin or Greek, but to the Old English words *caru*, 'a worry or care', and *carian*, a verb meaning 'to trouble oneself'. To care therefore meant to worry. Linguistic meanings change and develop over time. In nineteenth-century English philanthropic thought, 'care' referred to 'the means by which the conditions likely to produce danger [were] constantly monitored and kept under control' (Dean and Bolton, 1980: 82, cited in Dunlop, 1994: 30). Hence care for the sick referred to a form of public health intervention that involved preventing the spread of disease to the general population.

Conflicting sets of meanings – care as a 'worry', 'concern' or 'responsibility' and care as 'love' and 'charity' – seem to adhere to the word 'care' in the English language today. The word 'care', as commonly used today, may be either a noun or a verb. As a noun, *care* implies a state of intense attention or support, often as a sort of benevolent form of aid, as in such terms as 'community care' and 'nursing care'. It also indicates anxieties and concerns, as in the phrase 'without a worry or a care'. It may also refer to responsibility or guardianship, for example 'he was placed in the care of the state', or to a formal programme of specialized support, such as health care or child care. The verb, *to care,* is used as an expression of the activity of concern or worry as well as love, 'to care about' someone. It also indicates physical action, as in the phrase 'to care for', meaning to provide active help to someone or something. The word also retains a sense of expressing a preference, making it well suited to ambiguity and wordplay such as 'Who cares?'. *Caring* is both the adjective derived from care, used to describe someone who is kind and gives emotional support to others, and a present participle used to describe the practice of giving care.

Dunlop (1994) contrasts 'care' with the word 'cure', derived from French (and in turn from the Latin word *cura*). Following the Norman invasion of England in 1066, Anglo-Saxon was the language of the conquered, French the language of the victors. Old English words such as 'swine' and 'pig' survived and continued to be used by the common people, while Norman words such as 'pork' (from the French *porc,* meaning pig) supplanted them amongst the upper class. Such a difference can now be found between the meanings of 'care' and 'cure': the socially superior 'cured', while their subordinates 'cared', a division of labour suggestive of the social hierarchy encountered in health services in the division of labour between doctors and nurses.

Prior to the move of married women from the home into paid employment in the 1970s, care undertaken in the home was widely understood as women's domestic work, and subsumed within such descriptions as 'housework', 'homemaking', 'mothering' and 'care of the sick and invalid'. The recent (re)invention of the term 'carer' is a consequence of the need to name and make visible the hidden work of caring that occurred in the home. 'Carer' may therefore be considered a product of the cultural politics of the move of care from the private, domestic sphere, to the public realm (Bytheway and Johnson, 1998; Barnes, 2001; Fine, 2004). (Other recent examples of ongoing creativity in the application of the term include the introduction of concepts which concern personal maintenance, such as 'self-care' (Penning and

Chappell, 1990); 'care of the self' (Foucault, 1988a) and the term 'social care' (Daly and Lewis, 2000) used in British social policy.) Once clearly defined, carers/care-givers could be identified and counted in national statistics, their experiences documented by researchers, and incorporated into government policy. But there is a semantic cost. By stipulating what a carer is, others are excluded. Official definitions used in the collection of national statistics that equate the term 'carer' with primary care-giver, for example, serve to focus attention on one person regarded as the care-giver, and may obscure others, such as care networks, in the process. The definition used in both Britain and Australia for the purposes of national statistics and a number of specialized government programmes, for example, identifies carers as unpaid family members. Others who provide care are thereby excluded, including all paid careworkers, along with neighbours, friends, teachers, and others who might assist with care from time to time. Similarly, the mothers, fathers, step-parents, foster-parents and custodians of children who are not disabled or suffering a long-term health condition are also defined as not being carers (Fine, 2004). Grandparents providing care for grandchildren, and people with disabilities caring for their own or other children are also similarly excluded from the count.

As with the term 'carer', use of the terms 'care' and 'caring' to highlight particular activities and qualities must also be understood as being caught up in cultural politics. The deep linguistic roots and overlapping meanings and ambiguities attaching to the words (see Box 2) mean that, conceptually, 'care' and 'caring' are a long way removed from the sort of precisely defined technical term that is the hallmark of science. Instead, they refer to a value-laden concept that bespeaks a long association with human experience. Hidden beneath the idealistic, altruistic sense of the words *care* and *caring* is another, more disturbing meaning that can not be simply purged from the record. Both sets of meanings, that which suggests a positive concern for another and the performance of tender acts of kindness, and the more negative sense involving worry, control and self-sacrifice, are invoked in contemporary discourses on care. Even if the protagonists wanted to do so, these deeper layers of meaning could not be simply erased.

Attempts to define concepts such as care precisely nearly always end in frustration and dispute. The search for rigid definitions may be important for the purposes of scientific measurement, policy or legal reasons, but the attempt is prone to make controversial social questions into 'word games', that dilemma of social life that means that the harder we try to define the phenomenon under study, the more elusive it appears (Heller, 1990). Like other concepts concerned with social processes and values, care is not an objective material object with an independent existence of its own that can be brought into the laboratory to be examined and dissected. It is, instead, a social phenomenon that is constituted and reconstituted by our actions, so that its meaning can not be held still to study. While indicative of political and other struggles that have arisen in the wake of care going public, attempts to define the term 'care', to draw out or legitimize certain meanings, or to repress others, are important because they help to name and give form to the long-hidden processes involved. It is precisely these qualities that call for a sociologically informed analysis of its meanings and application.

In common with many other social concepts, such as community (Bell and Newby, 1971: 21; Bauman, 2001), the words 'care' and 'caring' are used, on the one hand, to provide a description of an existing reality and, on the other, to indicate a visionary ideal. As an ideal or vision of what can be achieved, care is necessarily normative and contested. When used in a descriptive sense, research on care often reports that actual practices fall short of or differ from the ideal. In the constant arguments about care there is evidence of a deep concern about the balance between the individual, our immediate others and the broader society.

A Labour of Love. Feminism and the Theorizing of Care

Beyond dictionary meanings and definitions lies the terrain of analysis and theory. It is here that care researchers, particularly feminist theorists and researchers, have done most to uncover the hidden character and potential of care in the contemporary world. By seeking to understand and explicate what had long been implicit, separating myths of the natural aptitude of the female for caring from the realities of domestic exploitation and denial of social rights, contributors developed a rich dialogue that links theory development with observation and political strategy. This has laid the groundwork for new approaches intended to remove the stigma and secrecy from caring and ensure that care is acknowledged and given the central place in social life that it requires.

An important entry point into recent theories on care is the distinction between dispositions and actions. As Joan Tronto (1998), Richard Hugman (1991) and others point out, care is typically understood in two quite distinct ways. First, the term 'care' can refer to a 'mental disposition of concern', a cognitive and emotional aspect that involves attentiveness and concern for the state of another. Second, care can be used to indicate the physical work of providing assistance, 'the actual practices that we engage in as a result of these concerns' (Tronto, 1998: 16).

It is not difficult to conceptualize a link between these two domains of care. In its initial stages, Tronto suggests, care may be thought of as involving a disposition towards others, an awareness of their need for support or attention that may, or may not, be subsequently put into action through the provision of care. This approach suggests that rather than there being two distinct domains or types of care, there is a sequencing of the two approaches, with care moving from thought to action. This approach, based on the staging of analytically distinguishable elements of care, is a crucial aspect of the logic behind Tronto's own more elaborated theory, which is considered shortly.

Focusing on the physical engagement involved in care, British researchers Janet Finch and Dulcie Groves (1983) eloquently formulated a link between the two domains. Care, in their words, involves 'a labour of love'. Both action and disposition, labour and love, are tied together, shaping the unique character of care as a vocation and identity pursued by women. Important as the hard physical work involved is, care can not be understood simply as a matter of physical labouring, the authors stress. The mental element, the love, worry and concern, the planning, anticipation and unselfish sacrifice of personal priorities and interests, is what enables the labour of care to continue without a revolt from the carers.

Breaking the concept of caring into two grammatically distinct sets of activities – *caring about* and *caring for* another person – Hilary Graham (1983) made a conceptual distinction to which almost all subsequent care research has referred. *Caring about* someone signals concern for another. This has traditionally been portrayed as involving a sense of duty, a moral commitment or a sense of personal affinity. Feelings of attachment or love have also been commonly considered to be a form of care. *Caring for*, in turn, refers to the work involved in nurturing, sustaining and tending another. Although it may be thought that the two aspects would always be found together, this is not necessary, argued Graham.

When someone is cared for, we would always hope that he or she is also cared about. Where they are cared for, but not about, we might consider it to be a form of depersonalized or 'uncaring' care. The opposite is not the case, however. It is possible to *care about* someone (a lover, for example) who does not need to be cared for. It is also possible to care about someone who needs ongoing help, but not personally to provide care *for* them. The distinction has been used to show that men often only 'care' in this more limited sense, leaving the hard work to their wives, mothers or daughters, but Graham also seemed to be thinking about women at home, suggesting that they should not feel paralysed by guilt if they did not undertake all the family care themselves. When care is organized it may be the result of a mother or daughter caring deeply about the particular individual, at the same time as recognizing that she is not necessarily able to provide all the hands-on care the recipient requires, that she lacks the necessary professional expertise, or that the sacrifice of career or personal opportunity involved in providing the care directly might not be appropriate.

Caring for another may also be considered to involve work. Although the effort and skills involved are often underestimated, we readily recognize the physical work of care through the activity and exertion involved. Emotional labour or 'emotion work', as Arlie Hochschild (1983) points out, is also involved. Hochschild first coined the term 'emotional labour' to describe the activities of flight attendants and bill collectors, occupations in which the ability to convince others of personal sincerity is vital. A key aspect of emotional labour is that it involves behaviour carried out in fulfilment of the requirements of the job. The emotional labour involved in care, for example as a personal assistant, care professional or close family member, typically involves being attentive to the needs of another, undertaking any duties in a responsible and caring manner. But it can also signal the extreme emotional exertions and discipline involved in helping another or many others, and the long-term costs arising from the suppression of self and of spontaneity required to undertake the work of caring. Along with Hochschild's own further studies involving both formal and informal forms of care (Hochschild and Machung, 1989; Hochschild, 1997, 2003) many other writers have since used the concept to analyse the provision of personal care, highlighting the short- and long-term emotional costs and stresses involved (James 1992; Sass, 2000; Franzway, 2001; Meagher, 2003).

An alternative approach to theorizing care has been to focus largely on one or other of the two domains. Examining care as a disposition, a way of thinking about one's identity and responsibilities in the world, proves to be an immense undertaking in its own right. This has been an domain of particular interest to psychologists and philosophers, as well as others, such as political theorists, whose primary interest in care is as an abstracted set of principles guiding moral action in the world. A substantial and very important body of theory has developed around this primary focus, building on Gilligan's innovative propositions concerning an 'ethic of care'. This strand of theory and research, which originated in the USA, sees care as a substantially positive value. It is examined in some depth in Chapter 3.

Similarly, research that addresses care primarily as a practice and activity, as a form of work, developed particularly strongly in Britain, Europe, New Zealand and Australia. In the UK in particular, feminist researchers and others with a background in social administration, social policy and social work laid particular emphasis on the practical and policy implications of the concept of care. An important aim of those working in this broad tradition has been to advocate for more effective policy measures, particularly concerning the plight of carers. This approach is reviewed in Chapter 4.

In a relatively recent and, in my view, important development, Mary Daly and Jane Lewis point to a third dimension of care. Care in these instances is seen as a product or expression of a social relationship between care-giver and recipient (Daly and Lewis, 2000; Daly, 2002). This identifies aspects of both the context and the form that care takes as implicit in the common understanding of the term, although in much of the earlier feminist work on care it was typically seen more as a one-way transaction between an active and a dependent party. Focusing on relational aspects of care is an important element of the approach developed by Eva Feder Kittay (1999), discussed in the following chapter.

Care as Practice and Process

Building a theory that attempted to link dispositions and actions, Joan Tronto set out a conceptual approach to care that is complex and sequential, building on and elaborating on the distinctions made by Hilary Graham. Care emerges not as a discreet or self-contained aspect of social life, but as ubiquitous and all-encompassing. Care, she insists, is a practice, an active way of being, something that involves a sense of work or effort, but also habit and disposition. Instead of trying to understand care as a single action or a state, she links the separate elements of care together as a process, with four distinct yet linked phases (Fisher and Tronto, 1990; Tronto, 1993, 1998):

1. *Caring about.* This first phase involves the development of an awareness of, and attention to, the needs for care in another person or thing.
2. *Taking care of.* This is the next phase, in which some responsibility for these needs is assumed and plans are made to respond to these needs.
3. *Care-giving.* This involves meeting some or all of the needs for care. This phase involves physical work by individuals and organizations, and usually requires direct contact between what Tronto calls 'care-givers' and 'the objects of care' (Tronto, 1993: 107).
4. *Care-receiving.* This is the final phase, which necessarily entails a response from the recipient, linking the two parties. Tronto notes that 'In a way, since any single act of care may alter the situation and produce new needs for care, the caring process in this way comes full circle, with responsiveness requiring more attentiveness' (Tronto, 1998: 16–17).

Because it draws together a range of different meanings of the word 'care' into a single process, this approach has considerable appeal, both at a conceptual/analytic level and as a set of normative guidelines spelling out elements of moral and political practice that go beyond the boundaries of the care hidden in the privacy of the home. Tronto's formulation of the process in this way is intended to show that care can function as a social value, an orientation to the world that goes beyond giving care to another person to a broader level of concern, demonstrating that care provides a general ethic for our being in the world. We can care for many other things, such as the environment, the plight of people in the Third World or world peace.

None the less, elements of the approach are suggestive of deeper questions that need to be considered in thinking about the value of a unified theory of care. By extension, these are also issues that might properly be traced back to other attempts to develop the concept of care as an ethical orientation to the world, or, perhaps even more disturbingly, to the very foundations of the concept of care. I focus here on three of these elements.

First, a feature of Tronto's formulation is the sequencing of the different aspects of the process of care. As she notes, these components are separable, both conceptually and in practice. While it is uplifting and analytically advantageous to think of care holistically, where each of the four phases is integrated into a single unified process, the phases identify an element of the approach that enables it to be broken up into component tasks and managed as part of a system of unequal power relations. 'Taking care of', she notes, is 'associated with more public roles, and with men rather than women' (Tronto, 1993: 115). The doctor, for example, takes care of his patients, although it is the nurses, orderlies and others who actually provide what Tronto calls 'hands-on care'. Similarly, a man, working as the breadwinner of the family, might be thought of as 'taking care of' his family. In contrast she notes, care-giving is an activity that has long been socially consti-tuted as a menial or devalued activity, and has 'mainly been the work of slaves, servants and women in Western history' (Tronto: 1993: 113). The critique implied is one of males who take care of the family but do not actually provide care. The division and sequencing of compo-nents, however, raises important questions about the relative value of each. Are those who give care more caring than those who care about and take care of another? Can people be considered caring if their involvement is confined to the first two stages of the process? If not, is it wrong for parents to place their children in child care, or for a senior nurse to supervise a more junior colleague on the ward?

Secondly, despite Tronto's assertions that care should not be defined as a dyadic relationship but one that is broader, social and shared (Tronto, 1993: 103), there is a sense in which her approach locates care as a process, a 'disposition' and 'activity', initiated by the care-givers and undertaken on their terms. The recipient is portrayed as a rela-tively passive object, rather than a subject actively involved in the construction of the relationship(s) of care. As shall be shown in the following chapter, this is one of the most contentious aspects of the way in which care has been conceived and one of the central concerns of those seeking to reconstruct care as meaningful practice for the contemporary world.

In developing a theoretical, metaconcept of care capable of generalization to a range of moral and political concerns, Tronto posited a generalized set of 'objects of care'. The approach to defining care was intended to show that the important values attributed to women but traditionally confined to the domestic sphere can provide a broad moral compass for public life. This may make sense when we think of things in the environment, such as trees, as passive objects needing advocates and support. But the approach is less satisfactory when applied to interactions between people. When care relationships concern people, each party, from the youngest infant onwards, can be seen to be actively engaged in the processes and relationship. Our capacity to initiate action, as recipients of care, our responsiveness to the attention and touch involved, our subjectivity and integrity, should be core factors shaping the process involved.

The third element that Tronto's approach exemplifies is the risk that the more specific attributes of care between different people and in different situations will be lost in the application of such a broad metaconcept of care. The need to acknowledge both the positive and negative aspects that providing or receiving care can involve, the very different meanings and practices involved in different contexts and for individuals from widely different social backgrounds and cultures, raises an important dilemma, as the philosopher Peta Bowden points out,

> Attempts to identify women's values or to produce a feminist ethics fail to resist the universalizing and exclusionary habits of modernism. Moves towards the inclusion in moral theory of values informed by intimate life practices seem only to create new exclusions. From the other side, however, both respect for the complexity and ambiguity of practices of care – their dark and their light sides – and attentiveness to the constitutive function of their different contexts and purposes, as well as to the personal biographies of their participants, appear to pose fatal limitations and insoluble problems for the 'ethic of care'. (Bowden, 1997: 11)

Bowden's own review of the concept of care is based on a review of literature on care in different contexts – mothering, friendship and the professional practice of nursing. In each of these contexts, care is shown to have a number of quite distinct characteristics. Maternal care for one's own children, for example, typically involves an intense level of personal identification between mother and child and a maternal preparedness to intervene in the most intimate details of the children's lives. Friendship, in contrast, is a much looser social bond, generally between equals, that requires a careful balance between personal concern and respect for another's autonomy. Rather than attempting to define a general concept of care, Bowden argues, we should recognize significant differences in these relationships and the way that ethical judgments in caring are shaped by the specific social contexts in which it is encountered. To do this, however, seems to suggest that we must at the very least acknowledge that care is a diverse phenomenon and carefully differentiate between the different forms that it assumes. A more radical proposition advanced by Bowden is that we must reject the notion of care as too vague a concept to be of serious analytic or philosophical value. Care, she argues, is not capable of a unitary analysis. It is, instead, a linguistic designation that gives an apparent unity to social and ethical phenomena that in reality are quite distinct.

Any empirically grounded analysis of the phenomena must recognize important differences between care in different contexts, at a certain level of detail. Not only is there a difference between identifiable types of care, such as care for young infants and care for older people, but the fine points of how care is conceptualized and brought to life will clearly differ between individuals, particular instances and different historical and social conditions. But does acknowledging the difference between specific forms and instances of care require abandoning attempts to identify common elements of these seemingly diverse phenomena? Unless we are to abandon all attempts at developing a general analysis of care and its significance in twenty-first-century social life, Bowden's critique of a unified analysis must be regarded as providing us with a warning. Attempts to develop an analysis of care must seek to provide a balance between, on the one hand, attentiveness to the uniqueness of specific cases and categorical forms and, on the other hand, a concern for the value of a general analysis that can identify common elements amongst a wide range of social activities.

Attempts to define and theorize care, I have argued in this chapter, have accompanied the move of care, along with women, from the private domain into the public arena in the final decades of the twentieth century. The search for new ways of conceptualizing and representing care is linked to the personal challenges which this has raised and the cultural and political struggles encountered as feminists and others have sought not only to develop an understanding of the problems experienced in existing ways of caring but also to support new forms of care and new ways of caring. Similar challenges have also been experienced within each of the more specialized subfields in which care is encountered. Within the fields of child care, mental health, disability support and aged care, for example, parallel debates have been taking place as older models of care have been found wanting and new ways of providing care have been sought. When we move the focus of the discussion towards the meanings that care has in specific contexts, therefore, we should anticipate that many of the same issues will be encountered. In the final section of this chapter, therefore, I examine one such field, that of nursing theory, in greater detail. As nursing concerns a paid form of care work, this is intended as a case study and test case of one of the most significant and contentious fields of care theory development.

A Profession of Care. Care in Contemporary Nursing Theory

Sioban Nelson, a nurse academic concerned with the historical sociology of the profession, defines nursing as follows:

> Simply put, nursing is the care of the sick. Nurses do not cure, although it has been believed since at least the time of Florence Nightingale that good nursing facilitates cure; nurses do not rehabilitate, although recovery and skilled nursing are interdependent: nurses do not treat illness, although increasingly there is a push to do so. Rather, nursing is the task of looking after people when they are too ill to look after themselves, and to wean them back to self-care as they recover.

> This endeavor is as old as any human activity one could mention . . . [but] care of the sick that is framed by domestic/household duty (slaves, servants) or love (family, friends) is not the same as the care of strangers – and it is with the care of strangers that the history of nursing lies. (Nelson, 2000: 1)

Nelson places two important qualifications on the concept of care as it applies to nursing. First, nursing is concerned with 'care of the sick', thus marking off nursing's territory as a discrete, although extensive, part of the human life course concerned with injury, disease and illness. Care in nursing therefore refers to activities that are confined to interventions that are time-limited and focused on particular aspects of the human condition. Second, as the phrase 'care of strangers' suggests, nursing care is not directed at particular individuals within the family but at those with whom a pre-existing, familial or personal tie need not exist at the time of the commencement of the interaction. Nursing, for Nelson and certain other writers on the topic (Shelly and Miller, 1999), remains an activity that, at its core, is concerned with care and spirituality. Although care in nursing bears many of the hallmarks of 'care' as it is more generically defined, it is marked out by its practitioners as bearing a number of distinct occupational characteristics.

The use of the term 'care' as a core characteristic of nursing has become emblematic of the professional claims made by practitioners. The title of one of the key nursing journals, the *International Journal for Human Caring*, produced by the International Association for Human Caring, a professional nursing association based in the USA, captures the sense of identification that many nursing theorists see as their professional domain. Care represents a core professional concept, central to nursing's claim to a unique body of knowledge and skills. For this reason there are few, if any, of the large number of theories of nursing developed since the 1960s that do not attempt to lay claim to the concept of care and to contrast this with the interventionist and depersonalized approach taken by medicine (Leininger, 1988; Marriner-Tomey, 1989; Gaut, 1993; Kottow, 2001; Boykin and Schoenhofer, 2001). Most of this work has been developed in the USA, but its influence has not been restricted to that country. Internationally, Dorothy Orem's self-care deficit nursing theory which identifies a general theory of nursing based on the concepts of self-care, self-care deficit and nursing system (Orem, 1991; Orem, Denyes and Bekel, 2001) has been particularly influential.

An important element of a number of the most influential of these nursing theories in the closing decades of the twentieth century has been the advocacy of an approach to care in which nurses learn to respond to the 'whole person', developing a capacity to empathize with the patient, by entering empathically into her 'life world' (Benner and Wrubel, 1989; Fjelland and Gjengedal, 1994). This understanding of care as involving a relationship based on empathy relies on what is frequently described in the nursing literature as the 'spiritual' elements of the relationship between carer and patient. According to Nelson

(2000), this is evidence of continuity between traditional Christian practices of penitence in nursing, and modern professional nursing. Yet the historical continuity which, Nelson asserts, should not be confused with recent changes in the understanding of care and the orientation of the profession. Nurses who trained before the 1970s (and many since that time), for example, report that they were warned during their training not to become 'too involved' with their patients. As Margaret Dunlop recounts,

> Benner (1994a) recalls being warned in nursing courses about becoming too involved. I, too can recall being repeatedly told this . . . but at the same time I can recall numerous occasions when I was asked, 'How would you feel if it was your mother, father, sister, brother, etc?' Thus, in a very theoretical way, nursing sought to teach me to maintain both separation and linkage in my practice: separation – 'you must remember that the other is a stranger' – and linkage 'you must think and act as if he were not'. (Dunlop, 1994: 31)

This sort of double message presented nurses with a difficult balancing act. While there was a place for compassion in the older approach to nursing, it was not boundless and there was a danger seen in over-identification with the care recipient. Rather, the emphasis in 'traditional' (ie pre-1970s) nursing practice was on nurses performing the functional tasks of clinical nursing under the direction of supervising medical staff; emotional detachment was stressed. Affective involvement was seen as potentially dangerous for the nurse, likely to compromise clinical objectivity and the effectiveness of the support and treatment she provided.

The Changing Meanings of Care in Nursing

In the 1960s, 'care', understood as the physical care of the body, was already seen as a crucial component of nursing, as evidenced by the influential theories of Lydia Hall (1966, cited in Dunlop, 1994: 31–2) amongst others. Hall's 'core, care and cure' model of nursing, published in the middle of that decade, identified care as the intimate activities of bodily care, such as feeding, bathing and toileting the patient (Marriner-Tomey, 1989). It was because nurses provided this bodily care, according to Hall, that they were able to effectively contribute to enhancing the patients' cure and the restoration of health and well-being.

The subsequent development of holistic nursing theories represent what Dunlop has termed the 'emergent sense of caring'. In this emergent sense, the concept of care is carefully and professionally reconstructed, attention shifting away from the tasks of body work to focus on the 'psychosocial' aspects of care. This is a concept of care, shared to a large extent by other established helping professions such as clinical psychology, social work, and counselling, that can be taught and acquired as a learned professional skill and which has demonstrably strong foundations in the behavioural sciences. In nursing theories developed from the 1970s onwards, this emergent sense of care was advanced as providing the profession with a scientific basis for claims to the specialized body of knowledge seen to be the basis for professional status.

One of the most successful nursing theorists to advance this new understanding of care was Jean Watson, whose highly acclaimed book *Nursing. The Philosophy and Science of Caring* (1979) asserted that care could be made into a systematic science and thus provide a sound professional basis for nursing. Watson argued that the 'day-to-day practice of professional nursing requires a grounding in a humanistic value system ... [that] must be combined with the scientific knowledge base that guides the nurse's actions' (Watson, 1979: 7).

Accordingly, the concepts and practices that Watson identified as constituting care were analysed using humanistic and other forms of scholarship. The results were then operationalized as guidelines for actions, often in an explicitly positivistic manner which utilized various scales and quantification procedures whereby various qualities of the nurse's capacity to care for her patients could be measured. Watson explained that just as *curative* factors were those that assisted patients' cures, so *carative* factors were those that assisted the caring process. Her approach led her to the identification of ten primary carative functions, listed as follows:

1.   the formation of humanistic–altruistic systems of values;
2.   the installation of faith–hope;
3.   the cultivation of sensitivity to one's self and to others;
4.   the development of a helping–trust relationship;
5.   the promotion and acceptance of the expression of positive and negative feelings;

6. the systematic use of the scientific problem-solving method for decision-making;
7. the promotion of interpersonal teaching–learning;
8. the provision for a supportive, protective, and (or) corrective mental, physical, sociocultural and spiritual environment;
9. assistance with the gratification of human needs;
10. the allowance of existential–phenomenological forces (Watson, 1979: 9–10).

As Dunlop (1994) has argued, this approach conceptualized care as an almost exclusively psychological phenomenon. Eight of Watson's ten carative factors can be seen as relating to care as a psychodynamic phenomenon. Number 6 is concerned with locating nursing as a profession based on scientific approaches to decision-making. Only one of them, number 9, is directly concerned with the nursing care as work involving the patient's body.

In her discussion of the ninth factor, Watson was concerned primarily with the importance of attending to what she termed 'assistance with the gratification of lower order biophysical needs' as the foundation for meeting the 'higher order' levels related to personality and social development. Lower order biophysical needs, according to Watson, following Maslow's schema of the hierarchy of needs, consist first of the need for food and fluids, the need for elimination and for ventilation, and secondly of the 'psychophysical needs', which she identified as 'activity–inactivity' and 'sexuality' (Watson, 1979: 105–74). In her discussion of these she dwelt almost exclusively on the supposedly deeper meanings of basic bodily functions, drawing strongly on psychological and psychoanalytic analyses of their symbolic meaning for the whole person's higher needs such as self-actualization.

Watson's approach emphasized caring as a process of personal and spiritual growth for both the nurse and the patient. As Fagermoen (1999) argues in a commentary on this work, if the theory is one based on humanism, it is a form of religiously inspired humanism. In addition to the use of spiritual concepts, there is a strong metaphysical intent in the approach to care, which was made quite explicit by Watson in much of her later work. While emphasizing a holistic approach that sought to recognize the unity of body and mind, Watson's approach effectively reinterpreted the concept of care in nursing. Instead of the physical tending of bodily needs, care came to be seen as a disembodied, psychological disposition. Supported by a scientific style of analysis, care also appeared as a mode of nurses relating to patients in which explicit and context-free standards could be established.

Patricia Benner and the 'Primacy of Caring'

The tendency to see care in psychosocial terms, drawing on the intangible quality of spirituality to explain some of the non-rational elements of interpersonal behaviour, is also evident in other works by contemporary nursing theorists, particularly those of Patricia Benner (Benner and Wrubel, 1989; Benner, 1994b), which first became influential around a decade later. Benner quite explicitly sought to advance an approach to a concept of care as one that recognized the embodied character of human existence (Benner and Wrubel, 1989). Yet, having stated this as a foundation of her approach, Benner seemed drawn towards an exploration of care as a question that primarily involved moral philosophy and issues of spirituality.

Benner based her approach on phenomenology and hermeneutics, drawing on and developing an approach to nursing theory that was 'informed by real-world experience and experiments, which are in turn subject to theoretical interpretation' (Benner and Wrubel, 1989: 5). Lessons were drawn from the explication of paradigm examples based on the lived experiences of nurses (and, only indirectly, their patients) in a variety of settings. As a result, the understanding of caring that emerged was one that eschewed the quantification sought by Watson and avoided the specification of any hard and fast characteristics. Rather, 'caring' (it is this form of the word, indicating activation and intentionality, that is used, never the word 'care') was seen as a form of generalized attitude, a 'way of being in the world' a form of 'involvement' highly contingent on context.

Benner and Wrubel (1989) outlined their approach to the 'primacy of caring' in the following terms:

> Caring as is used in this book means that persons, events, projects, and things matter to people. Caring is essential if the person is to live in a differentiated world where some things really matter, while others are less important or not important at all. 'Caring' as a word for being connected and having things matter, works well because it

fuses thought, feeling, and action – knowing and being. And the term caring is used appropriately to describe a wide range of involvements, from romantic love to parental love to friendship, from caring for one's garden to caring about one's work to caring for and about one's patients. (Benner and Wrubel, 1989: 1)

Benner and Wrubel argued that because caring is a way of being in the world, it determines what a person finds stressful, and how they can cope with stress. It enables action by individuals and is thus a primary form of connection with others. Caring is primary, in this view, because it sets up the possibility of giving and receiving help. This view has much in common with the ethic-of-care approach derived from the work of Carol Gilligan (see Chapter 3), and to whom she explicitly refers. Given that both authors have a background in university psychology in California, this is not perhaps unexpected. As in the approach taken by Tronto, the concept of care (or caring, in this instance) is writ large, so that it becomes an all-encompassing concept. As Benner argued in a subsequent publication, 'Without care, the person is without projects and concerns, is without story. Care sets up a world, and creates meaningful distinctions' (Benner, 1994a: 44).

Importantly, Benner and her colleagues see care as involving a form of collaboration between patient and nurse. The nurse attempts to understand the patients' worlds, responding to their fears and anxieties, acknowledging their problems. A degree of openness and personal revelation on behalf of the nurse is also required. A large number of sensitive and often quite moving case descriptions provided by Benner and Wrubel (1989) are used to illustrate the way that this approach can have a transformative effect, reducing the patient's feelings of vulnerability, dependency and distrust, establishing trust, personal integrity and dignity in their place. The value of this approach for the patient is not in doubt, although the extent of personal stress and emotional labour involved on behalf of the nurse is not, to my mind, fully acknowledged.

The intimacy involved in providing physical care frequently helps open up opportunities for communication between nurse and patient. But this also brings problems, not just those that come from the potentially sexualized misreading of such activities by some (generally male) patients, but from the ongoing demands that intimacy with a large number of strangers entails. At the end of the day's work, the nurse needs to be able to go home and live a life of her (or his) own.

Switching off from the demanding level of emotional engagement advocated by Benner is not easy. Indeed switching off is not the stance Benner advocates. Instead, she argues, there is a process of personal and spiritual growth open to the nurse who learns to develop caring as the central practice of nursing. The expertise required for this, she sought to show in an earlier work, can only be learnt through experience accompanied by (self-)critical reflection, in an environment in which inspiration and support from colleagues is forthcoming (Benner, 1984).

The admonition by Benner and other nursing theorists to claim caring as the central core of nursing needs to be understood as a reaction to over a century and a half of nursing practice. Training programmes had long reinforced the official advice given to nurses to keep their distance, to maintain a degree of formality and objectivity about their work and, above all, not to become emotionally involved. The organization of nursing in most hospitals along military-like task-specific lines helped reinforce that message. Nursing has been further confronted by the increasing commercialization of health care in recent decades, accompanied by the tendency to regard the treatment of patients, staff and care as commodities to be bought and sold at the right price. The practical translation in contemporary nursing courses of the approach advocated by Benner and others, the 'emergent sense of caring' to which Dunlop refers, is for nurses to develop an empathic, rather than a sympathetic, approach to care. Empathy, in this approach, comes to stand for a sort of cognitive recognition of the patient's pain and suffering, but not the personal identification with each patient encountered or a full emotional engagement with their pain (Bradley and Edinberg, 1986).

Similarly, the frequent reference to the spiritual dimensions of care suggests that care in nursing has a higher purpose than simply the service of Mammon and submission to the greedy demands of the market. On one level this has a subversive potential, undermining reliance on monetary incentives as the sole motivator of human action. Identifying the spiritual dimension suggests too the achievement of a greater good through acts of compassionate solidarity, for the nurse as well as for the wider community. At the same time, the message of spirituality resonates with the sense of personal duty and calling that have long seen care associated with women.

What emerges at the level of ideals at least, is a workable professional ethic of care, one that is informed by the ideals of caring as private, personal and particularistic practice, but not reduced to it. At the same time, the approach serves to enable the practitioner to develop and maintain her capacity to continue this work over time through engagement with a very large, and potentially unlimited, number of people with whom it would be simply impossible to sustain ongoing, deep personal relationships. This is not to say that, in prac-tice, nursing is always able to meet these ideals. As works cited by Bowden (1997) and many other accounts have demonstrated, the conditions under which nursing is practised, in which casualized and agency-based staffing arrangements have come to be of ongoing importance, frequently limit time for empathic caring. Further, as nursing has become increasingly professionalized, patients are increasingly likely to encounter other care staff, as the new divisions of caring labour have seen responsibility for many of the physical components of care transferred to less expensive, and less qualified, personnel.

Nursing Practice

Jocelyn Lawler's more recent and empirically informed account of nursing as a practice provides a valuable point of contrast with spiri-tualized, psychologically based approaches to nursing care. Lawler (1991) documents the different ways in which basic nursing care is involved with the care of the body, which includes intimate and regu-lar contact with aspects of the person (including the patient's skin and bodily products such as sweat, excrement, phlegm and blood) that are regarded as dirty, unpleasant or unspeakable in polite society. The association between nursing care and the body in this way, argues Lawler, has caused nursing to be seen as a form of 'dirty work', a lower-status form of work, traditionally assigned to women and often treated as invisible. Her commentary on the recent approaches to the (re)conceptualization of 'care' as nursing's specific domain of expertise and its great virtue are revealing:

> In recent decades, particularly since the 1970s, nursing writers have philosophized, theorized and proselytized 'holistic practice'. Such an approach to practice is promoted in the belief that it ensures more individualized and more personalized care. It is also believed to provide an avenue through which nursing could move away from

the dominant medical model . . . It is also a very 'clean' image of nursing to promote. The body care and dirty aspects of nurses' work disappear, to be replaced by neologisms and euphemisms. Body care is subsumed into a range of nurse-identified needs of the patient. This period in nursing can be seen as an attempt to overcome 'the problem of the body' in an occupation of dirty workers who deal with the messy details of physical being, and to scientize and sanitize nursing knowledge and practice. (Lawler, 1991: 216)

Lawler's detailed accounts of nursing work on the wards and her powerful analysis of the marginalization of nursing as a form of dirty work stand in contrast to those produced through most nursing theories of care. Her approach is based on careful observation of the actual work practices involved in nursing care rather than the development of an idealized vision of care as a set of abstract principles. It reminds us that nursing care, at least as it has been practised to date, remains a skilled activity based around the provision of care, which must be considered as a form of physical work involving intimate contact with the bodies of patients. (Further discussion of the approach to care as bodywork is found in Chapter 7.)

Care in Nursing Theory and Practice

Like other caring professions and forms of care work, nursing needs to be understood not simply in terms of the direct interpersonal relationships between those who provide care and those who receive it, but as part of the gender, occupational and class structure of high modernity. One of the consequences of the moves to increase the recognition of the professionalism of nursing has been the expansion of divisions and specialities within nursing and the creation and extension of a realm of subordinate occupations. There is a vast difference between the activities and prestige of novice student nurses, those who are qualified, and senior and more experienced nurses, as Benner (1984) points out. Further hierarchical differences are evident, and sharply marked out, in the occupational rungs of seniority of professional nurses and the realm of subordinate nursing occupations – enrolled nurses, nurses' aids, assistants in nursing, ward attendants and often other categories of care staff – all educated and paid less than professional nurses. As nursing's quest for increased professional status has proceeded, gains in the recognition of nursing at management level have typically been accompanied by an expansion of the work allocated to subordinate occupations. Employment for those adjunct nursing occupations seeking to provide 'holistic care' has, in a great many cases, only been available by accepting increasingly insecure conditions of employment. Accompanying this, organizational systems and structured decision-making protocols are increasingly threatening the decision-making discretion of those nurses still employed (Campbell, 1999).

Some developments in the theory of caring, applied to nursing, attempt to get around these problems by introducing policies and approaches that formalize and standardize care requirements in ways that support and encourage a more holistic caring approach. One approach, Bonnie Wesorick's *Clinical Practice Model of Nursing* (1991), for example, attempts to encourage emotional care by introducing training which emphasizes caring, upholding its values through policy, and by changing the formal procedures and authority structure of the hospital to give nursing staff greater authority to diagnose and treat social and emotional problems. There is a specific injunction, for example, for nursing notes to document a range of personal and psychological information on each patient's well-being. As Francesca Cancian observes, this approach attempts to adapt care to the workplace of the hospital by bureaucratizing and professionalizing it, while in the process, 'caring is treated as an "art and science" based on specialized knowledge that requires specific training' (Cancian, 2000: 147). The dangers of codifying care in this way are that caring interventions increasingly come to be seen as the terrain of supervisory staff with the support of clinical documentation of patients' caring needs. The professionalization of care in this way is a double-edged sword: it ensures that care is given greater recognition by according it a more explicit profile in the formal procedures and value systems of the institutions; at the same time it holds the danger of reducing the recognition of lower-level staff and curtailing their capacity to respond in a spontaneous and caring way of their own accord.

Dunlop (1994) argues that there has not only been a move away from a recognition of nursing care as an activity involving the physical care of patients, but also that there has been a conceptual slippage in much of the recent nursing literature through which the history of this bodily component of nursing care has been glossed over, conflated with attitudinal aspects of care, and ultimately removed. The result is that a clean, uplifting and professionally appealing self-image is promoted under the banner of holistic nursing care. Given the conditions in which less professional and often unskilled staff are increasingly undertaking the work once carried out by nurses, the approach to care as a form of interpersonal spiritual engagement that is enriching to both giver and receiver must, in turn, be considered, in Gillian Dalley's terms, as much an 'ideology of care' as a unique professional skill (Dalley, 1988).

Lawler's account of care in practice, like those of others discussed elsewhere in this book, reminds us that care can not be conceptually confined to a matter of sentiment or understood simply as an expression of moral disposition towards others, as spirituality or as religion. Care is a particular form of work, one that both responds to the vulnerability of the body and in turn requires physical and emotional exertion for its performance.

Attempts to define care, I have argued in this chapter, reflect the need to develop a public language with which to discuss problems that, until very recently, were confined to the domestic sphere. Language and theory can have the power to influence perception, shape understanding and direct actions, but the process of meaning-making is not a purely technical or disinterested process. 'Care' and 'caring' are words that have considerable power, derived in many ways from their history, and that can not be made to disappear. Claims to their virtues, therefore, must acknowledge the deep ambiguity that is built into the meanings of the terms.

Tronto suggests that the apparent ambiguity of the term 'care' can be made to work for feminists and others who wish to help create a more caring world:

> Care is both a complex cultural construction and the tangible work of care. It is a way of making highly abstract questions about meeting needs return to the prosaic level of how these needs are being met. It is a way of seeing the embodiments of our abstract ideas about power and relationships. By thinking about social and political institutions from the standpoint of this marginal and fragmented concept, we see how social structures shape our values and practices . . . The vocabulary of care is [the mechanism] . . . that offers the greatest possibility for transforming social and political thinking, especially in the treatment of 'others'. (Tronto, 1993: 124)

Much of the value Tronto sees in the concept arises because care refers simultaneously to both abstract ideals and tangible work, linking the theoretical with the specific and familiar. Yet, as the brief review of attempts to define and use concepts of care in contemporary nursing theory has shown, the social context of work shapes the meaning that care finally assumes. As the professionalization of nursing has proceeded, the concept of care has become more abstract, psychosocial and dispositional. In making claims for greater recognition and increased professional standing, nursing theories have not sought to emphasize the mundane, grinding, daily work of attending to sick bodies and ailing bodily functions, but instead have appealed to idealistic and uplifting sentiments. While they have sought to promote care as a general value, they have also sought to claim the expertise as their own. As Lawler's account of daily practice confirms, however, in reality hands-on care continues to be treated as marginal and subordinate work, despite the strong emphasis on the ideals of caring in nursing theories. The case study of nursing theory suggests, therefore, that despite several decades of intense theoretical work on the concept, care is likely to remain a contested and often ambiguous concept that will continue to evolve and accumulate meaning.

This chapter introduced some of the core concepts involved in the attempts to develop contemporary definitions and theories of care, but could not hope to do justice to the rich field of scholarship that has developed. To explore the approaches to care in greater depth, the next two chapters examine two of the major developments. Chapter 3 considers the concept of the 'ethic of care' and its link to gender and ideals of public virtue. This debate, taking place largely at the intersection of feminism, moral philosophy and political theory, has done much to invigorate our understanding of the complexity of the multiple phenomena termed care, opening new lines of imagination and discussion. In Chapter 4 I turn to consider the notions of care developed in the social policy field.

CHAPTER 3

Promoting an Ethic of Care for an Unjust World

One of the key problems faced by women as they entered the workforce in increasing and unprecedented numbers in the late twentieth century concerned the way in which neither employers nor public life more generally took account of issues of care. Beyond the immediate need to develop practical solutions, it was apparent that the dominant value systems in public life were blind to the issues of responsibility for the lives of others which women experienced in the home and which still kept many there. One of the approaches developed by feminist researchers and theorists to tackle this was to present care and caring as a distinct set of moral principles and as an alternative to the existing system of male privilege and impersonal standards that dominated public life. Following the work of Carol Gilligan, the ideal of caring as such a moral standard for the world became known as the 'ethic of care'.

This chapter reviews the emergence of proposals concerning an ethic of care and the intellectual disputes and controversies that accompanied it. The debate arose from a number of questions of fundamental importance. Is care a feminine value? Should women reject the values of care which have long been associated with their confinement to the domestic sphere? Or should these values be embraced and drawn into public life as a necessary and morally superior approach that could transform the world? The response to questions such as these have been largely philosophical and theoretical in character, with the ethic of care proposed as an altruistic, holistic and inspirational ideal. Comparison of the ethics of care approach with the approach advanced by advocates of social capital who see care as a civic virtue reveals a number of common features, despite important differences in the regard given to gender. By celebrating the altruistic value of care, presenting it as an inspirational ideal, each of these accounts ignores many of the problematic issues that attend care. In comparison, the approach to a public ethic of care introduced by Kittay, presented later in the chapter, is grounded on a more critical analysis and supported by a very different engagement with the standards of justice and equality that are held as ideals of public life in liberal democracies.

Origins of the 'Ethics of Care' Debate

The ethics of care debate developed within feminism initially as a result of the work of the American psychologist Carol Gilligan (1982) on the moral development of children. Research undertaken by the cognitive development psychologist Lawrence Kohlberg, with whom Gilligan had worked, suggested that the development of moral reasoning in children occurred through six distinct developmental stages. These extend from an orientation to obedience and punishment (stage one) to recognition of the universal ethical principles of justice (stage six). The sixth and highest level of moral capacity was said to involve the capability to make impersonal judgments using Kantian-like abstract principles of universal justice and respect for the dignity of all persons (Kohlberg, 1981, 1984). These stages had been developed largely in work with boys, based on their responses to vignettes posing moral dilemmas. Kohlberg's 'Heinz dilemma', for example, poses the question of what action a husband, Heinz, would be justified taking in order to save the life of his dying wife. There is an effective treatment available, but this involves the use of drugs which the husband would never be able to afford and to which he would not otherwise have access. Would it be right for him to steal them under these conditions?

Gilligan noted that in their responses to such vignettes, females typically seemed more concerned with preserving relationships and scored less well than males on Kohlberg's orientation towards universal standards of justice. This seemed to suggest either that females were less capable of achieving these standards of abstract moral reasoning, or (as Gilligan suspected) that the tests were somehow biased against them. To explore this issue, Gilligan undertook her own study amongst a group of 29 women who had sought counselling following the decision to have an abortion. Their responses, according to Gilligan, suggested that when confronted with such a moral dilemma, rather than appealing to the impersonal and abstract moral principles of justice, women commonly emphasized the responsibility they felt to maintain and strengthen personal ties between people (Gilligan, 1977, 1982). She termed this ethical concern for sustaining personal relationships an 'ethic of care'. It is distinctive moral logic, as she noted:

> the logic of an ethic of care is a psychological logic of relationships, which contrasts with the formal logic of fairness that informs the justice approach . . . The ideal of care is thus an activity of relationships, of seeing and responding to need, taking care of the world by sustaining the web of connection so that no one is left alone. (Gilligan, 1982: 73)

The essential characteristic of the ethic of care, according to Gilligan, is its relational quality. This can be understood as a sense of responsibility for the well-being of others, a concern for specific human relations rather than abstract or rarefied principles. Following Piaget's work on the development of cognition in children, the process of moral development for Kohlberg and Gilligan was understood as developing out of a process of growth and maturation. Experience, teaching and self-development through confronting the challenges of moral problems draws out the child's capabilities for increasing complexity and maturity of moral reasoning. Yet in subsequent debate about these ideas, it is not the psychology of cognitive development that has driven interest in the concept of an ethic of care, but the implications that such a concept has for feminist moral and political theory. In the process, two issues have emerged as central to both the propositions developed and the controversies that have ensued: the link between care and gender and the link between an ethic of care and that of justice.

On both issues, Gilligan's original writings have lent themselves to the support of quite opposite conclusions. Gilligan sought to demonstrate the existence of an ethical perspective among females that differed from that of males, while arguing that such an orientation towards others is capable of being developed by both females and males and is therefore not inevitably linked to gender. She clearly asserted the link with gender in some passages of her work, while in others she noted that the association was not exclusive. Some girls, as many as a third of her qualitative sample of those seeking abortion counselling, for example, adopted justice-style arguments. There was also evidence that some boys adopted the relational approach she regarded as characteristic of care. Hence, she also argued that this gender link was present but not inevitable: 'Development for both sexes would therefore seem to entail an integration of rights and responsibilities through the discovery of the complementarity of these disparate views' (Gilligan, 1982: 100).

Even more emphatically, she argues elsewhere,

> The different voice I describe here is characterized not by gender but by theme. Its association with women is an empirical observation, and it is primarily through women's voices that I trace its development. But this association is not absolute, and the contrasts between male and female voices are presented here to highlight a distinction between two modes of thought and to focus a problem of interpretation rather than to represent a generalization about either sex. (Gilligan, 1982, cited in Tong, 1998: 164–5)

Is an ethic of care, which expresses a concern for the well-being of particular others, inferior to, or simply different from, an ethic of universal justice? On this question, too, Gilligan was equally insistent on identifying a caring voice, a moral language in which concern for others can be distinguished from codes of abstract principles, while not necessarily conforming to the sexual and moral dichotomy inherent in imposing a judgement about the relative superiority of one approach over the other. In her best known work, *In a Different Voice* (Gilligan, 1982: 174–5), it is clear she regarded an orientation to care as in no way inferior to that to justice, but simply different. Further, she suggested that fully developed moral persons will be able to draw on both approaches, or, as Tong (1998: 158) describes it, 'display a marked ability to speak the languages of care and justice equally well'. In subsequent work Gilligan (1986) went further, arguing that a disposition to put other people's well-being first is a sign of women's moral depth, not of any possible moral inferiority.

Natural Caring

There are no such doubts about either the link between care and gender or its ethical significance for Nel Noddings (1984, 2002), an educationalist and key advocate of the ethic of care as a feminine attribute and feminist standpoint. Noddings regarded care as a distinctive orientation amongst women, one that, like women generally, has long been suppressed and devalued. The mechanism whereby the link between women and care occurred, for Noddings, was not genetics, but experience:

> An ethic based on caring is, I think, characteristically and essentially feminine – which is not to say of course, that it can not be shared by men any more than we should care to say that traditional moral systems can not be embraced by women. But an ethic of care arises, I believe, out of our experience as women, just as the traditional logical approach to ethical problems arises more obviously out of masculine experience. (Noddings, 1984: 8)

Responding to the perceived needs of others, the care response, she argues, is an outcome of a woman's moral reasoning that is less a 'rational' response and more an 'emotional' response than that of men. When faced with a decision about care for her child, for example, a mother is likely to refer to her 'feelings, needs, impressions, and . . . sense of personal ideal', rather than an abstract set of impersonal principles. Her goal will be to identify as closely as possible with the child, so that the decision taken is, in effect, one compelled by the child, by the other needing care, rather than by herself (Tong, 1998: 159).

While Gilligan appears to have some doubts about whether an ethic of care is simply different from, or even equivalent to, an ethic of justice, Noddings expresses no such doubts. An ethic of care is ultimately better than that of justice, she argues, precisely because it is particular and personal. Human relationships, for Noddings, are not based on abstract sets of rights, but on the concrete and particular experiences of individuals and their needs. Nevertheless, she claims, there is a universal experience, which she terms natural caring, underpinning the development of care ethics: 'In situations where we act on behalf of the other because we want to, we are acting in accord with natural caring' (Noddings, 1984: 79).

Noddings argues that memories of caring are possessed by every child, including males. These memories, however, can wither, suggesting to Noddings the need for an ethical education and upbringing which will develop these natural impulses and memories, enabling a deliberately chosen response of ethical caring to replace and complement natural caring. The process of the accumulation of the memory of receiving care thus suggests the importance of further education, not just to reinforce but also to develop the natural inclination of humans towards care. By understanding an ethic of care as not just different from a concern for justice but in many ways as more fundamental and important, she sought to turn the existing value system on its head. In her more recent work, she has continued this line of reasoning, insisting on the achievement of greater recognition of the importance of care as a principle not just for education but for all social policy (Noddings, 2002).

Although her interpretation of the approach brings her into conflict with many other feminists, an important aspect of Noddings's propositions is her claim to advance feminism through recognition of the ethic of care. In the early 1980s, feminists generally understood advancement for women as requiring an escape from the obligations of domesticity, replacing what they saw as the burden of responsibility for care with opportunities for women to seek employment and participation in public life outside the home. For Noddings (1984), the achievement of social, economic and political recognition by women should not have to mean abandoning the ideals of care in order to embrace the supposedly male values of competition, individual achievement and impersonal principles of justice. Instead, she proposed embracing the ideals of an ethic of care, seeking acknowledgement and greater recognition of the virtues of care and caring activities. This would thus involve extending the values of women's traditional domestic lives into the public sphere – feminizing public life, rather than forcing women to act just like men.

Like Gilligan, Noddings's approach links the values of care to women. But she sought at the same time to embrace them as universal principles for an era of human history in which care was no longer to be confined to the home. The audience for this work, however, was predominantly other feminists. Rather than embracing her philosophy, many sought to dispute Noddings's claims about care as a feminine value, challenging also the way in which it was portrayed as an alternative to an ethics of justice.

Extending the Moral Domain of Care

Following the work of Gilligan and Noddings, a number of feminist writers sought to develop the approach of care as a necessary ethical response to the human condition, while seeking to avoid the problems inherent in seeing care as necessarily linked to the female gender and opposed to universalist principles of justice. In perhaps the most important single contribution to the debate, the American political scientist Joan Tronto (1993; Fisher and Tronto, 1990) embraced the ideals of care as an alternative way of understanding our responsibilities as people. In her book *Moral Boundaries* (Tronto 1993) she argued that the values of care had long been excluded from public moral discourse, but needed to be recognized as providing a necessary alternative set of principles for both public and private life.

While Tronto was strongly aware of the conventional links between gender and responsibility for care in the domestic sphere, her intention was to advocate for the adoption of an ethic of care as a guiding principle for public life, one that is not intended to locate care as a value that speaks for women only, but as a statement of principles capable of appealing to, and motivating, all. She therefore argued that its traditional ideological associations as a value system linking care to women, and in particular to the work of reproduction, nurturance and domesticity, need to be challenged. This must involve going beyond the limits of the moral boundaries inherent in existing political thought by adopting an ethic of care in moral and political philosophy, and working to have this adopted as a guiding principle for public life (Tronto, 1993).

While highlighting the positive qualities and potential of care, Tronto also identifies the ways in which care-giving as a practice has been marginalized and contained. Not only is care typically portrayed as an 'emotional' rather than a 'rational' activity, it has also traditionally been devalued by being contained in the private sphere and by its assignment to low-status workers. As she notes, 'Care has mainly been the work of slaves, servants and women in Western history' (Tronto, 1993: 113). This continues to be the case, she argues, with caring work devalued, underpaid and undertaken disproportionately by subordinate groups, including women.

Tronto's approach goes further, identifying much of the dark side of the concept of care, as well as setting out definitional elements that, she argues, must form part of an ethic of care. Care, she points out, is a site of conflict (Tronto, 1993: 109). As an illustration of this, she discusses how those giving direct care are often caught up in bureaucracies or decision-making hierarchies and forced to give care in ways that they might not personally choose. Conflict also arises when caring for another leads to the care-giver neglecting her own needs. One might expect, here, a closer examination of conflict between care-giver and recipient, but this is, at best, implicit. For Tronto and many other writers in this field, the practice of care is understood as an active but largely one-way process initiated by the carer. Her writing is largely a celebration and appreciation of women as care-givers, and she misses few chances to criticize males for leaving this work to them. As suggested in the previous chapter, the voice of those who depend on care is invoked in the fourth stage of her approach to care, which concerns receiving care. But this voice is not given clear expression in Tronto's discussion, as she focuses on promoting care as a sort of cele-bration of the values of altruism and concern in the long-suppressed private lives of women.

Tronto's approach to care as a system of public and private ethics is evident in the following very extensive definition of care she proposes:

> On the most general level, we suggest caring be viewed as a species activity that includes everything that we do to maintain, continue and repair our 'world' so that we can live in it as well as possible. That world includes our bodies, our selves, and our environment, all of which we seek to interweave in a complex, life-sustaining web. (Tronto, 1993: 103; Fisher and Tronto, 1990: 40)

This definition is an attempt to extend the concept of care well beyond the domains of personal support and intimate relationships with which it is commonly associated. It is ambitious and bold, staking a claim that extends the concept of care into almost all aspects of human existence, and perhaps much beyond that. The approach suggests not only a concern with the well-being of others, but a responsibility for the broader social and natural environment and for our place in it. Tronto's approach also builds deliberately on Gilligan's notions of connectedness and responsibility, drawing once again on her image of 'taking care of the world by sustaining the web of connection'. The impression one is left with on reading this and other similar passages in Tronto's work is one of care as an extension of interpersonal concern and responsibility. The moral elements of an ethic of care, for example, are identified as attentiveness, responsibility, competence and responsiveness. For the care to be 'good care', she argues, each of the four phases of the care process (caring *about*, taking care *of*, care-*giving*, and care-*receiving*), discussed in the previous chapter, must fit together as a whole, along with the four moral elements (Tronto, 1993: 127–37).

While care is undoubtedly an important part of life, is it right to extend an ethic of care as the leading principle for all of social life? Viewing care as 'a species activity that includes everything that we do to maintain, continue and repair our "world" ' presents a definition that, according to Sybylla, is

> so broad that it can be used opportunely to mean whatever is convenient ... it can be used to support many kinds of policy, from benevolent, paternalistic policies to utilitarian or fascist ones, for 'to maintain ... and repair' and to 'live as well as possible' can be interpreted in many, many ways. (Sybylla, 2001: 78)

If care is more narrowly defined, though, might it not once again be made invisible?

Are Justice and Care Compatible?

Following Gilligan's initial identification of differences between care and justice, the values of care were often regarded as opposed to those of justice, or at least radically different. Justice is portrayed in many of these discussions as an essentially masculine value involving the application of abstract and impersonal principles to the public world, while the ideals of care are seen as values deriving from the personal and private world of the home and family, capable of providing an alternative basis for a public as well as private morality. In this dichotomous way, care came to be seen as an essentially feminine perspective, emphasizing the ties between people rather than their autonomy. Table 3.1 summarizes the main points of difference seen between the criteria of care and justice in Gilligan's discussion of the issue (Crittenden, 2001).

Chris Crittenden (2001) argues that care can provide the basis for universal moral principles that in many ways are superior to the current assumptions that justice is based on principles of competitive individualism. She points out that it is harmful to reduce thinking to dualisms or dichotomous oppositional pairs (such as male/female, independent/dependent, universal/particular, justice/care). The prin-

Table 3.1 Comparing the propositions of an ethics of care and of justice

Care	Justice
1 A sense of self that is connected and relational	1 A sense of self that is autonomous and independent
2 Responsibility determines the extent of proper moral activity	2 Rights and principles determine the extent of proper moral activity
3 The intricacies of context make it hard to generalize from one situation to another, limiting the usefulness of moral laws and principles	3 General formulas or universal laws are more important than minor contextual differences for determining moral actions
4 Narrative and dialogue-based decision-making	4 Decision-making features formal or logical procedures, abstracted from context and tending to homogenize (e.g. pleasures become interchangeable)
5 The agent's moral vantage remains personalized, historically and temporally situated and affective	5 The agent assumes an impersonal moral vantage point that attempts to escape subjectivity
6 Moral motivation stems from the virtues of care (e.g. those concerned with maintaining relationships)	6 Moral motivation impelled by rationally imposed duty
7 An emphasis on eliminating oppression and the psychological mechanisms of oppression	7 An emphasis on fair distribution of social goods and services, fair allocation of rights, and the preservation of autonomy

Source: Based on Crittenden (2001).

ciples of care should be able to provide universal moral guidelines if it can be shown that they meet two essential tests. First, the principles of care must be able to provide moral guidance on important decisions, both at a personal or private level and in the public realm. Second, they must be capable of being developed as a set of abstract principles that could be employed for regulating public life. Both conditions, she demonstrates, can be fulfilled by an ethic of care. But the question remains – is justice compatible with, or an alternative to, care?

For a decade following Gilligan's original work, discussion of the ethic of care was hampered by an obsession with considering the difference between approaches to ethics based on care or justice. If care was understood as an alternative to justice, then adopting care as an ethical principle would be seen as competing with, and perhaps displacing, principles of justice. A major concern was the idea that care was considered to be based on an orientation towards particular people, while justice (that is, liberal concepts of justice) seeks to treat all people equally. Parents, for example, are likely to feel a greater responsibility to care for their own child than for others. Adopting ethical principles based on particularity and abandoning the universal standards of justice, critics asserted, would be a major step backwards that would be more likely to harm the interests of women than to advance their cause. By the 1990s, however, a growing tiredness with the debate was evident, leading to a new call to explore the common links between care and justice.

Tronto (1993), for example, argued that the dichotomy between care and justice was false and unhelpful. Care should not be unjust, nor justice uncaring. Seyla Benhabib similarly took issue with the perspectives of writers such as Kohlberg and Habermas, who, she claims, saw care as 'personal matters of self-realization' rather than as moral questions involving justice. Considerations of care are genuinely moral, she argued, but their ultimate justification as a public (rather than private) virtue 'rests on their being able to be validated or affirmed from an impartial perspective' (Benhabib, 1995).

This line of debate was one taken up by others who contested the claim that an ethic of care must inevitably conflict with ethical principles based on the ideals of justice (Dudeley, 1994; Clement, 1996). Based on an analysis of care as 'necessary labor', Bubeck (1995, 2002) developed the argument that justice and care are not opposed, but are principles that presuppose, and should be made capable of informing, each other. If social life requires the provision of care, she argued, care itself must be regarded as essential. Those who are responsible for providing it, however, have become vulnerable to exploitation as a result of their involvement in what she terms 'the circle of care', where providing care requires forgoing other opportunities. A theory of justice is required that can address the potential of care while preventing the exploitation of those who provide it. Both care and justice should therefore be regarded as essential and complementary principles.

Other writers on the subject also came to reject the supposed dichotomy between justice and care. Perhaps the most persuasive case is the argument that rather than the two sets of values being opposed, the ideals of justice are embedded in those of care (Kroeger-Mappes, 1994; Held, 1995). Developing this line of reasoning, Margaret Moore (1999) has recently shown that the abstracted principles of justice advocated by John Rawls, which conform to the Kantian ideals of universalism and objectivity, presuppose a process of moral development based on the experience of a sense of justice and fair treatment within families and social networks. She concludes,

> If, as this argument suggests, we learn to value ourselves by experiencing valued treatment from others, then justice and care are reciprocal. On this conception, the beliefs, values, and relationships that people care about and are committed to should be seen as integral to the development of just people and a just society. (Moore, 1999: 14)

In other words, liberal conceptions of justice depend in important ways on the pre-existence of supportive care.

Care and Social Capital

Parallel to the work of feminist scholars on the ethic of care, a notion of care as a civic virtue has also recently been developed by third-sector advocates concerned with fostering the institutions and practices of civil society (Wuthnow, 1993; Bellah, 1994). The approach is closely linked to the concept of social capital, initially proposed by Pierre Bourdieu (1986), but modified and popularized by the work of James Coleman (1988) and Robert Putnam (1993, 2000).

Robert Bellah, for example, argues for the development of a sense of social responsibility through participation in community associations that reach out and provide care for community members who need assistance. This, he argues, is necessary to counter the extreme individualism and selfish-minded commercialism of modern capitalism:

> The greatest threat to our lifeworld, to real community and to genuine practices of caring, comes not only from a state whose

power becomes too coercive ... but from market forces that become too coercive, that invade our private and group lives and tempt us to a shallow competitive individualism that undermines all our connections to other people. (Bellah, 1994: 26)

For Bellah, care needs to be understood as a civic virtue. The bottom line for this is the development of a sense of responsibility which he terms 'attentiveness', being mindful of one's own existence and the responsibilities for others that this brings (1994, see also Bellah et al., 1991). To restore attentiveness, a change is required at all levels of American society. At one level this requires the moral regeneration of individuals and family life; at another the rebuilding of local communities; and finally it is necessary to work to restructure national and international institutions in ways that will foster a sense of 'attentiveness', responsibility, belonging and hope. Restoring caring in America, he argues, requires a major shift in the organization of work and public policy, so that it will be possible to 'regain a balance between job and family' (Bellah, 1994: 31).

While Bellah's calls for political reforms, couched broadly, offer a similar critique of the public culture of American capitalism to those advocating an ethic of care, his appeal to the family and marriage marks the approach out from that of feminists. Bellah argues for greater emphasis to be placed on the development of caring practices in the family:

Despite romantic fantasies, marital love is not a narcotic that soothes all wounds. Attending to each other, expressing our deepest concerns and aspirations and listening to those of the other, are fundamental in a good marriage and crucial to the satisfaction it provides ... Attention is important between marriage partners, but it is fundamental for children. Infants who do not get attention, in the sense of psychic interaction and love, simply cannot survive, even if they are fed and clothed. And the quality of attention that children get has a great deal to do with how they turn out ... In short, I think, attentive homes breed attentive children. (Bellah, 1994: 30)

The nuclear family is seen as the crucible, an ever-renewable source of care. In this respect Bellah's views might be seen as close to those of Noddings (2002) who also argues that we learn care as a form of 'attentive love' at home through our engagement with the family, and that we need to extrapolate that to the larger social domain. Men as well as women in the nuclear family are enjoined by Bellah to be attentive, but the issue of gender does not receive further attention, despite the penalty that women have paid of limited opportunities for social participation as a result of assuming responsibility for the ongoing care of children and other family members. This silence on gender means that he is open to the accusation, levelled by feminists at various policy proposals, that assigning care to the family means leaving care to unpaid women.

By regarding the family as the nurturing basis of attentiveness and care, Bellah's arguments follow the same logic as the communitarian Robert Wuthnow (1993). Both authors understand the capacity to care as being generated by early experiences of care received within the family. One of the accusations against this approach, it will be recalled, was that the familial, gender-bound approach to care as a value system was based on a particularistic approach to care. For Wuthnow, this sense of care is generalized from the family to become a public practice, through the awakening of concern for unknown others in volunteer situations and through other forms of civic engagement. As he claims, 'Somewhere in the past they learned the importance of caring for others; as volunteers they are developing new ideas about kindness' (Wuthnow, 1993: 5).

Extending this line of thinking, Wilkinson and Bittman draw on Putnam's approach to social capital to explore further how it is that a 'civic model of care' might be possible. The concept of social capital, they argue, draws on his communitarian legacy, which sees ethical behaviour promoted as a sense of civic duty through experience of social connections, especially connections developed through participation in voluntary and philanthropic associations (Putnam, 2000: 116–33; Wilkinson and Bittman, 2003). The approach draws on Putman's argument that social capital represents a form of 'generalized reciprocity'. As Kittay also argues, this is a form of reciprocity in which there is no direct expectation of immediate payback, but an understanding that self-interest is served, over the longer term, by acting altruistically now. Collective interests are thus reconciled with self-interest. Putnam explains, 'The touchstone of social capital is the principle of generalized reciprocity – I'll do this for you now, without expecting anything immediately in return and perhaps without even knowing you, confident that down the road you or someone else will return the favor' (Putnam, 2000: 134).

This communitarian approach to the development of a civic ethic is helpful for understanding care in some ways, but problematic in other, important ways. It is helpful in its critique of the sort of selfish individualism advocated by neo-liberals, and in its pointing to the ways in which co-operation between individuals provides generalized social benefits such as trust and shared protection. However, the emphasis placed on the heterosexual nuclear family with its gendered division of labour as the prime site for care, and its failure to acknowledge the realities of dependency and the relations of power that surround it, marks it out as obscuring the exploitative reality that care has traditionally meant (Kittay, 2001). Because it incorporates these positions, the notion of 'civic virtue' promoted by communitarians, finally, is likely to provide for the sort of community in which men and women participate, but in which men's participation is often achieved at the expense of women and other care-givers and recipients.

Care, Power and Social Justice

Common to each of the different formulations of both an ethic of care and the concept of care as a civic virtue is the typification of care as a value system. Within this frame, care is portrayed primarily as a philosophical ideal or 'disposition', not as a social relationship or exchange between care-givers and recipients. Further, the accounts are typically presented in generalized and often highly abstract terms, with the absence of a more grounded, critical account of the daily realities of care conspicuously absent. The low social status accorded to caregivers is typically acknowledged, but, rather than this being understood as a core feature of care, the analysis offered focuses instead on the positive and altruistic motives that lie behind the giving of care. The approach, in short, is often self-righteous rather than analytical.

Gilligan, Noddings and Tronto had sought to address the question of women going public by seeing in care a distinct set of ethics, one that they argued was morally superior in important ways to the existing male values that dominated public life. The 'ethic of care' became an accepted formulation for bringing this ideal of caring into the world. Care, in this formulation, is an inspirational ideal, a positive value that its critics suggests presents a romantic and sugar-coated portrayal of the problems faced by women as they seek to achieve equality. This led many feminists to challenge the approach, seeing in care a set of values that would threaten rather than enhance the new opportunities women had of achieving justice and equality in a world that had until then told them to be satisfied with responsibility for care at home. Not surprisingly, critics of the approach identified the failure to clearly diagnose the often exploitative conditions experienced by care-givers as a significant shortcoming.

One of the most strident of these critics is Sarah Hoagland (1991), who focused her attack on the analysis of care advanced by Nel Noddings. Hoagland argued that by basing her approach to care on what she claimed was a natural relationship, that between mother and child, Noddings had produced a moral paradigm from an essentially unequal relationship that is meant to be transcended, not maintained. Such unequal relationships require the 'cared-for' to submit to and trust the care-giver, and are therefore ethically problematic. Hoagland challenged Noddings's assumption that it is morally permissible for the care-giver to control the relationship with the one cared for, arguing that the cared-for must remain the best judge of what is for his or her good. This led her to challenge Noddings's assertion that a care relationship is unequal owing to inequalities in ability. Rather, she claimed, inequalities in power underlie such a relationship. Paradoxically, such unequal relationships work against the care-giver as well as the cared-for because the relationship is not based on true reciprocity but simply on the 'receptivity' of the one cared for. A moral life, argued Hoagland, can not be limited to being responsive to the needs and wants of others (Hoagland, 1991).

A related criticism was advanced by the philosopher Bill Puka, who identified Gilligan's ethic of care as a 'sexist service orientation, prominent in the patriarchal socialization, social conventions and roles of many cultures' (Puka, 1993: 217). He suggests that the approach to care serves to 'rationalize' women's moral victimization under patriarchy, producing a form of slave mentality in which the victims justify their submissive position (see also Torpey, 1988). Puka therefore proposed an alternative and critical approach, in which taking responsibility for care was seen as a form of coping mechanism for women under patriarchy. When she is not properly acknowledged in her own right, a woman learns that she can exercise her strengths, interests and commitments within the male power structure by expressing her concern and responsibility for those who can not care for themselves, he argued. The values of care, according to Puka's 'care as liberation' interpretation, present its bearers with an opportunity for cognitive liberation within the structures of patriarchy, but they can not be a means of achieving personal liberation.

These critiques, alongside those discussed earlier, raise fundamental questions about the viability of such a broad concept of care, as a moral ideal, to provide an alternative set of principles by which to order public life. Instead of seeking to valorize the values of care and rejecting those of justice, the assessments suggest the need for an alternative approach that might link care with justice. Maintaining a strong feminist orientation, the recent account of care as dependency work developed by Kittay has attempted to address the issues in precisely this way.

Doulia: A Public Ethic of Dependency Work

In addition to her background in feminist moral and political philosophy, Eva Feder Kittay (1999, 2002) draws explicitly on her own experience as the mother of a 'profoundly dependent' daughter, and on other empirical research in a personally grounded and experiential way that distinguishes her account from those that are confined to theorizing based on reflection on abstract principles. Her approach places dependency and considerations of power in the relationship between care-givers and care recipients, and between both parties and their broader social context, at the centre of the analysis. In contrast to the approach of defining care as an all-encompassing orientation to the world, in Kittay's approach the concept of care is writ small, its scope confined to specific activities embedded in concrete relations between specific individuals.

Kittay wrestles with a different problem to that of other writers on the ethic of care. Or, more accurately, she frames the problem differently. Kittay sees in care, and in the ideals of equality inherent in the principles of justice, a more complex and gritty reality. The need for care and the difficulties experienced by women attaining the recognition and opportunities inherent in the liberal ideals of equality provide a tension field within which she seeks to find a resolution. She does this not by abandoning the standard of justice and replacing it with the values of care, but by acknowledging the problems and disadvantages faced by those responsible for the direct provision of care and seeking just redress. Her view of care, therefore, while far from negative, is markedly less romantic and idealized than that advanced by care advocates such as Gilligan, Noddings and Tronto.

The decidedly unromantic term 'dependency work' was chosen by Kittay to describe the task of attending to those who need care. This is a term chosen quite deliberately to emphasize that 'care of dependents is work . . . traditionally engaged in by women' (Kittay, 1999: 30). Avoiding the contentious terminology of care and caring, she identifies those who directly provide such care (whether paid or unpaid) as 'dependency workers'. Those whom they assist she terms the 'charges', a term suggestive of a degree of personal incapacity that requires another to take responsibility for providing the necessary support.

Dependency is thus a key term in Kittay's approach to care. She distinguishes two broad forms. First, dependency is a fundamental condition of human existence strongly linked to the human life course. It is a condition encountered in early childhood, illness, disability and frail old age, moments that she notes Martha Fineman has called the 'inevitable dependencies' (Fineman, 1995 cited in Kittay, 1999: 30). These moments are grounded in our biology, in the body as sociologists say. Secondly, dependency can also be socially constructed. The distinction between these two forms, as we shall see, is crucial for Kittay's analysis.

Kittay proceeds by identifying a paradigm form of dependency work which she then uses as an analytic device to explore its complexities. Following Martin, she defines dependency work as labour that, when well done, involves the three Cs: *care*, the tending of others in response to their vulnerability; *connection*, building intimacy and trust or sustaining ties between intimates; and *concern*, giving expression to the ties of affection that sustain the connection (Martin, 1989, cited in Kittay, 1999: 31). In the paradigm case, the well-being of the charge is the responsibility and primary focus of the dependency worker. Importantly, notes Kittay, while the worker has responsibility for the charge, the dependency relationship does not authorize the exercise of power unless it is for the charge's benefit.

Examining the nature of power within and surrounding the care relationship, Kittay makes the useful distinction between the inequality of power and the exertion of domination. Inequality of power, she notes, is prevalent in dependency relationships, but this does not inevitably involve domination. The care recipient is vulnerable, by virtue of her lack of capacity, to the abuse of power by the care-giver. The charge may also have power over the worker, arising, for example, from his or her social position, wealth or control of employment.

These sources of unequal power do not necessarily mean that abuse is inherent in the relationship, as the relationship is one that, ideally at least, is built on mutual trust and responsibility. Domination can occur when either the worker or the charge abuses this trust. Kittay notes,

> Domination is an illegitimate exercise of power. It is inherently unjust. The moral character of a dependency relation and its nature as a caring or uncaring relation is determined, at least in part, by how the parties in the dependency relation respond to one another, both with respect to the vulnerabilities of the dependent *and* to the vulnerabilities created for the dependency worker. Inequality of power is compatible with both justice and caring, if the relation does not become one of domination. That the relation be a caring one is largely the obligation of the dependency worker. That the relation not be one of domination is an obligation that equally befalls the dependency worker and the charge. (Kittay, 1999: 34; emphasis in original)

The vulnerability of the care recipient comes from her lack of physical or mental capacity. This does not provide an excuse for the worker to abuse or dominate the charge, and any attempt to do so is likely to meet with strong moral disapproval and possibly legal sanctions. The vulnerability of the worker arises for a large part from her readiness to assist, from her identification with the well-being of the charge and from her inability to express annoyance or vent frustrations in interacting with the vulnerable charge in ways that would normally be acceptable in human relationships between equals. The recipient of care may exert a 'certain tyranny' by advancing false needs, by making exaggerated demands on the worker or by 'exploiting the worker's concern and need for the connection forged through the relationship'. Kittay notes how a care recipient may 'graft the substance of another to one's own', thereby failing to recognize the integrity of the one who undertakes the work of caring. The special vulnerability of care-givers thus arises as a result of the ties formed through the recipient's dependence on her, through which she experiences her substance grafted on to the other (Kittay, 1999: 34–5). In such a case, the carer has effectively become overidentified with the charge and is unable to assert an autonomous sense of self.

The analysis of power and dependency in the dyadic relationship between dependency worker and charge is only one part of the picture. Equally important is Kittay's analysis of how women as dependency workers, as mothers, sisters, wives, nurses and care attendants, 'have been made vulnerable to poverty, abuse and secondary status . . . and often suffer psychological, sexual and other physical abuse as well as economic exploitation' as a result of taking on this work (Kittay, 1999: 40–1). In what amounts to a theory of gender, Kittay seeks to explain this situation as involving a second, socially created, level of dependency. Both the charge and the dependency worker are reliant on a third party, whom she calls 'the provider'. In a familial situation, the worker, as wife or mother, may be dependent on the male breadwinner and head of the household. In a welfare state, the worker may be an employee and the provider the state, just as, in other situations, the worker may be a domestic employee of the household, or a private employee in a care corporation or small business. Kittay notes,

> The social esteem and control over resources enjoyed by the best established professions ensure a large measure of autonomy to the professional whose work may well demand that they put the interests of another first. In the case of the dependency worker, the provider's control of resources combines with a general social devaluation of the work of dependency to thwart the possibility of a comparable autonomy for the dependency worker. To speak of this diminished autonomy is another way of speaking of the dependency worker's unequal relation to the provider. (Kittay, 1999: 45)

Dependency, for Kittay, arises in the first instance from a lack of physical or cognitive capacities for daily survival and maintenance. The dependency worker, committed to the well-being of her charge, experiences a secondary dependency as a result of her dependence on the provider.

Drawing together Rawls's concepts of social citizenship and the work of Amartya Sen concerning human capabilities, Kittay argues that if we lack the capability to care for ourselves and therefore need support, we should be able to receive it without those who provide the assistance being penalized. Recognition of the inevitability of dependence at some stage of each of our lives, and of the need for care of those who are dependent, must involve an acknowledgment of human interdependencies. Such a concept is not an assertion of interdependency as an alternative to or negation of dependency, but rather one based on the recognition of 'nested dependencies' which link those who need support with those who help them, and in turn link the helpers to a set of broader supports. She terms this a notion of *doulia*, from the Greek word for service: 'Just as we required care to survive and thrive, so we need to provide conditions that allow others – including those who do the work of caring – to receive the care they need to survive and thrive' (Kittay, 1999: 133).

The approach to care taken by Kittay must, therefore, be properly regarded as one based on a concern for issues of justice. Justice is not served if those who provide care to those who are dependent are penalized, either directly or indirectly. Her focus on the issue of mental retardation, in which dependency can not be dismissed as a social construction, a by-product of some social convention (such as the failure to provide wheelchair access to buildings) that can be readily reversed given the right sort of social intervention, helps highlight the need to place the management of dependency at the centre of concerns for justice. Thus, she argues, a conception of justice is required that goes beyond the liberal conception of equality which eschews dependency and relies on a notion of reciprocal recognition extended between reasonable and rational adults:

> Those who are dependent (at least when, and to what extent they are) cannot reciprocate the care that they receive. In our dependence, we cannot pay back our caregivers and compensate them for their labor. Another must do so. I have called this form of reciprocation *doulia*, after the doula, the contemporary postpartum caregiver who cares for the mother so that the mother can care for her new infant. I have called for a public conception of doulia, by which the larger society supports those who care for the 'inevitably dependent' (dependent because of age, infirmity or severe disability). I conceive of this as a principle of justice, in fact, a principle of justice that embraces those excluded by the contractual model of reciprocation. We need a principle of doulia for a caring that is justly compensated, and a justice that is caring. (Kittay, 2002: 270)

Her analysis makes issues of power central to an understanding of care, just as it makes an understanding of the need for and provision of care a basic consideration for understandings of human society. Kittay shows, too, how a recognition of the complex nature and character of power and dependency can be used to understand both the dynamics of interpersonal interaction between carer and recipient and the injustice of exploitation and dependency experienced by carers. The analysis suggests that it is the gender-based responsibility for providing care that affects women more generally.

There is a possibility of confusion, however, about the concept of care used by Kittay. In my view this arises, in part at least, from her effort to avoid the use of the sentimentalized term of 'care' and to substitute instead the rather awkward term 'dependency work'. This linguistic strategy can be understood as part of her attempt to avoid the word games into which social analysis often degenerates, or it can be understood, in turn, as a form of word game that Kittay sought to make her own. (See Chapter 2 for a discussion of such word games and the problems linked to defining 'care'.) I have already explored the complexity of the meaning of the word 'dependency' in Kittay's analysis. But the word 'work' is no less important. Kittay (1999: 30) indicates that she chose the word deliberately 'to emphasize that the care of dependents *is work*' (her emphasis) that shares characteristics with other forms of labour in which women have traditionally been engaged. Significantly, the analysis identifies features common to both paid and unpaid forms of dependency work. Rather than portraying maternal care as the model from which lessons about care should be derived and generalized, the deliberate search for elements common to both the paid and unpaid work of care mark Kittay's analysis out as providing a detailed conceptual analysis of the issues that need to be faced in post-industrial societies in which women are more likely no longer confined to the home, have, formally at least, achieved equality:

> Those who do dependency work, be it familial or paid, garner the satisfaction of doing a labor of love. They watch an infant flourish; they comfort a sick person; they return the loving care they received from a person who cares for them. They also become vulnerable to economic deprivation, lack of sleep, disruptions of their own intimate life, loss of leisure and career opportunities, and so on . . . In their labors, dependency workers subject themselves to work conditions which are among the most emotionally and morally demanding. These demands are constitutive of the labor itself.

> There are additional hardships not essential to the labor itself: when the efforts of the dependency worker are not reciprocated by others, when they do not receive adequate release time, adequate

compensation, emotional support, and when they are not provided the social and technical services a particular form of dependency requires. These are the result of social and political inequities. (Kittay, 1999: 183)

Kittay's approach to the need to recognize care as a public concern is thus built on quite different assumptions to those underpinning the work of Gilligan, Noddings or Tronto. Care is most definitely not thought of in sentimental or idealized terms, but as a form of necessary labour. Hence, when Kittay discusses her concept of *doulia* as the basis of a public ethic of care, she invokes a concept of justice – the fair treatment of those who provide care such that they might enjoy the same opportunities and rights as those who do not take on this responsibility – rather than seeking to replace public standards of justice with those assumed to be the values of care. Care, in this view, is not opposed to justice or able to provide better principles than those of justice. For justice for women to be realized, however, it must be remade to support rather than penalize the giving of care, whether this is socially configured as paid or unpaid work.

The work outlined in this chapter on the recognition of an ethic of care was undertaken almost entirely by American feminists. In common with approaches to care as a civic virtue, much of the emphasis in the approach bespeaks this national origin, one in which direct concerns for political programmes are relatively muted in favour of the deeper moral principles underlying the action of individuals and their society. The agent of care, in this view, is typically a women within a family. The frequent references to her characteristics and disposition as an individual care-giver are further suggestive of the emphasis on individual responsibility in contemporary American culture (Bellah et al., 1985).

In a globalized world, national borders no longer confine ideas, if indeed they have ever done so. Importantly, the approach of an ethic of care has been taken up by European writers (including Knijn and Kremer, 1997; Sevenhuijsen, 1998; Morris, 2001; Williams, 2001), who use the concept of an ethic of care to call for a more directly political programme than their American counterparts had initially envisaged. This approach, which involves such specific measures as guarantees of service provision and the constitutional recognition of rights to give and provide care, is discussed in the following chapter.

CHAPTER 4

Carers and Care Work. Social Policy Analysts on Care

The Canadian researcher on care and caring labour, Sheila Neysmith, observed that the debate about the ethic of care has been conducted in highly theoretical terms in ways that have mostly seemed quite separate from, even irrelevant to, the real-life politics involved in the restructuring of care work experienced in welfare services, in health care and in the home (Neysmith, 2000: 7). But there is an alternative approach to theories and research about care in which those involved have explicitly sought to be relevant, to engage with the issues faced by ordinary people in their daily lives, to advocate for policies and practical interventions that will improve the life of those who depend on care and those responsible for providing care. The applied approach, examined in this chapter, looks at care as an activity, a form of work or practice. The theoretical ideas produced are quite deliberately political and strategic, intended to be directly applicable to the struggles around social policy.

Within this broad perspective, different voices, social movements and political forces are engaged in an often passionate struggle, producing debates that, despite differences, express a shared concern with issues of social justice and the development of social policy and an acknowledgement that the concept of care has fundamental political–economic importance. There is, none the less, a dialogue between writers, policy analysts and activists. This sense of common purpose is reinforced by the fact that those involved are primarily, although by no means exclusively, from Britain and other European nations. Some of the most important discussions of care have occurred amongst UK authors who have focused, quite deliberately, on policy developments in that country. But in the globalized world of social policy, as in other fields of scholarship, debate is increasingly international.

As care policies were repeatedly restructured over recent decades, the social policy research agenda came to shape theory development. Subsequently, the concept of care advanced in this policy research has been dramatically transformed. Three distinct changes are evident: first, the concept has moved from care as a form of non-work to one in which the work of care is central; secondly, it has developed from being defined as a distinctly female activity to one that seeks to define care as gender-neutral; thirdly, care is no longer thought to be a uni-directional activity of helping another but rather a bi-directional, multi-stranded system of relationships. The recasting of what is understood as care, evident in the works examined in this chapter, is incomplete, and, I argue, is unlikely to be finally resolved by the production of a single unifying definition. Instead, as Carol Thomas (1993) has argued, there is a disturbing lack of enduring consensus about the meaning of the term. While care provides a workable empirical terrain for policy and social research, it lacks the ontological and definitional characteristics that make it possible to utilize it as a reliable measure of social achievement.

An Alternative Vision of Care

The emergence of care as a key policy concept in Britain, as in many other comparable countries, is strongly linked to the introduction of community care policies and to the critiques of institutional care that accompanied them. To the post-war reformers who sought to use the welfare state to improve the lot of ordinary working-class citizens, the continuing reliance in the 1950s and 1960s on the provision of residential care for old people, the mentally ill and people with a disability was an intolerable extension of the 'history of neglect' that these 'Cinderella services' represented (Means, Richards and Smith, 2003). An impressive body of empirical research emerged in Britain documenting the problems of institutional care that undermined its legitimacy and compelled humane governments to find an alternative form of provision. Russell Barton, for example, diagnosed the problems of institutionalization encountered in mental health facilities

(Barton, 1959), while Peter Townsend's famous study, *The Last Refuge*, reported on a four-year study of residential aged-care facilities, most of which had changed little from their pre-war days as workhouses (Townsend, 1962). Their depiction of the formal care provisions available continue to have a haunting quality:

> In the institution people live communally with a minimum of privacy, and yet their relationships with each other are slender. Many subsist in a kind of defensive shell of isolation . . . they are subtly oriented towards a system in which they submit to orderly routine, lack creative occupation and cannot exercise much self-determination . . . (the result is) a gradual process of depersonalization. (Townsend, 1962: 3)

Research from the American sociologist Erving Goffman and the French historian Michel Foucault (Goffman, 1968; Foucault, 1965), as well as other British research (Meacher, 1972; Miller and Gwynne, 1972; Jones and Fowles, 1984) extended the criticism of the care available in formal settings, supporting the call for alternative forms of provision that would be more humane. As services were expanding to address unmet need, policy-makers were also searching for more affordable programmes than the existing system of formal care provisions. Community care seemed to fit the bill. Pointing to studies of community life such as Townsend's early research on the family life of old people in the working-class London community of Bethnall Green (Townsend, 1963), a body of research and theory emerged that set out the case for an alternative form of care, based in the community.

According to Qureshi (1990), the distinction between formal and informal care was first introduced in the later part of the 1970s by the sociologist Philip Abrams (Abrams, 1978). Abrams was highly critical of orthodox political authority and control and sought a more participatory, communitarian alternative to the professional model of care available in total institutions. In the anti-professional spirit of the time, captured by the work of Ivan Illich's influential attack on medicalization and professional health care (Zola, 1972; Illich, 1975), he sought to contrast the dominating, uncaring approach of professional medicine and the apparatus of the British welfare state with the organic, long-neglected sociability of neighbourhoods and families. Informal care could be distinguished from formal services, according to Abrams, on the basis of the criteria of eligibility for service, and the personal quality of the relationship that underlies assistance provided by those at home. A further distinction was evident in the specification of the form of intervention, its intended purpose, and the tendency towards the formalization of rules that apply to the interaction. The anti-bureaucratic conclusions he reached were clearly expressed in the terminology he chose. If the terms 'amateur' and 'professional' had been used instead of 'informal' and 'formal', the implicit choice might have been very different.

The search for a care alternative was also reflected in a range of other work on care published in the 1970s. Drawing on earlier research from Denmark and Sweden, Wolf Wolfensberger, a Canadian researcher and activist, sought to introduce the concept of 'normalization' into policy to enable people who need ongoing care as a result of disability to 'establish and/or maintain personal behaviors and characteristics which are as culturally normative as possible' (Wolfensberger, 1972: 28). Similarly, Hattinga-Verschure, the Dutch hospital services researcher, wrote about the need to develop alternatives to the 'hegemony of professional care' which was based on the monopoly power vested in medical practitioners and nursing staff by the welfare state. To enable those who depend on care to realize their potential as individuals, he argued, it is necessary to minimize their subjugation to the impersonal and bureaucratic rules that govern professional care, and to promote self-care and informal care (*mantelzorg*) (Hattinga-Verschure, 1977, 1980).

The vision of care articulated by those seeking an alternative to residential institutions, therefore, was powerfully argued and well supported by detailed research into the problems of such facilities. Accounts of alternative provisions, however, lacked detailed specification. Instead, a rather glowing picture of domestic and community life was presented, in which 'care' was provided spontaneously, generously and selflessly by family members, friends, neighbours and others. The vision of care implied in these propositions was one of liberation for care dependants, an acknowledgement of their human rights and dignity. The irony that this approach was introduced at precisely the same time that women were seeking to exercise their human rights, by seeking their own liberation from the unpaid domestic roles to which they had been assigned, was, however, not lost on feminists.

Care as Women's Work at Home

The starting point for the feminist analysis of care and the work of carers in the 1970s and 1980s, as Carol Thomas points out, was the social identity of the carer, a status equated readily with the position of women in society (Thomas, 1993). According to this perspective, care could be broadly defined as women's social role – the normative set of responsibilities and expectations of women that focused on reproductive and family activities, effectively confining married women to the domestic sphere. As Hilary Graham (1983: 16) wrote, the practice of care is not just tied to the identity of females 'but with those private places where intimate relations with women are found. Specifically caring is associated with the home and family.' Three key elements stand out in this conceptualization of care: gender, family and unpaid work. Care was, by this definition, the unpaid family responsibility of women. It was distinguished from paid work because it was informal and unpaid, motivated by a sense of normative duty which invoked the higher callings of unselfish personal concern and responsibility for family, rather than personal gain. This understanding of care as women's home-making responsibilities drew not just on feminist theory but on government policy and the increasingly influential human rights movement linked to deinstitutionalization.

The term 'care' was effectively defined as a product of the tension field at the point that acts of government, especially the development of community care programmes, intersected with both feminism and other social movements. Policy-makers in the UK began to develop programmes of community care as early as the 1950s. As these were expanded in the 1960s and 1970s, policy documents justified the move by pointing to the loving care available at home, contrasting it with the impersonal treatment available in more traditional institutional facilities (Abrams, 1978; Titmuss, 1979; Dalley, 1988: Chapter 1). The British Department of Health and Social Services (DHSS), for example, argued, 'The primary sources of support and care for elderly people are informal and voluntary. These spring from the personal ties of kinship, friendship and neighbourhood' (DHSS, 1981, cited in Dalley, 1996: 6). (Propositions such as these were not, of course, unique to the UK, as comparable Swedish reports from the same period document (see, for example, Lagergren et al., 1984).)

The concept of 'care' presented in these policy documents is that of ongoing and unpaid personal help and support provided at home by family members. The home was presented as a warm, cosy and supportive environment. In an uncritical, gender-blind sort of way, women were not identified in policy-makers' portrayals of the home. Nor was women's work distinguished from that of men. Despite the narrowness of the conception, Graham (1991) argues that feminist writers on care policy in the 1980s such as herself and Janet Finch, (Finch and Groves, 1980; Graham, 1983) adopted the concepts of care that underpinned such policies and pragmatically incorporated them into their analyses as commonsense analytic tools, alongside other concepts such as the gendered division of domestic labour. Care thus came to be considered in the British literature as support provided at home, informally, by unpaid female relatives of the recipients. Graham (1983) famously labelled it a 'labour of love'.

A critical and enduring interest in care amongst feminist social policy academics in the UK arose initially as a concern for the unpaid work carried out by women within the family. In the 1970s, Ann Oakley's pioneering analysis of the sociology of housework stimulated already burgeoning interest in the previously neglected area of the treatment of women and their work in the home. This was soon extended as feminist activists and researchers sought to explore the position of women in relation to the family and the state (Oakley, 1974; Wilson, 1977; Land, 1978). 'Care', in this context, came to be the term used to refer to the domestic duties undertaken by married women. These duties included 'caring for their children, their elderly or sick relatives and, of course, their husbands' (Land, 1978: 360). The term 'care' referred not just to the nurturing of children or to the assistance provided to an elderly relative, but to the full range of home-making activities, especially the domestic support a wife provided her husband.

In an important development, Finch and Groves (1980) extended this critical feminist analysis to community care policy. Community care, they argued, meant unpaid care by women provided in the home. Because responsibility for this care prevented their participation in paid employment and imposed many other hardships, the costs were hidden but none the less very real and borne by women who devoted their lives to caring for others. From the perspective of feminists seeking the liberation of women from unpaid domestic duties, such unpaid care was seen not as a philosophical ideal but as a 'burden' of responsibility holding women back.

In the process of advancing the argument a translation had been made. The concept of care came to mean the support provided at home to those who were dependent as a result of illness, disability or frailty due to age. This accorded with the meaning in policy documents such as that from the DHSS cited earlier, and with the terms used by the National Council for Carers and their Elderly Dependants (NCCED) and the Association of Carers (AOC) (Barnes, 2001). Informed by this paradigm, much of the subsequent policy research focused on the so-called 'burden of care' borne by those women identified by the new terminology as 'carers'.

Empirical research subsequently documented the large number of hours devoted to providing hands-on care as well as the even greater amount of time that caring took in terms of providing supervision, company and simply being available. The research also reported the hidden 'costs of care' in terms of the social isolation and psychological distress involved, and the lost earnings and careers foregone as a result of the care of elderly or disabled relatives (Nissel and Bonnerjea, 1982; Glendinning, 1983; Baldwin, 1985; Wright, 1986; Ungerson, 1987; Lewis and Meredith, 1988; Glendinning, 1989). Nor was this work restricted to Britain. Elaine Brody (1981) in the USA, for example, contributed to and extended the debate by drawing attention to the difficulties faced by women 'in the middle', providing care in their middle years simultaneously to both parents and children. Researchers in Australia, Canada, New Zealand and elsewhere subsequently documented similar patterns of women's care (Aronson, 1992; Briar, Munford and Nash, 1992; Watson and Mears, 1995; Baines, Evans and Neysmith, 1998; Watson and Mears, 1999). Defining care in this way led to a significant and impressive research effort, with a particular focus being the documentation of the long-neglected problems experienced by unpaid carers in the home (Pitkeathley, 1989; Parker, 1990b; Twigg, Atkin and Perring, 1990; Twigg and Atkin, 1994). Policy measures followed, however slowly and inadequately, in the UK and in other countries, such as Australia, Canada, New Zealand, Ireland and the Netherlands, where this approach was also influential.

Care Work and the New Social Divisions of Care

Despite these impressive practical outcomes, the definition of care as unpaid women's work in the home effectively obscured other forms of care and other groups of care-givers. Men were one significant group of domestic care-givers obscured by the definition, as analyses of national survey data soon found. While women predominated amongst family carers, British data from national census collections and other sources consistently identified a substantial group of male care-givers who constituted around a quarter to a third of all care-givers for frail older people and people with disabilities (Arber and Gilbert, 1989; Qureshi and Walker, 1989; Arber and Ginn, 1990). Where data sources permitted, similar findings were reported from comparable countries (Rossiter, Kinnear and Graycar, 1983; Chappell, 1985; ABS, 1990; Chappell, 1991).

Although men are under-represented as unpaid carers of children or parents, the male spouses and partners of older women are relatively prominent in community care (Orme, 2001). According to Michael Hirst's analysis of recent trends in informal care-giving, the extent of care-giving by men increased through the 1990s, while that of women declined, so that by 1998 in the UK men were proportionally as likely as women to provide care for a spouse (Hirst, 2001). Comparable Australian data also shows the proportion of male carers increasing with age. Males constituted 21 per cent of 'primary carers' aged 15–44, 32 per cent of those aged 45–64, and 35 per cent of those aged over 65. Thus, while women predominate amongst informal carers, men are not an insignificant group of carers at any age, while the proportion of men reporting caring responsibilities above the age of 65 is higher than amongst women (ABS, 1999a). At different ages, primary carers were more likely to be caring for a particular member of their family. Those aged 15–34 years were most likely to be a parent of a child (35 per cent), while those aged 35–64 years were most likely to be caring for their partner (36 per cent). Three-quarters of primary carers aged 65 years and over were caring for their partner.

Another important exclusion involved private, paid care-givers. Hilary Graham (1991) argued convincingly, from a social justice standpoint, that by confining the definition of carers to the performance of unpaid care, paid domestic staff (including maids, personal care assistants, nannies and private nurses), had been excluded from research and policy. By identifying private domestic staff from working-class backgrounds and ethnic or racial minorities as carers, Graham criticized the narrow definition of care that she and others had used, arguing that the approaches employed until then had been based too much on the experience of white, middle-class women and had failed to take account of social class and racial divisions. Graham's new definition went beyond the idea of care as an unpaid personal devotion, but continued to see it as an activity confined to the private domain of the home, strongly linked to women.

A more extensive critique of the definition of care as unpaid domestic work concerned the exclusion of paid staff and formal services. In Britain, Roy Parker (1981) had argued that it was necessary to regard care as a form of work and that there was no reason to restrict 'tending' to the format of reproductive activities undertaken within the family, nor to define it by gender. To draw attention to the physical work involved, the activity he termed 'tending' (as in 'care attendant') he claimed could be carried out by any person who provided such assistance – nurses, care attendants, housekeepers, child-care assistants and other formal staff, as well as family members, friends or neighbours. Parker recognized the sexual division of labour involved in tending, but this was not, in his formulation, an essential or defining characteristic.

Although it was used rhetorically by some authors, Parker's term 'tending' did not catch on at the policy level. Nonetheless, recognition of the importance of paid care work followed, and the common dimensions of paid and unpaid care were increasingly brought into focus in much of the work that followed in Britain and elsewhere (Lewis, 1989; Glazer, 1990; James, 1992b). One of the most influential of writers to have followed this path is Clare Ungerson, whose work I follow here for its rich insights into care and as an example of the development in theories of care taken by a range of contributors to the debates. (This work could be said to parallel a shift in the perspective of other UK researchers, such as Janet Finch: see Finch, 1989; Finch and Mason, 1990, 1993.)

In 1990, Ungerson noted the rather narrow definition of care prevalent amongst British researchers, which she contrasted with that used by Scandinavian colleagues. Her discussion of the problems encountered by British feminists seeking to confine the concept of care to the domestic sphere remains insightful:

> Both policy-makers, commentators on caring and even feminists, then, find themselves dealing with a central problem in the use of the word 'care'. The contemporary assumption is that the chief locus of love is the domestic hearth. Thus the location of the tasks of 'caring' within the domestic domain in itself means 'caring' as an

activity is also assumed to constitute a set of feelings between people which are appropriate to the private, rather than the public, sphere . . . It is then an easy step not only to presume that such care, based on affection, is qualitatively different from the rationality-based 'formal' care but, because of the loving feelings contained within it, it is *better* care. (Ungerson, 1990: 10–11)

Ungerson called for a rejection of this narrow conception and for the abolition of the 'false dichotomy' between formal and informal care. The distinction had in any case become increasingly difficult to sustain, she argued, not just in recognition of the case of paid domestic assistants, as Graham (1991) had suggested, but in response to new developments in policy that were blurring the previously sharp demarcation between family and paid sources of care.

The formal/informal distinction had already been critiqued strongly in the Scandinavian literature, observed Ungerson (1990). Kari Waerness, for example, had previously proposed a very different taxonomy of care based on the distinction she made between *care-giving work* and *care*, that identified not two but three basic forms of care:

1. *Caring for dependents.* This involves care-giving work, in which the recipient, through incapacity related to age or other causes, is incapable of self-care and is in a position of dependency and possibly helplessness in relation to the carer. This kind of relationship can be found in both formal and informal care, in public and private settings.
2. *Caring for superiors.* This may take the form of personal service care work, such as provided by a maid in domestic service. It is characterized by an unequal relationship in which the care recipient is more powerful than or superior in status to the care-giver.
3. *Caring in symmetrical relationships.* This kind of care work takes the form of balanced reciprocity, a give-and-take most commonly connected to relations of kinship and friendship which the participants might describe as 'caring for each other'. This has the potential quality of mutuality and balance, as between supportive partners. (Waerness, 1984, 1989)

Waerness's term 'care-giving work' referred to the activities carried out to provide support. 'Care', in contrast, was understood as involving a mental disposition, an attitude of concern and affection for the other.

To care in this second sense, she suggested, normally requires opportunities for the development of a personal relation between the giver and recipient of the support. Hence for Waerness, whether care-giving work actually involves care is a matter that would require investigation in any situation, whether assistance provided is paid or unpaid. One of the key implications of her approach is that the actual quality of the personal relationship should not be seen as predetermined by its form. Waerness's approach helped demonstrate that care at home may be less caring than is often portrayed, while that provided through other relationships may be imbued with a quality of personal affection obscured by the term 'formal'.

Drawing on the work of Waerness (1984, 1989), Leira (1990) and others, Ungerson was keen to show that it is simplistic to assert dichotomous differences between formal and informal support and implausible to assume that care is a characteristic that can be considered the monopoly of just one particular set of relations, the informal sphere which classifies family, neighbourhoods and community networks together. But did this mean that the concepts of formal and informal should be thrown out altogether?

While the policy debate was framed in ways that suggested formal and informal care were alternatives, others explored the relationship in more sophisticated ways. In the USA the sociologist Eugene Litwak contrasted the organizational characteristics of formal services with those of families and other primary social groups (Litwak, 1985), suggesting that rather than being alternatives, formal and informal sources of care are complementary. Formal services, which typically function as bureaucratic organizations, are well suited to undertaking specific, technically defined care tasks, such as nursing, that involve therapeutic interventions or require professional or technical expertise, he argued. Family members are considered unlikely to be displaced by such formal services as the main care-givers because their organizational characteristics enable them to offer forms of support, including emotional support, supervision and company, that formal services simply cannot provide. Litwak's approach has been used to suggest ways in which the division of responsibility between family and formal services can be incorporated into the design of community care programmes (Kendig, 1986; Whitaker, 1986). The nature and extent of complementarity between formal and informal care has also been tested by Neena Chappell and others (Chappell, 1985, 1991; Chappell and Blandford, 1991). The results of such empirical research confirmed the importance of formal services to assist and support care given by family members at home. Formal services, argued Chappell, neither replace such informal family care nor add to the burden of family carers. Informal care is not an alternative to the formal. In advanced societies, each is necessary.

A related approach, the 'hierarchical compensation model', was advanced by Marjorie Cantor (Cantor, 1979; Cantor and Little, 1985; Cantor, 1989) to explain the pattern of service use and the contribution of informal care-givers. Her approach emphasizes the social psychology of help-seeking by care recipients and their social networks, rather than the structural characteristics of the social group that provides care. Rather than rely on assistance provided by another, according to Cantor, most older people referred to community care prefer to maintain their independence. To sustain this, when care is required, people choose assistance provided by close family members or others with whom they have intimate and longer-term relationships over the support available from formal services. Help provided by spouses or partners (female or male, as available) is the most preferred, then that by daughters, sons and other family members (in that order of preference) over that provided by formal services. The model suggests that help is likely to be sought from formal services only when informal care-givers prove inadequate or need supplementation. The approach was found to explain community care use in the UK (Qureshi and Walker, 1989) amongst a sample of older people. Where help from spouses was available, that was most preferred, with the help from female or male depending on availability. But when this was not available or was inadequate, assistance from daughters was more prevalent than that from sons. Not all participants in the study had daughters who were able to help, however, and in these cases male offspring were likely to be involved.

Importantly, the model of formal and informal care suggests that the two forms of care are quite distinct. Yet empirical research suggests that the links between formal and informal care are more important than divisions between them, with the result that a hybrid form of care is now increasingly common, as research in Australian studies of community care amongst older people has shown (Fine and Thomson, 1995, 1997; Fine, 1999a). Research by Canadians Catherine Ward-Griffen and Victor Marshall (2003) also points to the importance of seeing family care and paid care as 'interconnected'. A detailed study of home nursing noted the 'bi-directional movement of the caring work between the public and private spheres' in which a process of work transfer between lay carers and professionals took place (Ward-Griffin and Marshall, 2003). Such hybrid forms of care, in which both paid and unpaid carers are engaged, negotiating and renegotiating boundaries and shared responsibilities in their work, suggest the importance of an understanding of care that does not assert a fundamental incompatibility or rigid task division between the two forms (Fine, 1994).

Rather than setting out a natural law, any hierarchy of preferences must be regarded as contingent, depending on the context set by the care recipient, the structure of their intimate relationships and the availability of services. Among disabled people, for example, the findings of a preference for care by close family members applicable to older people are not confirmed. One study which explored service use amongst recently disabled people living in Australia, New Zealand, the US and the UK, found that those who had access to paid personal assistants reported that they felt more comfortable and in control of their lives, while those who relied on family and informal care experienced a much higher degree of shame and frustration (Galvin, 2004). Access to formal services in this case enables the person reliant on care to develop a sense of independence and autonomy that is not possible where it is necessary to be ever dependent on and grateful to a mother, partner, child or other available family member.

Care as the Production of Welfare

In the final decades of the twentieth century, developments in policy and the market meant that the conceptualization of care needed to extend beyond the dichotomy of formal and informal forms raised by Abrams in the 1970s. By the mid-1990s research on care increasingly sought to address the new mix of provisions that arose at the point of intersection between cash vouchers, families, public services, voluntary and private services and the market. Understanding what influenced consumers to choose care from one or other of the sources available became a key focus of the new research in the field that Ungerson and her colleague John Baldock termed the 'social care mix'. (Baldock and Ungerson, 1994, 1996). Like the approach of Cantor discussed above, their research addressed the preferences, 'norms' and 'intermediate values' that might influence the choices of those who needed care. In one study looking at the care used by stroke survivors, they suggested that rather than there being a single hierarchy of preferences, a more complex decision-making matrix was evident which they sought to describe along two key axes: one measuring the degree to which a person sought individualized forms of care or sought help from some kind of collective provision; the other measuring the extent of participation in decision-making sought by consumers (see Figure 4.1).

Research on care has also needed to address the variety of service innovations and hybrid forms of support, such as payments for caregiving (Ungerson, 1997), that resulted from marketization and quasi-market reforms introduced in Europe and North America in the 1990s (Evers, 1994; Pijl, 1994; Wilson, 1994; Feinberg and Ellano, 2000; Glendinning et al., 2000). Along with other researchers, Ungerson has also been increasingly concerned with women responsible for providing paid care (James, 1992; Aronson and Neysmith, 1996; Ungerson, 2000), pointing to the way that the costs of paid care have been brought down through privatizing services and expanding competition

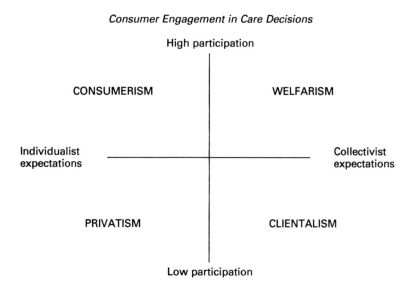

Source: Baldock and Ungerson (1996: 181).

Figure 4.1   Modes of participation in the market for care

between providers, reducing the job security and wages paid to the female staff, an increasingly large proportion of whom are paid as casual, part-time workers, unable to save for their own future care needs. As Ungerson's ongoing research shows, economic concepts and analyses, once sharply excluded from the analysis of care, are increasingly understood as necessary tools for this research (Ungerson, 2003, 2004). In the context of ongoing economic restructuring and the propensity for the demand for care services to outstrip supply, an understanding of economic perspectives on the funding of services, both public and private, has proven vital for any analysis of policy developments in the field of care. Increasingly, an understanding of the economic dimensions of care has been incorporated into its very conceptualization.

Although there is a plethora of work by health economists and others on the finance of health care and welfare, few if any economists had written systematically about unpaid work or care until the 1980s (Gardiner, 1997; Jenkins, 2001). As Nancy Folbre has argued, the lack of interest in activities outside the market has served to reinforce the marginal position which care is seen to have in national affairs (Folbre, 2001a, 2001b). At a macro level, a review of economic perspectives on care includes attention to political economic analyses of the place of services in the new post-industrial economic order (Iversen and Wren, 1998; Esping-Andersen, 1999). Macro-economic analyses have also been used to justify the expansion of care services, as occurred, for example, with an important study commissioned by the Australian government (Anstie, 1988) which showed that public revenue from tax paid by women dependent on formal child care for their jobs far exceeded the government subsidies on child care which enabled them to take up employment (Brennan, 1998). Following the pioneering work of Sally Baldwin and Caroline Glendinning in the 1980s on the costs of care in terms of both the income foregone and the expenses incurred in providing unpaid care (Baldwin, 1985; Glendinning, 1989), there have also been an increasing number of studies attempting to cost the value of informal care and the contribution it makes to national economies (Parker, 1990a; Clifford, 1992; Mutschler, 1993; Smith and Longino, 1994; Moore, Zhu and Clipp, 2001). In line with Folbre's injunction to make the accounting of informal care visible, time-use data and an understanding of the time involved in caring-use data has also become increasingly important (Land, 1991; Bittman and Thomson, 2000; Bittman et al., 2003; Folbre and Bittman, 2004).

Attempting to use the tools of micro-economics to cost services and to develop innovative new approaches to meeting human needs, Bleddyn Davies and colleagues including Martin Knapp and David Challis from the Personal Social Services Research Unit (PSSRU) at the University of Kent drew on the concept of a production process. This was a model they borrowed from industrial economics and applied to the field of human services. The result is a theoretical framework they termed 'the production of welfare' model, widely used today as a research tool in the design of large-scale evaluations and research studies.

The economic and social theory underpinning the approach were spelt out in an early publication concerned with care in residential institutions (Davies and Knapp, 1980). Davies and his colleague Martin Knapp proposed an approach to care and human services that broke the care-giving process into a series of analytically distinct stages, as set out in Figure 4.2. The essence of the production of welfare approach is the identification of three distinct points in the provision of services – inputs, outputs and outcomes – that enable

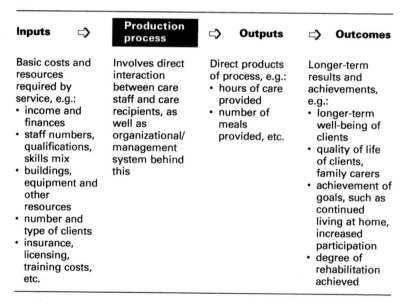

Figure 4.2   A schematic overview of the production of welfare approach

services of different sorts with qualitatively different ways of working to be accurately compared using quantitative measures. The approach also provided an economic cost function analysis that helped conceptualize care as a form of productive work and enabled it to be systematically compared with other forms of employment.

A key achievement of the approach was the introduction of a wide range of non-economic concepts and measures, such as measures of client happiness and well-being, physical function and the need for help amongst clients, into an economic analytic framework. Using these concepts, a series of groundbreaking studies and evaluations of service provision for older people were conducted. Perhaps the best known of these is the Thanet case management project established in Kent. Using a quasi-experimental design with a matched control group, 74 frail, elderly individuals, who would otherwise have been placed in residential care, were supported at home, receiving an individualized package of case-managed social services (Davies and Challis, 1986). Results after a year, and later after two, three and four years (Chesterman, Challis and Davies, 1987) showed conclusively that the lives of those in the intervention group were considerably enhanced in comparison with those in the control group. The intervention, which delayed institutionalization for about two years for most and prevented it for others, did not, however, come cheaply, as the cost of supporting those at home, including medical care costs, was approximately the same as for those in the control group, most of whom had been provided with residential care during the course of the study. Subsequently, this approach was applied to a range of other interventions (Davies et al., 1990) including large-scale analysis of community-based home care interventions (Davies, 1994).

What is of most importance here is the conceptualization of care as a process of production, involving a number of conceptually distinct phases or components. Although clearly absent from formulations of care in feminist-inspired research in the early 1980s, within twenty years many of these concepts had become so familiar to all researchers, through their application to policy, that they became central to the ways of thinking about care in terms of policy. The gradual infiltration of micro-economic analyses into the literature and research on care is also indicative of a deeper transformation in the way that care is understood. From a policy perspective, it is clear that it is no longer desirable to consider the importance of care to be self-evident. Nor is it tenable to consider it as an altruistic act that is above the market, morally superior to economic transactions. As care has been increasingly understood as a form of work, it has needed to be valued and analysed in ways comparable to other forms of work.

The Disability Critique

A significant voice in the British and international policy debate about care since the early 1990s has been that of disability advocates who have argued that in drawing attention to the 'burden of care', feminists and others had assumed the passive dependency of the recipient, excluding them from the debate and aggravating their dependent position in policy. Care had come to be seen as a one-way process in which concern is shown for the plight of carers while the recipients of assistance have been portrayed solely as a burden.

Recognizing that feminism has emancipation as its basic value and had therefore sought to lift the cloak of 'invisibility' from women carers, disability activists such as Jenny Morris and Lois Keith attempted to extend the strategy, calling for recognition and empowerment of the recipients of care (Morris, 1993a and b, 1994, 1996; Keith, 1992; Keith and Morris, 1996). Drawing on principles articulated as part of the 'social model of disability' (Oliver, 1990; Barnes, 1998) as well as those of feminism, Morris argued that the problems with the then-prevailing feminist conceptions of care can be traced to a failure to examine the factors which underlie the need for assistance in the first place:

> By taking the need for care for granted and by assuming the dependency of older and disabled people, feminist research and carers as a pressure group have not only failed to address the interests of older and disabled people but they have, unwittingly, colluded with both the creation of dependency and the state's reluctance to tackle the social and economic factors which disable people. In doing so they have failed to challenge either the poverty of older and disabled people, or the discrimination and the social prejudice which characterizes their interaction with individuals and social institutions. (Morris, 1993a: 49)

Morris went further, calling also for a recognition of the complexity of care-giving. As a mother, responsible for the care of her own children, she sought recognition of the fact that 'disabled women' are not just recipients of care, but are care-givers in their own right. In the process, she chastised feminists such as Clare Ungerson, whom she accused of portraying care recipients purely as a burden:

> This separating out of disabled and older women from the category 'women', comes about because these feminist researchers fail to identify with the subjective experience of 'such people'. The principle of 'the personal is political' is applied to carers but not to the cared for ... Ungerson's failure to identify with those who need care is then carried over into her feminist analysis while she considers only one part of the caring relationship. Yet again disabled and older women are marginalised – but this time by those who proclaim their commitment to 'women-centred issues'. (Morris, 1993b: 157)

Other writers from a disability perspective have been even harsher in their criticism of the focus on the plight of care-givers in policy debates about care:

> The discovery of the 'carer' in the late capitalist welfare state has sharpened the contradictions imposed by the approach to families of welfare state policies. Constructing the category carer and developing policies in respect of this group has neither enabled disabled people to become independent nor freed other family members from their 'caring' duties. In fact, apart from inventing a new word and giving employment to yet more welfare professionals and opportunistic voluntary organizations, nothing much has changed and the contradictions of family life remain. (Oliver and Barnes, 1998: 8)

These critiques of the feminist concepts of care confront the tendencies towards self-righteousness that at times seem pervasive in the care literature. They also remind us that care is not simply an act of giving, undertaken by those who assume responsibility. Rather, care involves transactions between two or more people and can not be understood simply from the perspective of the giver of care alone. By calling for a voice for those reliant on support and for deeper attention to the factors underlying what they see as the social construction of disability and dependency, disability activists draw attention to what they see as the social causes underlying the need for care. In doing so, they seek the implementation of policies and approaches to care, such as attendant care schemes, which tackle the causes of their dependency on others and provide recipients with funds and resources they lack, which will provide them with control and agency.

The social model of disability, as Corker and Shakespeare (2002) point out, has its roots in historical materialism and incorporates many elements of a modern socialist critique of capitalist society. The model makes a conceptual distinction between impairment (a bodily deficit) and disability (a socially constructed limitation) in a manner similar to the feminist distinction between sex and gender. Disability is seen as social, constructed on the basis of impairment, placing 'the explanation of its changing character in the social and economic structure and culture of the society in which it is found' (Corker and Shakespeare, 2002: 3). Clearly, this suggests a number of useful ways in which the need for care can be reduced. At a practical level this can be achieved by the appropriate use of technology and the principles of good design, for example by making buildings wheelchair-accessible and removing the need for a wheelchair-bound person to rely on carers to provide access. Other social causes, such as discrimination in employment, may also be removed through legislation or other provisions. Providing those reliant on care with access to sufficient resources may also place them in the position of being in charge of the labour required for their ongoing care. More radical solutions for dealing with social causes of dependency and exclusion can also be imagined. But problems remain which the social model alone can not deal with. Not surprisingly, some writers from within the disability movement have called recently for a recognition of the lived reality of the body and of embodied determinants of physical or mental incapacity (Crow, 1996; Morris, 2001; Price and Shildrick, 2002; Thomas and Corker, 2002).

Despite these critiques of the way that care has been conceived and constructed, recognizing the validity of the disability critique does not require abolishing the concept of care (Fine and Glendinning, 2005). However, it is clear that if care is conceptualized primarily in a way that is designed to draw attention to the oppression of women, it can not provide a model for future social solidarity or for a wider form of social emancipation (Parker and Clarke, 2002).

Some idea of what such a more inclusive approach might involve is evident in recent writings that seek to incorporate the perspectives of those reliant on care. As Margaret Lloyd argues, caring is an activity that disabled women themselves can do and like to do, even as they demonstrate that the capacity to provide physical care need not be equated with the capacity to take responsibility for care (Lloyd, 2001). Rather than seeing care as the sole responsibility of the carer, this emergent approach stresses the view that caring needs to be understood as a 'widespread activity in which we are all implicated', with a need to 'balance the rights of both people in the caring relationship' (Lloyd, 2000: 148). In calling for more attention to care as a 'relationship-based' activity, Henderson and Forbat (2002) similarly seek not just to incorporate the views of care recipients and service users in care policy, but call for an open acknowledgement of the conflict often involved in care policy and transactions.

Care as a Citizenship Issue

As the survey of policy approaches to care presented above makes clear, attempts to define care tightly in a rigid and definitive manner have, at best, proven elusive. Beneath the shifting definitions, however, is a suggestion that the concept has an intuitive and enduring appeal as an inspirational and political ideal. Drawing together the key strands of the social policy approaches outlined in this chapter and the ethics-of-care approach considered in the previous one, a new conceptualization of care has recently been proposed. According to this approach, as Knijn and Kremer (1997) argue, care needs to be understood not as a women's issue but as an issue of 'inclusive citizenship'. The core of the approach, the two Dutch authors emphasize, is a recognition of the right of each citizen to be able to give and to receive care:

> At some point within a citizen's life, people have to care for young children, and at other times close friends or elderly parents need personal care. Such demands of 'significant others' can nowadays only be fulfilled at the cost of what is perceived as the most vital aspect of social citizenship: labor participation. Hence, caregiving leads to a reduction in citizenship status. Rather than focusing on labor-participation alone, we argue for a reconceptualization of citizenship which acknowledges that every citizen will be a caregiver sometime in their life: all human beings were dependent on

care when they were young, and will need care when they are ill, handicapped, or frail and old. Care is thus not a women's issue but a citizenship issue. (Knijn and Kremer, 1997: 332)

This approach serves to emphasize the links between unpaid giving of care and paid labour in ways that enable the debate on care to engage with those taking place about the restructuring of employment and the economy. Care should no longer be seen as a form of work comparable to, and often performed as, employment. The approach serves to make care a concept of central importance for contemporary welfare states.

The Dutch political theorist, Selma Sevenhuijsen, similarly draws out the practical and political implications of care as a political demand. As it is no longer acceptable to regard women as the domestic dependants of men confined to the home, she argues, there is a need for a public ethic of care. Although traditional gender roles have made it seem that way, care and the adoption of a caring approach to life, should not be seen as a role or capability exclusive to women. Drawing upon the work of Tronto and others, Sevenhuijsen argues that care is fundamentally 'a relational activity' and a person's feelings about themselves and about their connections to others must be central. This is especially so when caring involves intimacy and closeness to strangers or when the care-giver's own well-being is threatened. However, the particularity of care should not be seen as diminishing its ethical significance. Moral questions need to be faced, for example when providing care involves threats to or exploitation of the care-givers, when resources to support care are inadequate, or when there are situations involving inequalities, dependence or significant differences in access to power between the recipient and the giver of care (Sevenhuijsen, 1993: 142).

In arguing for the incorporation of an ethic of care as a principle of modern citizenship, Sevenhuijsen (1998) also explores ways in which care can also be seen as providing a more universalistic set of ethical principles for public life. The public recognition of a democratic ethics of care, she claims, should complement principles of justice (which tend to be framed in terms of individual rights) and add a significant additional ethical dimension to advanced modern societies. Hence, in addressing the limited notions of 'care and protection' in Giddens's (1998) proposal for a social investment state as part of 'third way' politics, she argues,

We are living in a period of change that could perhaps best be characterized as a transition from modernist forms of care politics,
based on familial care, to a politics that is better attuned to postmodern caring practices situated in different social domains and in
a diversity of lifestyles. A notion of 'philosophical conservatism' [for
example, by legally enforcing familial responsibility for care] does
not suit this situation since it frames these politics too much in a
backward looking way. It would be better to question how social
policies can adapt to 'postmodern kinship practices' and to the need
for caring to be integrated into democratic agency at different loca-
tions. This provides a solid starting point for further substantiating
the notion of caring as a democratic practice. (Sevenhuijsen, 2000:
30)

Sevenhuijsen points out that while Giddens advocates a political
programme that would balance citizens' 'rights' with 'responsibilities',
he has missed the political message of feminist theories of labour and
care in democratic societies. This, she argues, is that 'as many individuals as possible should have the opportunity to combine paid work and
informal care in their life course' because 'caring should be valued as
an important human practice', not just a response to the continuing
need for care.

A democratic ethic of care starts from the idea that everybody
needs care and is (in principle at least) capable of care giving, and
that a democratic society should enable its members to give both
these activities a meaningful place in their lives if they so want.
(Sevenhuijsen, 2000: 15)

Illustrating how such an approach might be implemented, she argues
for a 'life-plan approach' which would enable individuals (both male
and female) to have 'more extended time for caring', while participating in public life through paid work and through the 'intermediate
institutions of civil society', such as 'neighbourhoods, welfare offices,
women's centres, self-help groups, consumer groups, etc.'. Social
participation, for Sevenhuijsen, thus includes voluntary community
work as well as paid work. In these contexts, caring is no longer seen
as limited to a private, particularistic concern with individuals from the
one family, but becomes a means of public engagement and a process
for the development of social responsibility. As she points out, 'These

citizen initiatives are often motivated, not by self-interest, but rather by a desire to find channels for social commitment that come close to the values of the care ethic' (Sevenhuijsen, 2000: 25–6).

Importantly, Sevenhuijsen does not see care simply in terms of moral virtue. Like Knijn and Kremer (1997), she speaks of the ethic of care in hard political terms, as one in which constitutional recognition is sought not just for the right to give care, but for a right to receive care, including access to health care. It hardly needs to be said that this is far from a Utopian notion. Jenny Morris has also made a recent appeal for an inclusive ethics of care built on the concept of human rights:

> We need to challenge the social construction of dependency, but we should not at the same time deny the experience of our bodies and the consequences for the provision of assistance. Vulnerability is created by one person having a greater need for physical assistance than the person who is in a position to provide it and by the nature of the assistance required. This is why a focus on human rights is so important in our challenge to the meaning of care . . .

> Whatever 'care' is – whether it is in the form of formal services, cash payments, or personal relationships – if it does not enable people to 'state an opinion', to 'participate in decisions which affect their lives' and to 'share fully in the social life of the community', then it will be unethical. We need an ethics of care which is based on the principle that to deny the human rights of our fellow human beings is to deny our own humanity . . . Most importantly we need an ethics of care which, while starting from the position that every-one has the same human rights, also recognizes the additional requirements that some people have in order to access those human rights. (Morris, 2001: 14–15)

Such an ethics of care, based firmly on ideals of human rights, it should be clear, differs in important ways from the ethics of care proposed by feminist moral philosophers working in the tradition of Gilligan, Noddings and Tronto, as Morris is aware when rejecting the appeal by her fellow disability researcher (Shakespeare, 2000a) for an endorsement of the values of 'interdependence'. The pursuit of autonomy and independence, it will be recalled, were strongly criti-cized as male values by a number of those who proposed a feminist ethic of care. But, for Morris, abstract theoretical differences between the concept of justice and the values of care should not stand in the way of an inherently sensible idea: an ethic of care conceived of as a measure of justice based on understanding access to care as a human right.

Illustrating the appeal of a practical approach that links a concern for care with principles of justice and citizenship, the British social policy analyst Fiona Williams has called for the adoption of what she termed a *new political ethics of care* which could be taken up as part of a new welfare strategy under the New Labour government (Williams, 2001). Williams is keen to demonstrate that a political ethic of care should not be regarded as idealistic or abstract principles, unlikely to be attained in real life. Instead, she constantly connects issues of care to the real-life difficulties experienced by those living in post-industrial Britain. She thinks carefully, too, about the economic viability of care. Rather than seeing care as an alternative to, or outside, the economy, Williams argues that care needs to be understood as a form of work structured by economic forces. She points to the emergence of a new political discourse based on concerns for *work/life balance*, in which people nowadays seek to combine the pursuit of careers and employment with opportunities to provide care. Drawing lessons also from the disability critique, she argues that care must be made available in ways which support, rather than diminish, the personal autonomy of those reliant on personal support provided by others. To enable people to achieve a balance between work and care in the twenty-first century means that there needs to be the space and time for people to map out their work/life needs within three different but connected spheres of their lives. Putting these demands directly, she argues we each need:

- time and space to engage in work;
- time and space to engage in care;
- time and space to engage in activities concerned with self-care, personal relationships and other meaningful personal pursuits (Williams, 2001).

Like Morris, Sevenhuijsen, Knijn and Kremer, Williams articulates a realistic approach to care that involves a rethinking of family policies and their intersection with work and welfare. But more emphatically than the other writers, Williams links care to contemporary concerns about employment and personal life and the different forms of social

disadvantage – social, economic, and cultural, as well as gender and
disability status. Her approach calls for a political recognition of the
values of care, just as it emphasizes that issues of care should be seen
as integral to the pursuit of social justice as part of a pragmatic,
progressive and holistic socio-economic orientation to social life in the
twenty-first century.

Advocacy of a political ethic of care by British and European care
researchers draws together two quite distinct approaches to the
concept of care. The first, the ethic-of-care debate, derives originally
from psychology and was subsequently taken up by feminists working
in the fields of moral and political theory. It was developed as what has
been referred to as a 'depoliticized' debate on care (Knijn and Kremer,
1997) that focused on care as an attribute of female identities and
responsibilities. It would be wrong to deny the larger, longer-term
vision of the political importance of theories and ideas that clearly
underlies the elaboration of the ethic-of-care approach, but this was an
abstract and philosophical concern and not one conceived of in terms
of immediate impacts on policy. The second approach, which can
claim a heritage linking British and European feminism with the broad
field outlined by the discipline of social policy, developed largely as a
practical and politically aware critique of policy. Engagement between
competing perspectives within this approach was possible through a
common interest in the practical politics and political economy of care
and human services within the system of the welfare state.

   While building on these bodies of earlier work, recent proposals for
the introduction of what Williams terms a political ethics of care are
an important landmark in the contemporary debate. This emergent
approach involves a conceptual reconciliation of a number of
elements that have long been regarded as distinct. It also represents an
important practical initiative, moving beyond the idea of care as
women's work while at the same time recognizing the link between
gender and the allocation of responsibility for undertaking the physical work of ongoing care. Importantly, the emergent positions are also
an extension of attempts since the mid-1970s to capture the emotionally resonant meanings of the term 'care' and to deploy it for broader
political purposes.

   This approach is not without detractors. As Carol Smith points out,
care has been seen as morality requiring personal commitment and
the development of qualities such as trust and responsiveness (Smith,

2002) once seen as in many ways quite distinct from a codified right. An approach based on the enforcement of codified rights, in contrast, is argued to distance individuals further from moral responsibility for their own actions, and hence to result in a reduced rather than an increased responsiveness to care as a social value (Bellah, 1994; Bauman, 1995). There is also a danger of romanticizing the term, so that the darker aspects of care – including the potential for the abuse of power, the dependencies of the care-givers, the cloaking of personal ambition with self-righteousness, the exploitation of care-givers – are no longer visible. Indeed, after the early identification of care as a burden, attention to these elements of care is noticeably absent in the policy discussions. Placing too great an emphasis on the positive aspects of care risks emptying the concept of care of its meaning, making it once more a term, such as that of 'welfare' has become, that is used for largely ideological purposes of denigration and control.

Yet care has the potential to be a rallying cry for a set of human values and practices that counterpoise the domination of life by global corporations and the never-ending search for increased profits. In the possibilities of a political ethic of care lie not just the demand to meet the needs of those who are unable to support themselves, but the hopes of many for fostering social justice and the strengthening of recognition and mutuality between people of different genders, ages and ethnic, national and racial backgrounds by ensuring that there will be an opportunity to both give and receive care.

PART 2

The Politics of Care in the Twenty-First Century

For the post-industrial societies of the twenty-first century, two interlocking social trends cause policy-makers, advocates and others enormous anxiety about the viability of future care arrangements.

The first social trend, described in hard mathematical terms, concerns *demographic changes associated with the ageing of the population.* This calls forth fears of unprecedented numbers and proportions of older people, economically dependent on a relatively small and decreasing working-age population and unable to care for themselves. These demographic anxieties of ageing are increased by historically low fertility rates that have now fallen below replacement levels in every Western country and all but a handful of OECD member states. Changes of this order are interpreted to mean not only that the total population size will fall, but that there will be a negative feedback process through which the numbers of people of working age needed to support the ageing population financially and in terms of care and other services over the twenty-first century are shrinking at precisely the time that greater numbers are required.

The second social trend, more amorphous but more immediate and real for most people, concerns the emergence of *work–life pressures* linked to changes in the household and family system and their relationship, through paid employment, with the market and the state. The decreased capacity of the home to provide unpaid care, flowing from the engagement of women in paid work, is exacerbated by the increasing stress of paid employment. Added stress at work feeds into conflict in the home through the spiral of increasing hours of work and rising insecurity in both employment and social programmes. Other changes at the household level, such as the increased rates of divorce and family re-formation, the prevalence and recognition of same-sex partners and the emergence of alternative, often fluid domestic forms, including the increasing numbers of people who live alone, also cause concern. Together, changes in the state, market and family raise doubts about both the future viability of informal care and the availability of formal services.

These circumstances have been seen by some contemporary analysts as producing a 'care deficit' (Hochschild, 2003) or even 'crisis in care' (Lewis, 2002). Nadine Marks argues that the effect of these demographic and social trends will be 'to increase the likelihood of becoming a caregiver' (Marks, 1996: 27) because there will more older people needing care but fewer of those of working age to assist them. Yet is it not also possible to argue that the reduced birth rate and increased longevity might signal a reduction in the need for care of children and a further shift towards older carers and systems of mutual or shared care between partners? The debate, far from being settled by demographic figures or financial calculations, raises fundamental questions. Is it possible to predict the future of care-giving? What are the likely consequences of known demographic, social and economic developments for the availability of care? What are the sorts of policy responses that will need to be promoted to enable us best to meet these challenges?

To address these questions, I explore the extent to which demographic pressures provide evidence to support the predictions of a future crisis in care and human services in Part 2. I also consider the impact of the changes in households and domestic support in the context of increasing imbalances in what is now commonly referred to as the work/life balance and examine some of the broad directions that policies on care will need to assume to adjust to the new circumstances of an ageing, post-industrial society. Comparison of the need for aged care and child care shows that changes in the demand for care can not be simply extrapolated directly from raw population figures. Reduced fertility and replacement rates which have seen a reduction in the number and proportion of children in advanced societies have been accompanied by an increase in the demand for child care, not a reduction as the raw figures might suggest. While women within families have been the major source of care in the past, we must understand that which is able to be provided and shaped by a range of other sources – most importantly through social provisions, underpinned by civic associations, the state, the market or combinations of these.

Careful attention therefore needs to be given to the political economy of contemporary 'welfare regimes' in low-fertility societies (Esping-Anderson, 1990, 1999), particularly the part played by decisions made by individuals, families and governments.

CHAPTER 5

Demography, Ageing and the Need for Care in the Twenty-First Century

The view that we are facing a crisis in the capacity to provide care for the ageing population in the twenty-first century is widespread. A background paper prepared by the National Health Policy Forum (NHPF) in Washington for the benefit of federal health policy-makers, for example, sets out the facts and well-known arguments:

> The number of elderly with activity limitations will more than double, from 8.5 million to 21 million by 2030. By 2050, over 25 million elderly will be limited in their activities and need assistance ... Beginning in 2025, the number of persons aged 65 and older will exceed the number of women aged 25–54. Moreover, due to greater opportunities for education and workforce participation by women over the past four decades, fewer new workers are entering the long-term care workforce. In the past, women had many fewer avenues of employment; today, work opportunities less difficult and better-paying than long-term care are abundant.

These sociodemographic factors have affected the availability of informal care-givers as well. More women are working outside the home, making them less available to care for family members in need of assistance. Marriage and reproductive trends, such as an increased number of childless couples, smaller family sizes and higher divorce rates, have also decreased the pool of potential family care-givers. According to the National Family Caregivers Association, the number of potential family care-givers for each person needing care will decrease from 11 in 1990 to an estimated 4 by 2050. (Super, 2002: 2–3)

In making these predictions, the author of the NHPF paper, Nora Super, draws demographic and epidemiological projections alongside a consideration of the 'sociodemographic' factors currently affecting women and families. Although much of this may appear to the author and perhaps others to be a uniquely American set of problems, the risks and dilemmas described, in broad outline, are like those projected for most comparable societies. Many of the systems of care are already portrayed in the media as dangerously close to crisis. When an impending demographic shift towards a much older population profile is added to the mix, it is not hard to question the viability of future care arrangements.

The NHPF is not alone in relying on this data. Focusing on the future of care for older people in the twenty-first century, I look more closely at a number of these predictions in this chapter. I consider first the demographic and epidemiological transitions and their outcomes, before moving to consider shifts in the balance of care projected for the future, drawing on a number of detailed, country-specific studies from Sweden, the UK and Australia that look at the need for or availability of care.

The Demographic Transition

The historian Peter Laslett's description of the 'demographic transition' helps to capture the dramatic and historical nature of the enormous shift currently under way in the population balance of the advanced societies of high modernity:

> Within the last hundred years, and to a considerable degree within the last fifty years, the populations of Europe, North America, Australasia, and Japan have become far and away the oldest human populations of which we have knowledge. These populations are older – and still getting older – in two important senses: average individual lifetimes last for very much longer than they ever have before anywhere or at any time, and these populations have among them quite unprecedented numbers of elderly people. [While] it is obvious that the situation could not always have been like this . . .

[knowledge of] the historical demography of aging is evidently necessary to recognize how novel the situation is in the advanced countries. (Laslett, 1995: 3)

The demographic transition can not be understood as just the lengthening of life expectancy, historically significant as this achievement is. A second and equally important component of the transition is the reduction in fertility, evident in the equally dramatic reduction in the birth-rate that began to be evident once death rates began to fall (van de Kaa, 1987; McMichael, 2001). Together, longer lives and fewer births have led to an increasingly aged population. This has impacted on individuals and families as well as populations. The process has been a gradual one in countries such as Britain and France, where it commenced in the mid-nineteenth century (Golini, 1997). In others, most notably Japan and China, these same developments have occurred in a much more compressed time frame.

Demographers also identify the second demographic transition as commencing at the point when the birth-rate began to fall below the death-rate towards the end of the twentieth century (van de Kaa, 1987). The dramatic fall in fertility, when compared with the fluctuations and gradual reduction that had been occurring over the past two centuries, appears to be a result of increased education and the creation of life options for women outside motherhood, along with the widespread availability of reliable contraception. Its effects are evident across the advanced world, although these are most pronounced in the former Eastern Europe, in Western Europe (especially Spain, Italy, Greece and Germany) and in Japan, as can be seen from the figures presented in Table 5.1. One of the basic causes of the fall in fertility that marks the second demographic transition is the incompatibility of the breadwinner family model, which Duncan terms 'housewife marriage', with women's economic and social aspirations (Duncan, 2002). Inadequate external support and the enforcement of a model of familial care would appear to be one explanation for why countries such as Italy, Spain and Japan currently show such low fertility rates while in Sweden and Denmark, where care services are far more 'women-friendly', birth-rates are among the highest in the post-industrial world (Duncan, 2002: 32). The result is a population that is no longer growing or even self-sustaining, but that over time reduces in size without immigration (Lesthaeghe, 1995; Golini, 1997; Sleebos, 2003).

Table 5.1 Fertility rates[a] and life expectancy[b] in OECD countries, 1970–2000

	Fertility rate				Life expectancy males				Life expectancy females			
	1970	1980	1990	2000	1970	1980	1990	1998	1970	1980	1990	1998
Australia	2.89	1.91	1.84	1.75	67.4	71.0	73.9	75.9	74.2	78.1	80.1	81.5
Austria	2.29	1.65	1.45	1.34	66.5	69.0	72.3	74.7	73.4	76.1	78.9	80.9
Belgium	2.25	1.68	1.62	1.66	67.8	70.0	72.4	74.8	74.2	76.8	79.1	81.1
Canada	2.33	1.68	1.71	–	69.3	71.9	73.8	75.8	76.4	79.1	80.4	81.4
Czech Republic	1.90	2.10	1.90	1.14	66.1	66.8	67.6	71.1	73.0	73.9	75.4	78.1
Denmark	1.95	1.55	1.67	1.77	70.8	71.2	72.0	73.7	75.7	77.3	77.7	78.6
Finland	1.83	1.63	1.78	1.73	65.9	69.2	70.9	73.5	74.2	77.8	78.9	80.8
France	2.47	1.95	1.78	1.89	68.4	70.2	72.7	74.6	75.9	78.4	80.9	82.2
Germany	2.03	1.56	1.45	1.36	67.2	69.9	72.7	74.5	73.6	76.6	79.0	80.5
Greece	2.40	2.22	1.39	1.29	70.1	72.2	74.6	74.6	73.6	76.6	79.4	79.4
Hungary	1.98	1.91	1.87	1.32	66.3	65.5	65.1	66.1	72.1	72.7	73.7	75.2
Iceland	2.83	2.48	2.30	2.08	–	73.7	75.7	77.0	–	79.7	80.3	81.5
Ireland	3.87	3.24	2.11	1.89	68.5	69.5	72.1	73.0	73.2	75.0	77.6	78.6
Italy	2.43	1.64	1.33	1.23	69.0	70.6	73.5	75.3	74.9	77.4	80.0	81.6
Japan	2.13	1.75	1.54	1.36	69.3	73.4	75.9	77.2	74.7	78.8	81.9	84.0
Korea	–	2.80	1.60	1.47	59.0	62.3	67.7	70.6	66.1	70.5	75.9	78.1
Luxemburg	1.97	1.49	1.60	1.79	67.0	68.0	72.3	72.9	73.9	75.1	78.5	79.4
Mexico	6.82	4.71	3.35	2.40	59.7	64.0	68.8	72.4	63.6	70.0	74.0	77.0
Netherlands	2.57	1.60	1.62	1.72	70.8	72.5	73.8	75.2	76.5	79.2	80.1	80.7

New Zealand	3.28	2.12	2.12	2.00	68.3	70.0	72.4	75.2	74.6	76.3	78.3	80.4
Norway	2.50	1.72	1.93	1.85	71.0	72.3	73.4	75.5	77.3	79.2	79.8	81.3
Poland	2.26	2.26	2.05	1.34	66.6	66.0	66.5	68.9	73.3	74.4	75.5	77.3
Portugal	3.01	2.25	1.57	1.52	65.3	67.7	70.9	71.9	71.0	76.6	77.9	78.8
Slovak Republic	2.41	2.31	2.09	1.29								
Spain	2.88	2.20	1.36	1.24	69.6	72.5	73.4	74.8	75.1	78.6	80.5	82.2
Sweden	1.92	1.68	2.13	1.54	72.2	72.8	74.8	76.9	77.1	78.8	80.4	81.9
Switzerland	2.10	1.55	1.58	1.50	70.3	72.3	74.0	76.5	76.2	78.8	80.9	82.5
Turkey	5.68	4.36	2.96	2.52	52.0	55.8	63.9	66.4	56.3	60.3	68.5	71.0
UK	2.43	1.89	1.83	1.65	68.6	71.0	72.9	74.6	75.2	77.0	78.5	79.7
USA	2.48	1.84	2.08	2.13	67.1	70.0	71.8	73.9	74.7	77.4	78.8	79.4

Notes: (a) Mean number of children per adult woman; (b) Mean number of years a person is expected to live, at birth, based on age-specific death rates found in life tables; — Data not available. Fertility rate: Turkey, refers to 1972 and 1982; Life expectancy: Ireland, Luxemburg 1995 data for 1998.

Source: OECD Social Indicators and Tables, 2002, Tables GE4.1 and C1 General Health Annex. Downloaded from http://www.oecd.org/dataoecd/

The longer-term demographic impact of this development is difficult to predict with accuracy. Indeed, it would be foolish even to
predict that existing trends will continue, as there are strong historical
precedents for longer-term fluctuations in the birth-rate in the past.
However, projections based on existing trends are widely used by
politicians and other policy-makers. These suggest that the very different population balance that is emerging will affect the need for care,
the availability of informal and formal care-givers, and the affordability and provision of social provisions. A vignette from Italy, one of the
countries with the lowest fertility rates, provides a useful illustration of
the emerging demographic balance: 'In Italy in 1950, there were 8.5
children under five for every 80-year-old. In 1995 the ratio had fallen
to 1.3, while by 2050 there may be 6 over-80-year-olds and 18 over-60-
year-olds for every [Italian child] under five' (Golini, 1997: 54).

The same demographic transition also affects other countries,
although the pace and, importantly, the extent of change differs significantly between, as well as within, countries (Golini, 1997; Sleebos,
2003). According to Golini's calculations, the population ratios in the
UK, for example, changed from 6.1 children under five for each
person aged 80 or over in 1950 to 1.7 by 2000. In 2025 the numbers
are likely to be approximately 1.4 children under five for each 80-year-
old, while by 2050 this is projected to become 1.25 of those aged over
80, and 4.6 of those aged 60 or over for each child aged five or less
(Golini, 1997: 53, Table 5).

Imagining a change of this magnitude, from a situation in which it
has been traditional for grandparents to expect to be outnumbered by
their grandchildren to one in which potential grandparents far
outnumber grandchildren, helps bring alive the common impact of
both reduced numbers of children and increases in the elderly population. But there is also experience, in both the USA and Scandinavia,
of birth-rates 'bouncing back' after a decade or two and similar developments are possible in other countries, possibly reflecting the decisions of women who had delayed birth for a decade or longer. The
inability of demographic projections to identify this move, as well as
the well-recognized limitations of previous demographic projections,
including those that underestimated the extent of current population
ageing, suggests, therefore, that even strong demographic predictions
need to be treated with caution. But, given that even the 'bounce-back'
of fertility levels is unlikely to reverse the trend towards population
ageing, the question still needs to be asked: what is the significance of

demographic change for understanding changing patterns of care and human services?

Shifting the demographic balance of care?

Despite the apparent attractiveness of presenting factual quantitative data about the past, present and future, basic demographic figures need to be treated with some caution, as they present only a limited and one-dimensional picture of a very complex reality. The predictions of population ageing could, for example, be interpreted as indicating a potential reduction in the support provided to young children and an increase in the support needed for older people. But such a trade-off is not as simple as it first sounds. Where the resources are exclusively financial in nature (for example, in the form of financial benefits or allowances), it is possible to envisage an exchange taking place relatively simply. But care for those in an older population who require it demands quite different skills, resources and personal relationships than that required for children.

Data comparing the ratio of those aged below 15 and those aged 65 and over to those of working age (16–64) in countries that are members of the Organisation for Economic Co-operation and Development (OECD) is presented in Tables 5.2 and 5.3. The data need to be interpreted with some caution, particularly the figures from 2010 onwards which are projections based on assumptions about the likely continuation of existing trends. Figures for the final decades of the twentieth century (1980–2000) demonstrate the impact of the demographic transition to date. Across the OECD there is a trend evident towards fewer children and greater numbers of old people in relation to the population of working age. The rate of demographic change over this period, however, varies considerably between countries.

Newly industrialized countries, in particular Mexico, Turkey, Korea and Ireland, started from a far more youthful population profile in 1980 than other, more affluent, earlier industrialized members of the OECD. The pace of the demographic transitions they have been experiencing over a period of approximately fifty years represents a very dramatic compaction of a much slower process of transition that has taken over one hundred and fifty years in the lands of North West Europe, North America and Australasia. Equally dramatic are those countries such as Italy, Spain, Greece and Japan, as well as a number

Table 5.2 Young age ratios in OECD countries, 1980–2050 (population aged under 15/population of working age 15–64)

	1980	1990	2000	2010	2020	2030	2040	2050
Australia	38.8	32.7	30.5	27.3	27.2	28.2	28.7	29.5
Austria	31.8	25.8	24.5	19.1	17.1	19.8	20.7	21.2
Belgium	30.5	27.1	26.3	22.0	21.3	23.7	24.4	25.0
Canada	33.5	30.4	28.0	23.6	24.2	26.3	26.6	27.5
Czech Republic	37.2	32.5	23.5	18.4	18.7	18.9	20.9	25.2
Denmark	32.2	25.3	27.4	25.0	22.4	25.4	27.3	25.7
Finland	30.0	28.7	26.9	22.3	22.8	25.6	25.3	26.3
France	34.9	30.8	28.7	27.1	27.0	27.1	27.8	27.9
Germany	28.0	23.3	22.8	19.3	18.3	20.7	21.4	21.9
Greece	35.6	28.7	22.4	20.1	18.9	19.6	22.0	24.9
Hungary	33.9	30.5	24.8	19.9	19.6	20.3	21.8	25.4
Iceland	43.9	38.7	35.8	29.3	27.8	29.5	29.1	29.3
Ireland	52.2	44.6	32.1	31.9	33.4	29.4	29.4	32.3
Italy	34.5	23.1	21.1	19.5	17.4	18.2	21.0	21.8
Japan	34.9	26.4	21.6	21.7	21.3	20.5	22.9	24.5
Korea	54.7	37.4	28.9	25.3	23.4	25.1	28.1	29.3
Luxemburg	28.2	24.9	27.9	26.3	26.4	28.5	28.4	28.3
Mexico	88.4	67.1	53.3	43.3	36.4	32.9	31.7	31.1
Netherlands	33.7	26.5	26.9	23.2	21.5	24.1	25.5	25.0
New Zealand	42.2	35.7	35.1	30.0	27.1	27.8	28.7	28.5
Norway	35.1	29.3	30.5	25.7	23.9	27.2	28.4	27.8
Poland	37.0	38.7	27.9	20.5	21.8	22.2	22.7	27.9

Portugal	40.8	30.1	24.7	24.1	21.6	21.5	24.2	25.8
Slovak Republic	41.2	39.2	28.3	21.3	20.9	19.9	20.0	22.7
Spain	42.4	29.0	21.5	19.3	17.5	17.1	19.7	22.4
Sweden	30.6	27.9	28.3	19.8	20.2	24.1	24.0	25.1
Switzerland	29.7	24.6	24.7	19.9	18.8	22.5	22.9	22.5
Turkey	70.0	57.6	46.8	39.3	33.5	32.7	31.0	31.2
UK	32.6	29.4	29.1	24.1	23.0	25.6	26.0	26.0
USA	34.0	33.3	32.9	28.6	28.5	30.1	30.3	30.7
OECD	**39.1**	**32.6**	**28.8**	**24.6**	**23.4**	**24.5**	**25.4**	**26.4**
EU	**34.5**	**28.3**	**26.0**	**22.9**	**21.9**	**23.4**	**24.5**	**25.3**

Source: OECD *General Social Indicators, 2002, Data Chart GE2.1.B,* derived from United Nations (2001), *World Population Prospects: The 2000 Revisions,* New York. Downloaded from http://www.oecd.org/dataoecd/

Table 5.3 Old age ratios in OECD countries, 1980–2050 (population aged 65+ / population of working age 15–64)

	1980	1990	2000	2010	2020	2030	2040	2050	Actual 2000[a]
Australia	14.7	16.7	18.2	19.9	25.9	32.3	36.1	37.5	26.3
Austria	24.0	22.1	22.9	26.9	32.4	46.4	59.8	62.5	33.5
Belgium	21.9	22.3	25.9	27.2	33.4	43.4	49.7	51.2	42.6
Canada	13.9	16.6	18.5	20.4	27.7	37.5	40.2	40.9	26.4
Czech Republic	21.1	18.9	19.8	22.3	32.4	38.4	47.8	60.8	30.4
Denmark	22.3	23.1	22.5	25.7	32.7	40.0	46.3	43.8	29.6
Finland	17.7	19.9	22.3	25.7	37.2	45.7	47.1	48.8	33.3
France	21.9	21.3	24.5	25.4	32.7	39.8	45.3	46.7	40.9
Germany	23.7	21.7	24.1	30.2	34.4	46.3	54.3	54.7	36.4
Greece	20.5	20.4	26.0	30.0	34.6	42.5	54.7	64.6	48.5
Hungary	20.8	20.1	21.4	23.0	29.5	33.3	40.8	51.2	38.1
Iceland	15.7	16.5	17.9	18.5	24.2	32.2	36.7	39.7	21.7
Ireland	18.3	18.5	16.9	17.8	22.4	26.3	30.0	37.2	26.3
Italy	20.4	22.3	26.7	31.1	36.8	47.3	63.8	68.1	49.7
Japan	13.4	17.2	25.2	34.8	46.9	51.7	63.6	71.3	29.3
Korea	6.1	7.2	9.8	14.0	19.3	31.3	43.3	48.8	16.5
Luxembourg	20.0	19.3	21.5	22.6	26.0	31.1	31.9	31.4	35.0
Mexico	7.4	6.9	7.6	9.0	11.7	16.2	23.5	30.0	12.9
Netherlands	17.4	18.6	20.1	22.3	30.0	39.6	46.7	45.0	28.0
New Zealand	15.7	17.0	17.9	19.1	24.8	33.7	38.6	38.5	25.3
Norway	23.4	25.2	23.7	24.0	31.0	39.1	46.2	45.3	30.8

Poland	15.4	15.5	17.7	18.0	26.0	33.4	37.3	49.5	33.1
Portugal	16.4	20.5	23.1	25.4	29.0	35.3	46.0	53.5	33.8
Slovak Republic	16.4	16.0	16.5	17.0	23.4	30.4	36.9	49.8	29.3
Spain	17.0	20.7	24.8	27.1	31.8	42.3	59.9	73.8	44.1
Sweden	25.4	27.7	27.1	29.6	37.8	46.0	52.9	54.5	37.1
Switzerland	20.8	20.9	23.8	29.2	38.3	53.0	59.5	57.3	30.4
Turkey	8.4	7.1	9.0	9.8	12.0	16.5	22.0	28.7	19.4
UK	23.5	24.1	24.1	25.3	31.1	40.4	47.2	47.3	34.2
USA	16.9	18.9	18.6	19.0	25.0	32.9	34.6	34.9	26.6
OECD	**18.0**	**18.8**	**20.6**	**23.0**	**29.3**	**37.5**	**44.8**	**48.9**	**31.9**
EU	**17.4**	**17.8**	**19.5**	**21.1**	**26.7**	**34.6**	**41.7**	**46.1**	**34.4**

Note: (a) Actual old-age ratio: population aged over 65 / total employment for the age group 15–64.

Source: OECD *General Social Indicators, 2002, Data Chart GE2.1A and GE2.2*), derived from United Nations (2001), *World Population Prospects: The 2000 Revisions*, New York. Downloaded from http://www.oecd.org/dataoecd/

of Eastern European countries, in which sudden and dramatic reductions in fertility have led to relatively rapid reductions in the young age ratio (Table 5.2) and subsequent striking upsurges in the old age ratio in the following decades (Table 5.3). The demographic transitions will also have a differential impact on the longer-term industrialized nations, with the migration countries of Canada, the USA, Australia and New Zealand experiencing a slower transition with a lower proportion of older people than the countries of North West Europe (Economist, 2002). Even here there are important differences, with the Nordic countries, the Netherlands and the UK ageing less rapidly, and less extensively, than most of their neighbours.

Taken together, the data in Tables 5.2 and 5.3 demonstrate the link between an ageing population and the reduced number of young children. The data also underline the longitudinal impact of the population changes already achieved, with the population of working age in the first half of the twenty-first century projected to continue to fall, ensuring that increased pressure will be placed on people of that age group, females as well as males, to undertake paid employment. Yet assumptions made about the meaning of basic demographic numbers are often misleading. One example of this is the calculation of age ratios as a percentage of the population of working age, assumed to be those aged between 15 and 64. Since the proportion of this population that is actually in paid work differs considerably from the total, a more accurate calculation is the ratio of dependent age groups to the actual working population. The final column in Table 5.3, therefore, presents calculations by the OECD that are based on the actual numbers of people in employment in the year 2000.

Comparing the actual rates in 2000 to the unadjusted rates for the same year in each country, it is clear that the old-age population was already a much higher proportion of the employed population than the unadjusted rates suggest. Similarly, the figures in previous years can also be misleading insofar as they assigned the population aged 15–64 to the category of working age. Much of this group was likely to be outside the labour force for one reason or another – some as students, others as unemployed or part-employed, and importantly, many as homemaker and unpaid carers. Many of those aged over 65 were also providing care or were employed in some form of other. The figures, which lack any indication of gender or employment status, are at best suggestive of the likely challenge to be faced in achieving a care balance. Employment, productivity and social policies emerge as significant. The basic demographic figures on the age composition of the population, in other words, are at best part of a much bigger and more complex picture.

Due to the high levels of employment, and especially the levels of labour-market participation by both males and females, Sweden, the country for which the highest old age ratio was reported for 2000, fell well below the adjusted old age ratio of Italy, Greece, Spain, Belgium, France and Hungary, all of which had more youthful population profiles but poorer employment records. Yet here, too, difficulties in interpretation arise owing to inconsistencies between countries in the definition of employment, as this measure groups together all people who report receiving income in return for labour, regardless of whether their employment was full-time, part-time or casual, or indeed employment at all. To be registered as employed may involve as little as one hour a week of paid employment in countries such as the USA and Australia. Participation in higher education or training and other activities, such as military service, are also typically reckoned as employment for the statistical purpose of calculating the employment rate. Hence the adjusted old age ratio, while in some senses preferable to raw population ratios, should not be regarded as providing an entirely accurate picture either. Without probing the realities of the changing patterns of workforce participation, household formation and social support that underlie them, reliance on raw demographic projections produces a picture that is, at best, incomplete.

As the European Commission recently set these out, there are four different dimensions of the impact of an ageing population, each of which directly impacts on the potential development of care. The first concerns *the ageing work-force* and the relative decrease in the population of working age, the second the growing *pressures on the pension* and income support systems of member states. The third dimension involves expanding and adapting the requirements of *age care and health care* for the elderly, while the fourth is concerned with *growing inequalities* between elderly people (European Commission, 1999; Walker, 1999). The effect of these dimensions will be experienced through the restructuring of employment required to accommodate the emerging demographic profile with its reduced numbers of young people and mature-age adults, and increases in those of older ages. It will also be expressed through the economics of financial support for an ageing population, though the provision of benefits and the taxation of assets and income.

The Epidemiological Transition and the Need for Care

To understand the need for care linked to population ageing, it is also necessary to consider the pattern of disease and its impact on the need for intervention and care. The prevalence of disability is known to increase sharply with age, as does the likelihood that an individual will need assistance in at least some area of daily living as a result of acute or chronic illness. Rates of severe disability, those in which restrictions require assistance on at least a daily basis, are generally relatively low until the age of approximately 55. From this point they continue to increase with age, so that over the age of 85 the likelihood of needing such assistance, either on an acute or ongoing basis, is in many cases greater than of remaining independent in the performance of activities of daily living (Jacobzone et al., 1998b; AIHW, 2000; Freedman, Martin and Schoeni, 2002). Yet although the number of people expected to have reached the age of 65 by the middle of the twenty-first century is relatively simple to estimate, because all of those who will be that old in the reference period were already born before the century began, accurate estimates of those who will survive beyond that age are more difficult. Estimates of the type and amount of care required are more complex still. Predictions based on current disability prevalence rates simply reflect the unlikely assumption that the prevalence of disabling conditions in the future will be the same as it is today.

Population health and the level of disability is bound up with what is called the 'epidemiological transition', a term used to indicate the changing patterns of disease that have accompanied, and to a significant extent shaped, further demographic developments. Historically, the epidemiological transition has seen a transition from societies characterized by short life expectancies, in which infectious diseases and epidemics were the main cause of death, to ones in which life expectancy has increased dramatically and the main cause of both mortality and morbidity has become non-communicable conditions, the diseases of later adulthood such as coronary heart disease, stroke, diabetes, arthritis and cancer (McMichael, 2001). These sorts of conditions are often described as 'diseases of affluence' because of their link to modern industrially developed societies and their first appearance amongst the more affluent upper classes and later amongst the middle classes. However, in the affluent societies of the West, the contemporary socio-economic distribution of these diseases is no longer one of affluence. Smoking, diets rich in fats, sedentary lifestyles and exposure to stressful and insecure employment have now become more prevalent amongst the working class and welfare-dependent than amongst those with higher education and income levels (McKeown, 1976; Wilkinson, 1994).

As McMichael (1993) emphasizes, ecological and environmental conditions are fundamentally important for determining population health. The epidemiological transition was initially achieved by reducing the rates of pestilence and mass disease in cities and surrounding areas, then by improving the survival rates and hence life expectancy of infants and children. Most of the changes in the patterns of disease affecting advanced societies can be traced to improved urban environments, and healthier social and economic conditions, such as better housing, more plentiful, hygienic and nutritious food, improved occupational health and safety, and the effect of widespread successful public health interventions, especially the extensive and reliable provision of fresh water, sewerage and rubbish collection in urban areas (McKeown, 1976; Powles, 1992).

In the late nineteenth and the early twentieth century, significant improvements in medical care, housing and working conditions reduced infant and child mortality and enabled greater numbers of adults of working age to survive. The consequence was that increasing numbers of people lived on into early old age, at which point they were vulnerable to the accumulated assaults on their body of a lifetime that often involved hard physical work and high-calorie, high-fat diets. The disease and mortality profiles of older people in the immediate post-war period, dominated by heart conditions and stroke, is indicative of these effects. By the final decades of the twentieth century, more extensive improvements were achieved in the health of the working-age population, with the consequence that increasingly significant numbers of people now survive into advanced old age. The emergence of 'delayed degenerative diseases' such as Parkinsons disease and Alzheimer's dementia is identified by Olshansky and Ault as marking a further stage in the epidemiological transition (Olshansky and Ault, 1986). As a consequence of these transitions in disease profiles, traumas, including the results of motor vehicle and occupational accidents, diseases of lifestyle and late-onset conditions are now the predominant causes of longer-term disability.

The success of medicine in dealing with acute and terminal conditions has ironically contributed to the burden of chronic illness
amongst survivors. This pattern is evident in early twentieth-century
success stories, such as the use of insulin to treat diabetes, where a
previously terminal condition became a chronic illness as a result of
medical intervention. It is also evident in more recent success stories,
such as the use of anti-retroviral medications to treat what was until
very recently the terminal condition of HIV/AIDS. This re-
emergence of epidemics of infectious diseases such as HIV/AIDS,
Hepatitis B and C, tuberculosis, SARS (severe acute respiratory
syndrome) and the annual development and rapid global transmission
of new forms of influenza and other respiratory infections such as the
avian flu viruses originating in Asian poultry also serves as a rejoinder
to the optimism of those public health officials who, in the 1960s, had
declared mass infectious diseases to be a thing of the past (McMichael,
2001).

The broad sweep of the epidemiological transition has thus been to
reduce mortality at all ages. But while this has extended life expectancies, it is not simply translated into reduced morbidity or lower needs
for care. Somewhat paradoxically, the epidemiological transition
appears to have accompanied an increase in the need for ongoing
support amongst those with chronic health conditions and disabilities.
These improvements include an extension of service coverage and
improved quality of care. However, as David Thomson's important
historical research has shown, the proportion of older people reliant
on residential aged-care institutions in the UK was virtually identical
in the 1970s to the proportion reliant on residential institutions (mainly
workhouses) more than a century before (Thomson, 1983).)

Estimates of the need for ongoing care

Going beyond demographic figures, disability prevalence rates are
widely used as measures of the need for care in a given population.
Howe and Schofield (1996: 5), for example, note that 'the underlying
determinant of the need for care is the level of disability in the
community', which, they point out, is closely associated with age.
Attempting to apply this approach to measure future needs for care,
however, is problematic as there is no consensus about the direction of
future trends in morbidity. Instead, three conflicting hypotheses have

currency (Mathers, McCallum and Robine, 1994; Lagergren and Batljan, 2000):

1. a *reduction in the need for care* arising from a reduction in morbidity and the overall levels of disability;
2. an *increase in the need for care*, that will result from further increases in morbidity and disability levels, compounding the basic population increase;
3. *a continuation of the existing pattern.*

Each of these is claimed by its advocates to be supported by the evidence.

The first theory, described by its originator, Fries, as the *compression of morbidity* hypothesis (Fries, 1980; Fries, Green and Levine, 1989), is that the increased longevity enjoyed by older people will translate into reduced needs for ongoing care. This hypothesis argues that while most of the achievements associated with increasing life expectancy to date have derived from preventing premature death in childhood or early adulthood, there is considerable scope for improving positive health through the adoption of health promotion practices such as improved dietary and exercise regimes, and by ending smoking. Adopting these sorts of measures will lead to an improvement in the health and activity levels of older people, with the result that the years added to life will be extra years of robust and active health, not extra years of disability. There is empirical support for this hypothesis, particularly from the USA (Mathers, McCallum and Robine, 1994; Costa, 2000; Manton and Land, 2000; Costa, 2002) where there is strong evidence that functional limitations amongst older men, in particular, have been declining. However, there is also evidence to the contrary from a number of other countries (Jacobzone et al., 1998b).

The second approach is an alternative hypothesis that posits the *expansion of morbidity* (Gruenberg, 1977; Kramer, 1980; Olshansky et al., 1991). This asserts that increased life expectancy has been accompanied by an equal increase in the number of years of ill health. This paradoxical development arises, according to its proponents, from the very success of medicine in keeping older people alive. By extending life through the successful treatment of a number of what were terminal conditions, the average duration of illness and disability experienced will also increase. Medicine has successfully intervened in a large number of what were once terminal illnesses, but has not been so successful to date in ending chronic conditions that arise in their place. The result is disability, and hence the need for care increases.

A third hypothesis, the *postponement of morbidity* (Manton, Stallard and Corder, 1995; Manton and Land, 2000), suggests that the extension of life expectancy has been accompanied by a comparable postponement of disability and chronic disease. Broadly speaking, this means that the amount of disability will remain approximately the same as it was at the end of the twentieth century, although disability as a proportion of the actual life course will reduce somewhat. There is strong, although inconsistent evidence from the USA in particular that disability amongst the elderly has been consistently decreasing in recent years, although evidence of the decrease is strong only for IADL (Instrumental Activities of Daily Living) activities, reducing the need for help with general domestic activities such as shopping, cleaning, cooking and geographic mobility, not for the more intensive ADL (Activities of Daily Living) level of activities indicating the need for assistance with personal care, personal movement and communication (Freedman, Martin and Schoeni, 2002).

Lois Verbrugge's critical commentary on the link between different forms of social and health intervention and longer-term trends in the need for care is helpful in understanding how each of these three scenarios could plausibly be encountered. Verbrugge distinguishes the differential effects of advances in primary, secondary and tertiary prevention (Verbrugge, 1991). Primary prevention, she reminds readers, reduces both mortality and morbidity by eliminating the development of the disease before it has an impact. The impact of successful preventative measures of this kind could lead to the reduction of morbidity, as hypothesized by Fries and his colleagues (Fries, Green and Levine, 1989). Secondary prevention, which takes place through the early detection of acute or chronic conditions and helps control or delay their outcomes, has a less dramatic but none the less significant impact on population health and the need for ongoing care. Where this is the main form of intervention, a pattern of need for support along the lines of the postponement of morbidity hypothesis could be expected. Tertiary prevention, which is based on interventions intended to treat or manage an established illness or condition; may prevent death but help keep alive a person needing high levels of care. The consequences would be likely to resemble the expansion of morbidity hypothesis advanced by Olshansky et al. (1991). Since each of these approaches is deployed to some degree in each of the OECD countries, part of the difference in the evidence of reported need for assistance amongst older people could be due either to the outcomes of the different mix of interventions employed over time or to the nature of the evidence used in deriving the estimates of prevalence.

The issue of whether epidemiological developments are likely to result in an increase or a decrease in need appears at first to be capable of being resolved simply by reference to the available data. However, this is precisely the problem, as data from different sources can be found to support each of the above hypotheses. A comprehensive study that examined trends in the prevalence of severe disability amongst men and women at different ages across the OECD (Jacobzone et al., 1998b) reported that comparisons were difficult as they involved comparing national data collected for different purposes using a variety of different definitions. Even within one country, comparisons over time are difficult, as gender differences as well as differing expectations amongst survey-respondents make interpretation difficult. For example, Collin Mathers concludes, on the basis of an extensive analysis of Australian data focusing on the impact of specific diseases, that 'For older Australian men, elimination of neoplasms, circulatory system disorders and genito-urinary conditions results in a relative expansion of morbidity, whereas relative or absolute compression occurs for elimination of each disease group for older Australian women' (Mathers, 1999: 53).

Different trends also appear over time, even within one country, as is evident from the data in Table 5.4, which uses the measure of disability-adjusted life years (DALYs) to condense information from a wide range of measures into a single figure.

On the basis of their review of a wide range of data covering the final two decades of the twentieth century in a subset of OECD member nations for which 'cross-sectional evidence is available for at least two points in time, five years or more apart' (Jacobzone et al., 1998b: 4) and comparing the data for Australia, Canada, France, Germany, Japan, the Netherlands, Sweden, the UK and the USA, the authors identify three distinct clusters as follows:

- *countries with very moderate or no gains in disability* on the whole – Australia, the Netherlands and the UK;
- *countries with mixed or moderate results* – Canada, Sweden;
- *countries with significant gains* – Germany, France, Japan and the USA. (Jacobzone et al., 1998b: 16)

Table 5.4 Disability-free life expectancy at birth[1]

Country, year of survey	Men			Women		
	Life expectancy	Disability-free life expectancy	% years free of disability	Life expectancy	Disability-free life expectancy	% years free of disability
Australia[2] 1981	71.4	59.2	82.9	78.4	65.0	82.9
Australia 1993	75.0	58.4	77.9	80.9	64.2	79.4
Australia 1998	75.9	57.5	75.8	81.5	63.3	77.7
Austria[3] 1992	72.7	69.0	94.9	79.2	72.4	91.4
Canada[4] 1986	73.0	66.8	91.5	79.7	70.0	87.8
Canada 1991	74.6	67.7	90.8	80.9	70.5	87.1
France[5] 1981	70.4	60.8	86.4	78.6	65.9	83.9
France 1991	72.9	63.8	87.5	81.1	68.5	84.5
Germany (6) 1986	71.8	66.3	92.3	78.3	71.2	90.9
Germany 1995	74.6	68.9	94.0	79.7	74.0	92.8
Japan [7] 1980	73.4	70.9	96.7	78.8	75.9	96.4
Japan 1990	75.9	74.2	97.8	81.9	78.7	96.1
Netherlands[8]1983	72.9	60.1	82.4	79.5	60.8	76.4
Netherlands 1994	74.6	62.7	84.0	80.3	60.8	75.7
New Zealand[9] 1996	74.3	57.7	77.7	79.6	60.9	76.5
Poland[10] 1988	67.2	59.8	89.1	75.6	62.6	82.8
Spain[11] 1986	73.3	60.8	82.9	79.7	62.6	78.5
Switzerland[12] 1981	72.6	65.9	91.0	79.3	69.7	88.2
Switzerland 1992	74.3	68.2	91.8	81.1	74.1	91.3
UK [13] 1981	70.8	58.7	82.9	76.8	61.0	79.4

UK 1992	73.4	59.7	81.3	78.9	61.9	78.5
USA [14] 1980	70.1	57.2	81.7	77.6	62.8	81.1
USA 1990	71.8	58.8	81.9	78.8	63.9	81.1

Original Notes: (1) Disability definitions and measurements are only partly harmonized across countries. When interpreting the table, attention should be paid to the country footnotes. (2) Disability defined as a person having at least one of fifteen conditions lasting more than six months related to: impairments, functional limitations (e.g., loss of sight, hearing or speaking abilities), activity restrictions (e.g., restriction in physical activities or in doing physical work), chronic and recurring pain that restricts everyday activities, or breathing difficulties. (3) Disability defined as any functional limitation. (4) Disability defined as one or more limitations in ADL or IADL (Instrumental Activities of Daily Living). (5) Disability includes those persons who are limited in their daily activities (working, schooling, etc.). (6) Disability based on reported days unable to fulfill their usual tasks or perform their usual activities due to ill-health or injury. Classified as occupational handicap-free life expectancy. Data refer to West Germany (Old *Länder*). (7) Disability defined as bed-free (including institution-free) disability; a very strict definition of disability. (8) Corresponds to long-term disability calculated with respect to 10 items from OECD indicator and short-term disability (inactivity due to illness). (9) Disability defined as having one or more functional limitations. (10) Disability not defined along any distinguishable section of the ICIDH. (11) Disability defined as having one or more functional limitations. (12) Disability includes long-term disability (with respect to 10 items from OECD list) and short-term disability (13) Based on any long-standing illness, disability, or infirmity which limits activity in any way. (14) Corresponds to both major and secondary activity limitations. Major activities include able to go to work, go to school, keep house. Secondary activities are activities such as going to church and recreational activities.

Source: OECD *Social Indicators and Tables, 2002, Table C.4.* Original table based on OECD Health database, 2000. Downloaded from http://www.oecd.org/dataoecd, January 2004.

The complexity of the results provide some support for each of three major epidemiological hypotheses outlined above. None the less, a report released by the OECD in the same year concludes, on the basis of cautious reviews of the data and research across the OECD (Jacobzone et al., 1998a, 1998b), that most evidence indicates a clear trend towards improved health, and hence a pattern of reductions in the total need for care amongst the elderly (OECD, 1998) that is likely to continue well into the twenty-first century (see also Waidmann and Manton, 1998, 2000; Mathers, 1999; Freedman, et al., 2004).

Predicting Future Needs for Care

Despite their limitations, demographic and epidemiological projections are widely used to provide information about the need for and availability of care now and in the future. On the demand side, they are used to provide a measure of the numbers of people receiving care and extrapolated to predict the numbers likely to need to receive it in the future. On the supply side, demographic projections are also widely used to forecast future care-giving scenarios. As the comparison of three studies of future care needs and provisions presented below shows, political, economic and cultural assumptions strongly shape the character of the final projections.

Sweden: Formal care services for an ageing population

Concerns arising from two quite disparate sets of demographic projections led to the commissioning of a major enquiry into the costs of care for the ageing population, the results of which have been published in English with the provocative title *Will There Be a Helping Hand?* (Lagergren and Batljan, 2000). The research was assigned to the same project leader responsible for an earlier report, published in English as *Time to Care* (Lagergren et al., 1984), undertaken by the Swedish Secretariat for Future Studies in the late 1970s and early 1980s. A key premise of the earlier report had been that care requires time, with the result that much of the earlier discussion had focused on ways in which lives might be organized in order that there would be 'time to care'.

The new study, undertaken as part of a larger study of prospects for the Swedish economy, was intended to provide a systematic and rigorous analysis that examined a wider range of considerations than had been the case with the demographic projections released earlier. The cost trend, the authors noted, could not be simply extrapolated from existing expenditure patterns. Consequently, a research methodology was devised which would extend the analysis beyond demographic projections to consider the following mediating factors:

- trends in health and functional ability;
- the need for help, support and care, given morbidity and social conditions;
- the availability of help and support from the family and social network;
- the propensity of older people to seek public health and social care, given changing expectations, charges and the probably private alternatives;
- the structure of care services, in particular the balance between the provision of health and social care in recipients' own homes or in institutions;
- the impact of care on the health and functional ability of recipients, especially the effects of preventative measures, of iatrogenic (medically induced) care needs and of rehabilitation;
- the staff requirements for given care inputs;
- the cost of staff and other expenses, considering salary rates, living standards, medicines, technical aids, and so forth. (Lagergren and Batljan, 2000: 14)

The study also assumed that the ongoing viability of the provision of health and aged care as a system of formal services was to be maintained at such a level 'that elderly people do not have to depend on help from family members, such as the spouse or adult children' (Lagergren and Batljan, 2000: 126). The authors, from the Swedish Ministry for Health and Social Affairs, noted a number of Scandinavian studies demonstrating the extensive involvement of family members (these include Johansson, 1991; Lingsom, 1997), commenting that the 'willingness to help elderly relatives is consistently high in Swedish society' (Lagergren and Batljan, 2000: 76). They note that while this informal help has not been displaced by formal services provided as part of the Swedish welfare state system, and that the demands on informal family care-givers increased significantly over the 1990s, there is none the less a 'lasting and ingrained expectation that in Sweden the public sector will assume primary responsibility for social care' (Johansson, 1991, cited in Lagergren and Batljan, 2000: 75).

The researchers concentrated, therefore, on the issue of the cost of sustaining a system of services that will provide a comparable level of care to that available during the 1990s, based on what they admit is the 'dubious assumption' that the proportion of public-financed assistance will remain unchanged (Sundstrom, Johansson and Hassing, 2002). Their analysis was conducted with the aid of demographic projections linked to projections of existing and likely future costs. These were then further elaborated into four 'scenarios' that allowed the researchers to examine the impact of variations in a number of their assumptions:

1. an assumption of unchanged health amongst the elderly + unchanged labour force participation;
2. improved health + unchanged labour force participation;
3. unchanged health + improved labour force participation;
4. improved health + improved labour force participation.

On the basis of calculations made using these scenarios, it was concluded that the total costs of all care for the elderly were likely to rise to between 10.7 and 13.1 per cent of GDP by 2030, compared with 9.9 per cent in 2000. The additional costs likely to be experienced by 2030 are in the order of approximately 10–12 per cent, not the higher figure of up to 20 per cent that would be derived from simple extrapolations of existing trends (Lagergren and Batljan, 2000: 108 ff.). There will also be a need to recruit approximately 100,000–180,000 extra personnel by 2030, raising the total employed in the care sector from 12.5 per cent of the labour force in 2000 to 14.9–17.4 per cent. According to the projections, this increase in demand for care labour is capable of being met by the Swedish labour market. The authors argue that higher pay may be required to attract the additional numbers required to care, and in their higher cost scenarios this was factored into their final cost projections (Lagergren and Batljan, 2000: 114). Because it is not just a question of labour supply but of the economic costs involved, a number of further measures to facilitate the future adjustment were also canvassed, including encouraging older workers to continue in employment by ending early retirement and other measures, and extending support to and encouragement of a certain level of immigration to supplement the relatively small number of people of working age, both as staff for care services and as tax-payers.

In the Swedish study, the attempt to answer the question posed in the monograph's title *Will There Be a Helping Hand?* leads to care being placed at the centre of an extensive social and economic analysis. The approach adopted in the studies of future pressures on care in England and Australia are, in contrast, far more limited. Importantly, in each case the assumption is made that it is informal care and the family, rather than formal services, which must be the priority for analysis.

England: Projecting future informal care for an ageing population

The study of the care for older people in England (Pickard et al., 2000) was concerned with projections covering the period 2000–31, comparable to the time frame adopted in the Swedish report. In contrast to the Swedish study's focus on formal services, however, the authors argued that a focus on informal care was necessary because evidence from the General Household Survey demonstrates that 80 per cent of older people (those aged 65 or over) who receive assistance with domestic tasks rely exclusively on informal help. Having regard for both demographic and social changes, the study sought to address the deep and widespread concern expressed about the longer-term viability of informal care.

The study developed projections, based on data from the 1994/95 General Household Survey (GHS), concerning patterns of need for assistance amongst older people and the availability of informal care received from others. The modelling also used projections of the existing probabilities of the need for care, which assumed that the age-specific dependency rates derived from the 1994/95 GHS will not change. As in the Swedish study, the basic projections varied slightly as a result of the use of three different scenarios, two of which examined the impact of different patterns of service provision, and one that projected further declines in the availability of co-residential care provided by children. A further assumption, technically necessary for calculations although as a forecast it may be barely credible, was that there will be no significant changes in patterns of family, marriage, partnering, household formation and social support over the period 1996–2031.

Some of the key results of the basic projections are summarized in Table 5.5. These projections run contrary to the widespread fears that there will be a reduction in informal care. One of the most striking projections was that there will be a fall in the number of widowed women living alone and a corresponding rise in the number of older women living with partners, suggesting a marked increase in the number of older people living together (Shaw and Haskey, 1999). A key implication of these findings, according to the authors, is that by 2031 more elderly people with substantial care needs will have access to a co-residential 'spouse carer' (which includes de facto partners) than is currently the case (Pickard, et al., 2000: 759). Insofar as the availability of care from a co-residential partner is considered positive, the nature of the change identified in the projections is likely to be especially beneficial for elderly women.

The picture of care in the twenty-first century which emerges from this study is strongly at variance with the crisis-of-care scenario that emerges from most simple demographic projections. Rather than there being a massive rise in demand for formal care services as a result of population ageing, the study suggests counterintuitively that there will be an increase in informal care. This new care will come from partners, themselves old, rather than from younger generations. But this does not mean that formal services will no longer be needed. Instead, more services will be required to support carers, according to the researchers, as spouse carers tend to be elderly and are often in poor health.

Much of the focus in discussions of informal care to date has been on assistance provided by the 'family'. With survey data showing fewer older people living with their family than previously, and increasing rates of family breakups due to divorce and non-marriage, it has been widely believed that informal care as it was known in the twentieth century would continue to decrease in importance. This study shows that these beliefs can be countered by adopting a rather different perspective, firmly grounded in findings from existing data that show the most intensive levels of informal care being provided by partners.

Importantly, the results show significant differences when the calculations are conducted using the marital status figures from 1992 and those from 1996. This difference highlights one of the most important

Table 5.5 Projected numbers of dependent elderly people in private households, by household type and dependency, 1996–2031 in England (x'000)

Household type	IADL problems only[a]	One ADL problem[b]	Two or more ADL problems[b]	All dependent elderly people	
	N	N	N	N	%
1996					
Living alone	205	355	335	895	42.7
Living with others	310	436	453	1198	57.3
Total in 1996	515	791	787	2094	100.0
2031 (using 1996-based marital status projections)					
Living alone	287	509	500	1296	38.3
Living with others	533	771	781	2085	61.7
Total in 2031	820	1280	1281	3381	100.0
2031 (using 1992-based marital status projections)					
Living alone	337	592	555	1484	44.0
Living with others	483	688	715	1886	56.0
Total in 2031	820	1280	1270	3370	100.0

Notes: (a) IADL – Instrumental Activities of Daily Living (domestic tasks); (b) ADL – Activities of Daily Living (personal care tasks)

Source: Pickard et al., 2000: 759, Table 5.

aspects of the use of demographic projections: the results are strongly dependent on the initial assumptions made by those responsible for the models. In this case, the sensitivity of the final figures to relatively minor changes in marital status between 1992 and 1996 also raises very serious problems for any long-term projections. If such changes occur over a period of just four years, how secure is an assumption that there will be no further change over the following 35 years?

Projections of informal care in Australia

Detailed projections of patterns of informal care-giving have also been provided by recent studies based on the modelling of demographic data on care-giving in Australia (Jenkins et al., 2003; Percival and Kelly, 2004). The first of these studies explored four possible care-giving scenarios over the relatively short period of the 15 years from 1998 to 2013 (Jenkins et al., 2003). Based on information reported in the Australian Bureau of Statistic's 1998 *Survey of Disability, Ageing and Carers* (ABS, 1999a, 1999b), the study relied on data concerning both the need for support and the availability of informal care by those defined as 'primary carers' to people of any age with a disability.

In developing the projections of informal care in 2013, Jenkins et al. (2003) outline four possible scenarios:

- a *baseline projection* that assumes that the 1998 pattern of informal care, along with the same sex and living arrangements, will be sustained throughout the 15-year projection period. Under this scenario the supply of carers would increase by around 47 per cent between 1998 and 2013, largely as a result of population growth in key 'caring' age groups through population ageing and the associated increase in the number of spouse or partner carers (Jenkins et al., 2003: 20–4).

- a *converging-life-expectancies scenario* that assumes an increase in the proportion of spouse or partner carers aged 60 or more years in line with an expected increase in the number of surviving couples among older ages due to the narrowing of the gap in life expectancy between men and women, while 1998 patterns of care continue for older people in other living arrangements. The results projected show an increase in the availability of care provided by partners, from 91,000 in 1998 to 160,300 in 2013, of which there would be 83,800 female and 76,500 male spouse carers (Jenkins et al., 2003: 25–6).

- a *decreasing-propensity-to-care scenario* based on the assumption that there would be a 'linear decrease' in the numbers of informal carers of working age (25–59 years) reaching a 20 per cent decrease by 2013. The results indicate that this would lead to 12,500 fewer primary carers in 2013 than there were in 1998 (Jenkins et al., 2003: 20–7).

- a *women's-career-preference scenario* based on the concern about the impact on the availability of carers of the trend towards greater workforce participation by women, with the implication that women of working age would be increasingly less willing to forsake paid work to provide unpaid care. These results showed that, despite a reduction of 20 per cent in the proportion of women willing to reduce or cease paid employment to provide care, the number of female primary carers in each labour force category would continue to increase as a result of population growth (Jenkins et al., 2003: 22).

A summary of the final results of the projected figures for all age groups based on these different scenarios is presented in Table 5.6.

Despite differences in the results obtained using different scenarios, the figures for the availability of informal care remain relatively robust. With the exception of the 'overall decreasing propensity to care' scenario, in which a deliberate reduction in informal care of up to 20 per cent was introduced, the results of the projections presented in Table 5.6 show the number of primary carers as likely to increase in line with population. The projections suggest that there are no sound demographic reasons for predicting a crisis in informal care for older people in the limited time frame considered.

The results of the second Australian study, which covers a more extended 30-year period, 2001–31, presents only one set of projected figures, not a number of different scenarios. This data-modelling exercise, commissioned by Carers Australia, forecast that the numbers of older persons with a 'severe' or 'profound' disability in Australia would increase by around 160 per cent (Percival and Kelly, 2004: 27). The numbers of likely informal carers of older persons, in contrast, was forecast to increase by a much lower rate, only 57 per cent. However, this general or headline figure disguises a substantial shift within the mix of carers, with numbers of non-co-resident carers projected to

Table 5.6 Estimated and projected numbers of primary carers aged 10 or more years, by sex, and people with severe and profound activity restrictions, Australia: 1998, 2003, 2008 and 2013

Scenario	1998	2003	2008	2013
Male primary carers				
Baseline propensity to care	133,500	148,700	163,200	175,700
Converging life expectancies	133,500	151,900	170,600	188,500
Decreasing propensity to care	133,500	138,800	141,400	140,600
Women's career preference	133,500	148,700	163,200	175,700
Female primary carers				
Baseline propensity to care	317,300	344,000	371,600	398,200
Converging life expectancies	317,300	347,600	379,600	412,200
Decreasing propensity to care	317,300	321,100	322,000	318,600
Women's career preference	317,300	342,400	368,100	392,900
All persons, primary carers				
Baseline propensity to care	450,900	492,700	534,800	573,900
Converging life expectancies	450,900	499,500	550,200	600,700
Decreasing propensity to care	450,900	459,900	463,500	459,200
Women's career preference	450,900	491,100	531,300	568,600
Estimated number of people with a severe or profound activity restriction[a]				
Females, all ages	598,100	671,800	746,300	816,700
Males, all ages	441,000	497,200	554,500	609,300
Persons, all ages	1,039,100	1,169,000	1,300,700	1,426,100

Ratio people with severe or profound disability: primary carers[b]

Baseline propensity to care	2.30	2.37	2.43	2.48
Converging life expectancies	2.30	2.34	2.36	2.37
Decreasing propensity to care	2.30	2.54	2.81	3.11
Women's career preference	2.30	2.38	2.45	2.51

Notes: (a) Severe or profound activity restriction – requires assistance with self-care, mobility or communication; n.a. – not applicable.

Source: Jenkins et al, 2003:29, 36 *(Tables 12; A1)* 1998 ABS Survey of Disability, Ageing and Carers (1998 baseline estimates); (b) author's calculations, based on data presented in Jenkins et al, 2003.

increase by about 34 per cent while co-resident carers, generally partners, were projected to increase by more than twice that rate, 71 per
cent. Importantly, the growth in the numbers of informal carers was
projected to occur amongst older persons, with those aged 65 and over
growing by 110 per cent, compared to just 19 per cent growth for
those aged less than 65. By 2031, it is forecast that 56 per cent of
carers will be older carers, compared to just 42 per cent in 2001
(Percival and Kelly, 2004; 27–9). None the less, in contrast to the study
of informal care in England (Pickard et al., 2000) the modelling
projected that the proportion of those living with a partner amongst
those aged 65 and over would decrease slightly between 2001 and
2031 (Percival and Kelly, 2004: 32–3, Figure 12).

The differences between the results of the two Australian studies and
the English study are indicative of the importance of the assumptions
and trends introduced into the modelling exercise. In addition to
national differences in the prevalence of disability and the availability
of carers, there are significant variances in the definitions of disability
used in the British and Australian data, as well as differences concerning the assumptions about marital status and household formation in
each of the studies. While Pickard and colleagues have used relatively
optimistic figures that show an increasing trend for older people to live
together, the Australian statistical data from the mid-1990s suggests a
trend moving in a different direction, with older people increasingly
likely to live alone. A further important qualification for each of the
studies concerns the identification of carers in the national data sources
used. As the figures on the 'Ratio of people with severe or profound
disability: primary carers', presented in Table 5.6 suggest, for Australia
there is no correspondence between the numbers of primary carers and
those requiring assistance as a result of disability. In each study it is
clear that the number of people needing care as a result of disability
exceeds the number of available carers. The projections suggest there
will continue to be a shortage of carers in 2013 and 2031. There is no
clear correspondence between levels of disability and the availability of
primary carers evident in either the Australian or the English data.

Jenkins et al. note that the relationship between demand and supply
for care is both 'complex and multi-faceted' and observe that 9 per
cent of primary carers in the 1998 Australian survey also experienced
a severe or profound core-activity restriction themselves (AIHW, 2002:
43, cited in Jenkins et al., 2003: 5). They also point out that informal
care is often provided by more than one person, that different levels of

intensity and forms of assistance are evident depending on the type of help required and that an individual's personal assessment of his/her need for care is sometimes at odds with what might be considered to be needed by a more objective observer. More fundamentally, however, the mismatch between the identification of demand, as expressed in the prevalence of disability, and the availability of informal care provided by primary care-givers suggests that any attempt to assess the viability of informal care that relies on epidemiological projections must at best be questionable.

In each of the three studies analysed here, reservations have been expressed about the capacity of existing data to provide detailed forecasts of either future demands for care or the likely availability of care. While, in general, there has been sufficient information generated from the extrapolation of existing data and the application of different scenarios to enable the researchers to reject talk of a coming crisis in care, doubts remain about the soundness of relying on predominantly demographic trends in making these forecasts. As Jenkins, et al. acknowledge towards the end of their report,

> The plausibility of a scenario in which there is a broad decline in carer availability is difficult to assess, not least because of the multitude of variables relevant in determining the carer supply, many of which are not well understood. This report has investigated the impact of only some of these factors and even then only in the artificial circumstance in which all other factors are held constant. Developing a detailed predictive model to address fully the question of the future supply of carers would require a level of detail in the data that is not currently available. (Jenkins et al. 2003: 33)

Apocalyptic Demography and the Limitations of Care Projections

Are the limitations of demographic projections in aged care simply a matter of too much missing data, too much complexity in the way that 'relevant variables' interact? If this were the case, we could expect that at some stage in the near future the relevant data might become available, and that the complexity of the relationships between the variables would be better understood. Yet while the focus of the debate is on projections from statistical indications of the outcomes of past trends, it is not possible to anticipate new or unexpected directions that might be taken.

With the advantage of hindsight, it is difficult not to concur with Lagergren and Batljan (2000) who note that studies based on demographic projections have in the past overestimated the level of services used by older people because they have extrapolated from existing trends and have not anticipated the impact of policy reforms, improved system efficiency, the robust contribution of informal care and improvements in health on the total picture. Even the demographic predictions have tended to be wrong, as predictions have consistently underestimated the total number of older people surviving into advanced old age, largely because demographers have failed to predict the continuing decrease in mortality in the final decades of the twentieth century. Further difficulties, they note, need to be faced in estimating the morbidity and need for assistance from the elderly population, whilst attempts to gauge future changes in the availability of informal and formal care is far more contentious and politically loaded (Lagergren and Batljan, 2000: 19–26).

The proposition that an aged population brings with it skyrocketing costs of care that must lead to financial instability and ultimately crisis is one of the key tenets of what Evans et al. (2001) have termed 'apocalyptic demography'. These costs are likely to be experienced most directly in the field of health care. As studies have consistently demonstrated across a number of countries (Evans et al., 2001; Anderson and Hussey, 1999; Reinhardt, 2000; Reinhardt, 2001), the profile of cost increases in health care is not determined by the age profile of the population (see Table 5.7). Nor is ageing likely to be the main driver of costs in the future. Other developments, including the increasing costs and sophistication of high technology medicine, the strategic power of the medical and other health professions, and, importantly, the extent to which health care is subject to strong public regulation or allowed to operate as a market, appear to be more important determinants of total service cost than the demographic changes affecting potential users of health care.

To reject demography as the major determinant of the cost of health and aged care is not, however, to dismiss the demography of ageing societies as unimportant for future developments in care. Underlying the demographic trends of population ageing and reduced fertility is a change of historic proportions in the formation of families and households. This is the aggregate result of a decline in marriages

Table 5.7 Health spending and demographic structure in selected countries, 1997

	Per capita health spending			Health spending as % of GDP		% of total population aged 65+
	All persons	Older persons	Ratio spending 65+/0–64	All persons	Older persons	
Australia	$1,805	$4,348	4.1	8.3	3.0	12.2
Canada	$2,095	$6,764	4.8	9.3	3.6	12.9
France	$2,051	$4,717	3.1	9.6	3.4	16.0
Germany	$2,339	$4,993	2.8	10.4	3.5	16.8
Japan	$1,741	$5,258	5.3	7.3	3.4	17.5
UK	$1,347	$3,612	4.0	6.7	2.8	16.1
USA	$3,925	$12,090	4.4	13.5	5.0	12.5

Note: Expenditures expressed in $US, adjusted for purchasing power parities.

Source: Anderson and Poullier (1999) and Anderson and Hussey (1999), adapted by Reinhardt, (2001: 193). By permission of University of Toronto Press. www.utpjournals.com

and an increase in cohabitation and divorce, lone parenthood, the age of marriage and the age at which mothers first give birth. The 'sexual revolution' that has accompanied the availability of reliable contraception means not just that sex has been liberated from procreation, but that heterosexuality can no longer be assumed to be the sole basis of household formation. As Gonzalez-Lopez and Solsona (cited in Duncan, 2002: 309) point out, fertility, even more than ageing, is a 'highly gendered' issue, for 'after all we are talking about [women] getting pregnant' (Duncan, 2002: 309). The impersonal, technocratic language of demography seems to deny choice and human agency, portraying fertility and ageing as if they were the end result of some supernatural, mechanical process. Yet what we are seeing is the result of people responding to the opportunities, demands and constraints of the world around them, reshaping over time not just their own lives but the broader social landscape as a result.

When it comes to discussing issues of child care, far less weight is given to matters of demography, as this, it appears, is not central to the issues of care that need to be faced. To explore the factors that do shape policy, therefore, the following chapter turns to consider debates in this field.

Work/Life Conflict and the Politics of Child Care

As women have turned their backs on unpaid domestic work in favour of employment and careers outside the home, the employment conditions encountered in increasingly deregulated systems of paid employment have emerged as major threats to the capacity of the family and friends to provide care. With employment more competitive and insecure than at any time since the Great Depression of the 1930s, the level of work in almost every field has intensified, affecting the lives of both women and men and severely compromising the caring capacity of families.

Pressures on the gender-based household division of labour, implicit in the breadwinner/housekeeper model of familial care prominent in the industrial societies of the mid-twentieth century, reflect too the changing character of primary groups in the social order of high modernity. This has seen the emergence of 'flexible' and 'democratic' families (Giddens, 1993; Inglis and Rogan, 1994) in which a single male breadwinner per family is no longer the sole normative ideal nor divorce and family reformation exceptional (Janssens, 1998; Williams, 2004). Divorce and remarriage, families based on cohabitation without marriage, sole parenthood, the recognition of cultural diversity and the wide variety of forms of family and marriage that this entails, and the acknowledgement of same-sex relationships as recognized civil unions or as legal marriages, raise further doubts about the capacity of the family to function unaided. Finding new ways to increase the contribution of men to caring in the home and to support women by recognizing their rights as citizens, workers and mothers has become more urgent than ever before.

Despite the rise of the market, the public emphasis placed on employment, the work ethic and individual achievement, the more traditional domestic exigencies of care, especially the need to care for those in infancy and old age and those suffering from disability or illness, have not disappeared. With fewer children than ever before, parents are caught in a bind, attempting on the one hand to devote ever greater amounts of time and personal attention to their offspring, while on the other seeking to maintain or improve their lot in the increasingly insecure and fickle modern workplace. The significance of quality care for the well-being of those who depend on it is more recognized than ever, and the tensions that surround the giving and receipt of care are made much sharper by the clash between the demands of paid work outside the home. Arguments for child-care services are increasingly framed in terms of the need to respond to these pressures.

This chapter examines the emergence of widespread demands for child care at a time when the capacity of families to care for children is directly confronted by the increasing ascendancy of market values, changing patterns of work and employment, and shifting systems of family relationships. I provide first an overview of the rationales for the development of child-care services, then turn to the increasingly urgent debate on work/life balance. This leads to a discussion of the evidence concerning the caring capacity of families in the twenty-first century and the significance of social policy in shaping the capacity of the family to continue to respond to the dual challenges of caring for those who require ongoing personal support and of earning an income through working outside the home. The need for child care and other forms of family support, it is argued, reflect the search for a resolution of the increasing conflict between work and family life. While private solutions such as the employment of nannies may be possible for members of high-income elites, and then often only through the exploitation of cheap, immigrant caring labour, a more stable and universal solution requires a social approach. Demands for child care must be understood as a product of the changed family system and indicative of the need to forge new sets of relations between the market, the family and the state.

Understanding the Demand for Child-Care Policies

Like aged care, a need for child-care services has emerged as a key political demand in the post-industrial societies of the twenty-first century. But, unlike care provisions for older people, the need for child care is seldom if ever justified as a response to increased numbers of children. To the extent that demographic indicators are used in planning or justifying child care, it is the falling numbers and proportions of children as evidenced in the fertility rates (Table 5.1) that are most commonly invoked. More pointedly, the arguments for child care are framed in terms of the employment rates of parents, (especially those of mothers), of changing family patterns as evidenced by divorce and family re-formation and, increasingly, of the need of children to receive an enriched early education (Lewis, 1998; Rostgaard and Fridberg, 1998; McDonald, 2002; Anttonen, Baldock and Sipila, 2003; Kamerman et al., 2003).

Despite decades of advocacy from feminists, controversy continues to surround claims about the need for child care. Opposition typically arises on the basis of conservative claims that children are best cared for in the home, as well as on the grounds of public affordability (Fox Harding, 1991; Folbre, 2001a; Hill, Waldfogel and Brooks-Gunn, 2002). Arguments for expanding public support for child care are seldom straightforward, with coalitions of interest developing that are shaped by the historical context and the opportunities available. It is nevertheless possible to identify five different types of argument for child care (see Table 6.1). Each has a characteristic logic and appeal to a political constituency, and is likely to shape the forms of provision that result (Mahon, 2002b).

The first and most frequently heard argument today is the feminist argument for *gender equality*. If mothers with young children seek employment, some form of child care is deemed essential to meet the deficit in care that would otherwise arise. The primary beneficiary of child care, according to this logic, is not the child who receives the care but the mother enabled to realize the benefits of income, career and social participation obtained by paid employment. The child and other members of the family benefit also, through the increased income in the household. More extensively still, the broader economy and society is held to benefit from the economic consequences of the increased rates of labour-force participation. Child care, in this representation, is seen as a necessary service if women are to have children and be able to be employed while any of their children requires ongoing care or supervision. The need for financial support for this arrangement arises from the cost of the child care and the need for supervision, licensing and an

Table 6.1 Rationales for public support of child care

Rationale	Intended beneficiary	Time orientation
1. Gender equality, female employment	Mother, democratic justice	Short-term, immediate
2. Early childhood education	Child, wider society	Long-term, future
3. Promoting fertility	Family, economy	Long-term, future
4. Social equality: early intervention	Child, community	Medium to long-term
5. Workfare: overcoming welfare dependency	Employers, Government (through reduced payment of benefits)	Short-term, medium to long-term

assurance that the care received by the child will be quality care. Unless the mother earns a high income or the child-care staff are paid at well below the level she receives, there would be no economic purpose served if she were to pay the full cost of child care. Hence an arrangement for the social sharing of the costs is necessary.

A second representation concerns the educational potential of child care. The main beneficiary is seen to be the child, who benefits from the early educational opportunities. It is also considered to benefit the broader society, as early educational opportunities help prepare a flexible and educated workforce. Child care in this form is part of a broader pedagogic strategy of *Early Childhood Education and Care* (ECEC) (Press and Hayes, 2000) which has been important in developing child-care services in most countries, but particularly so in a number of European countries. In Denmark, Sweden, France and Italy this rationale remains central to the operation of child-care services. In other instances, such as the Australian case, it has been historically important, although de-emphasized in the policy debate in the years of child-care expansion in the final two decades of the twentieth century. By arguing the benefits of quality education, the approach supports the development of educated, professionalized staff, but may not always provide child care with the availability and convenience sought by working women.

Overcoming the historically low rates of *fertility* currently encountered in advanced societies provides a third, and much newer, rationale increasingly cited as a justification for the expansion of child care. According to this rationale, closely related to the first, the unequal burden of care on potential mothers provides a disincentive to having children, preventing the mother from pursuing employment or other life goals and aggravating the effects of the demographic crisis said to be affecting ageing societies. Substituting formal care for that provided by the mother removes this disincentive to reproduction and will help encourage women to have children and restore a more youthful population profile.

The fourth and fifth rationales serve to justify a targeted rather than a universal approach to child care. Each is concerned with child care as a means for realizing goals of broader social policy, dealing with problems of social inequality and poverty. The fourth rationale, the achievement of social equality through early intervention, can be thought of as a variant of the educational goal discussed earlier, with *early intervention* in the lives of children from socially disadvantaged backgrounds seen as providing a means for overcoming potential educational deficits. This approach has been strongly associated with the 'Head Start' programme developed as part of the 'War on Poverty' in the 1960s and early 1970s in the USA (Adams and Rohacek, 2002). It is far from a historical curiosity, however, and increasingly important in early intervention programmes in Blair's Britain, in certain states of the USA, and in some Australian states (Randall, 2002; Baldock, 2003). The fifth rationale, using child care as a means of enforcing a requirement to engage in paid work to overcome reliance on welfare payments, in contrast, is the use of child care as part of a *workfare strategy* for poor single mothers. Child care is seen in a near-punitive light, as a means by which single mothers and women from other low-income households can be released from household care and required to accept low-paid employment (Levy and Michel, 2002; Kurz and Hirsch, 2003). Where this rationale has been used in the USA it is often the cost, rather than the quality of the care, that is crucial for policy-makers. This approach may also be dovetailed in to a broader strategy of social policy reform, as has occurred in Quebec, where it has been used as part of a broader anti-poverty strategy but made available on a universal basis (Jenson, 2001). The 'five-dollar-per-day' policy of affordable, publicly supported child care was introduced in Quebec in 1997, as the result of decades-long campaigns in which feminists, together with provincial 'femocrats', trade unionists and educationalists worked through a series of provincial government enquiries, promoting child care as a way to counter poverty and promote gender equality. Child-care reform was eventually embraced by policy-makers as part of a wider strategy for improving educational outcomes across the province, providing a means for addressing the demands of women to seek work and allowing the provincial authorities to enforce new employment requirements imposed on low-income mothers (Jenson, 2001).

In practice, demands for child care are likely to involve an appeal to more than one of these rationales. There is also a common concern, with each acknowledging the importance of paid work and the limited capacity of the family to meet unaided all of the demands for care, education and labour. Rather than being seen as an alternative to, or outside, the economic sphere, child care is increasingly acknowledged as a form of work, structured by economic forces and requiring significant levels of public support and management if it is to be optimal and to contribute to, rather than undermine, the child's subsequent development. The performance of paid work depends on care being available, and the availability of care at home, in turn, is increasingly contingent upon the conditions under which paid work is undertaken. Yet while the availability of publicly supported child care has long been a key demand of feminists (Bertone, 2003), paid services at best ameliorate, rather than overcome, the conflicting pressures of paid work and family life and the gendered division of labour evident in both the home and the workforce (Franzway, 2001: 119).

Employment and Work/Life Conflict

The emergence of pressures on families and households that limit the viability of care in the home is now a persistent theme in debates about care and work (Scarr, 1984; Hobson, 1993; Watson and Mears, 1999; Wheelock and Jones, 2002). The Canadian demographer Roderic Beaujot expresses what he sees as the key concerns as follows:

> On the level of the society, a demographer's main interest is in understanding the relationships between economic production and demographic reproduction, to use the terms of political economy. On the level of families, the central issues are earning and caring.

These functions include the *instrumental* activities, especially making a living and maintaining a household, and the *expressive* activities of caring for each other, especially for children and other dependents. Thus, the key question . . . is how to understand the changing links between earning and caring. (Beaujot, 2000: 21; emphasis in original)

Beaujot's analysis of the changing links between earning and care in Canada shows that pressures on the capacity of the family to care and the rising demand for child care can not be accounted for using the traditional quantitative population indicators commonly associated with demographic projections. It is not increasing numbers of children that have driven the demand for more formal child care but the changing social, economic and political conditions that these numbers reflect which shapes perceptions about the need for child care in various forms.

Beaujot argues that family models based on a patriarchal division of labour, which depend on 'complementary and specialized activities for women and men', are no longer adaptive in contemporary Canadian life and, as a consequence, there has been a move towards family models 'based on a collaborative approach – of two earners who are co-providers and co-parents' (Beaujot, 2000: 24). In these circumstances, the rise of dual-earner families, he argues, is inevitable. The wife's employment provides a form of back-up insurance in the event of the male losing employment or earning capacity, and proves adaptive in cases of divorce or family breakdown. In the context of the widespread economic restructuring and social changes that have led to the 'deinstitutionalization of the family', family life is no longer dependent on the institution of the traditional family but has become instead an expression of the continuation of interpersonal relationships between family members. In this sense, he stresses, 'families are now based more on expressive than instrumental interdependence' (Beaujot, 2000: 24–5).

The rise of female employment, documented in Table 6.2, shows a substantial increase in female employment in all countries belonging to the OECD between 1980 and 2000. The increase is attributed in particular to an increased participation rate amongst married women and mothers of young children, and is indicative of the increasing pressure put on the capacity of the family to provide unpaid care to children and others in need of ongoing personal support. Comparative international data available on the relative contribution

Table 6.2 Evolution of the female employment/population ratio
since 1980 in OECD countries, 1980–2000

	1980	1985	1990	1995	2000
Australia	48.0	49.4	57.1	58.9	61.6
Austria	–	–	–	58.9	59.4
Belgium	–	37.0	40.8	45.4	51.9
Canada	52.5	56.0	62.7	61.7	65.8
Czech Republic	–	–	–	61.0	56.9
Denmark	–	67.4	70.6	67.0	72.1
Finland	66.1	69.8	71.5	58.9	64.5
France	50.0	48.5	50.3	51.6	54.3
Germany	49.6	47.7	52.2	55.3	57.7
Greece	–	36.1	37.5	38.0	41.3
Hungary	–	–	–	45.9	49.7
Iceland	–	–	–	76.8	81.0
Ireland	–	32.4	36.6	41.5	53.3
Italy	33.4	33.4	36.2	35.4	39.6
Japan	51.4	53.0	55.8	56.4	56.7
Korea	44.6	44.1	49.0	50.6	50.1
Luxemburg	–	39.7	41.4	42.2	50.0
Mexico	–	–	–	36.5	40.1
Netherlands	34.2	35.5	46.9	53.4	62.6
New Zealand	–	–	58.5	61.7	63.5
Norway	60.8	65.6	67.2	68.8	74.0
Poland	–	–	–	51.8	48.9
Portugal	45.8	49.4	55.4	54.8	60.3
Slovak Republic	–	–	–	53.0	51.5
Spain	28.5	25.5	31.6	32.5	42.0
Sweden	73.4	76.9	81.0	70.8	72.2
Switzerland	–	–	–	66.0	69.3
Turkey	–	–	32.9	29.9	25.3
UK	–	55.6	62.8	62.5	65.5
USA	55.4	59.3	64.0	65.8	67.9
OECD countries	**49.6**	**49.1**	**52.8**	**53.8**	**57.0**
EU countries	**47.6**	**46.8**	**51.1**	**51.2**	**56.4**

Note: – Data not available.

Source: OECD (2002), Labor Force Survey database; *OECD Social and Economic Indicators, 2002. Data Chart SS1.1.* Downloaded from http://www.oecd.org/dataoecd/

of females and males to household activities including care points to the fact that women continue to be responsible for the majority of unpaid care in the home. Small rises in the proportion of domestic work undertaken by men are evident in the final decades of the twentieth century, but the bulk of familial care continues to be contributed by women (Bitman, Craig and Folbre, 2004; Ironmonger, 2004).

The need for viable new arrangements for the care of children is part of the search for a new balance between paid employment and unpaid family care. Although moral and religious conservatives may seek a return to the model of the breadwinner family in which men were responsible for earning while women assumed the duties of family care, the solution of a widespread return to the older patriarchal division of labour is no longer possible. To do so would not only require draconian moves against women's choices, but would also have significant fiscal consequences as a result of the reduction in working taxpayers. However, the continued association of caring with women places women in the family at the 'junction' between work and family, at the point of conflict between production and reproduction (Kemperneers, 1987, cited in Beaujot, 2000: 42), while 'women's caring' continues to be crucial for understanding gender inequality (Baines, Evans and Neysmith, 1998). What is required to resolve the tensions inherent in the current imbalance between employment and care is a new social settlement that will enable both women and men to earn and to care. This, argues Beaujot, must involve social supports that will enable families to achieve a more equal division of labour, overcoming the separation between public and private spheres (Beaujot, 2000: 351). As Beaujot's extensive discussion of changing fertility trends shows, the rebalancing of earning and care may have some impact on falling fertility levels, but this is far from certain.

Time for Care

The search for a new balance between paid work and family life is based on the premise that time is a limited and scarce resource for families. Time is essential for care, just as it is fundamental to the way it is valued (Land, 1991). No less than employment in care work, caring within families requires time. With just 168 hours each week available for paid employment, family life, leisure and sleep, time spent in paid employment inevitably reduces the time available for other activities. But while employment, including employment providing paid care, can be measured, remunerated, documented and compared according to the units of staff time devoted to the task, care in the family home remains unpaid and unquantified, and is excluded from national accounts and measures of economic well-being (England and Folbre, 1999; Folbre, 2001b). Because unpaid family care is understood as having no economic value, it has been easy to ignore in the push for economic growth, with children often portrayed as just another discretionary choice made by parents. Studies of time-use attempt to overcome the problem of the hidden character of domestic work by documenting the time spent on different activities.

Australian time-use figures analysed by Michael Bittman illustrate the impact that employment has on the time which parents are able to devote to housework and child care (see Table 6.3). These show that the total time available to families in which both parents worked full-time was at least two hours per day less than for families in which the wife worked part-time or was not employed. Similarly, the time available to families in which the wife worked part-time was markedly less than amongst those in which the wife remained at home as housekeeper and homemaker. Over the decade 1987–97, the proportion of families in which both parents worked full-time increased significantly, from approximately a quarter to a third of all households, while those in which the husband was the only breadwinner fell by an even greater amount. Indicating the trend towards casualized and part-time work, there is also evidence of a greater proportion of males not in full-time employment over the same years.

Barbara Pocock reminds us that the effects of the changing patterns of employment and the dominance of paid work on the patterning of family life became a concern to social researchers and commentators as women began to pursue more active engagement in the labour market in the final decades of the twentieth century (Pocock, 2003). This is especially so in the relatively strong growth economies of English-speaking countries – the USA, Canada, the UK, Australia, and New Zealand – where the regulation of work hours has been weakened or is non-existent, and where increases in women's employment have not been matched by an equally significant expansion of public support for child-care services or maternity (Hochschild and Machung, 1989; Schor, 1992; Hewitt, 1993; Lewis and Lewis, 1996; Hochschild, 1997). Many northern European countries, in contrast, have acted on concerns about family life by limiting working hours,

Table 6.3   Time devoted to family care of children: total hours per week devoted to unpaid housework and child care, married and de-facto couples, Australia[a]

Parents' employment	1987		1992		1997	
	Hrs	%	Hrs	%	Hrs	%
Husband full-time/ wife full-time	45	25.5	44	29.8	46	32.5
Husband full-time/ wife part-time	60	27.4	63	30.6	64	29.9
Husband full-time/ wife not employed	71	37.6	67	25.2	72	23.4
Husband not full-time	70	9.5	64	14.4	66	14.2
All couples	61	100.0	58	100.0	60	100.0

Note: (a) Reference person in household aged 25–54 years.

Source: ABS Time Use Surveys 1987, 1992, 1997, from Bittman, 2004: Tables 8.3 and 8.4: 157–8.

making high-quality child care widely accessible, developing parental and other carer leave provisions, and attempting also to support family life in a range of other ways (Lewis and Lewis, 1996; Hakim, 2000; Duncan, 2002; OECD, 2002).

Recognition of the issue of work/life balance is evident in the discourse about the need for 'family-friendly' policies from government and employers (Ackers, 2003; Kay, 2003). In seeking to identify the fulcrum point of the current imbalance, it has become common to speak of problems occurring at the 'intersection' of employment and family. Pockock takes her cue from an American journalist to describe the meeting point as producing the 'work/life collision' (Pocock, 2003: 6). The effects of this collision, she argues, are evident daily, with growing hours of work and pressures on employees to work longer hours with unpaid overtime, together with increasing insecurity in employment, placing families and carers under continual pressure.

Pockock sees these issues as manifesting a collision of the 'values' and 'logics' of market and family, production and reproduction. The workplace, she notes, is increasingly a site in which women and men work alongside each other. At home, however, the unpaid work of care and homemaking is still done mostly by women (Pocock, 2003: 7) While the founder of neo-classical economics, Adam Smith, was able to calculate the direct economic benefit to families of having children in the eighteenth century, in the early twenty-first century these benefits have disappeared and the economics of family care and of the market no longer align. Employment, generated and located in the market, is subjected to the principles of competition, self-interest and cost–benefit calculations. Care, she argues, has a very different logic – that of 'selfless mothering' (Pocock, 2003: 7). Pocock notes,

> The basic assumptions of neo-classical economics – of 'Economic Man', weighing economic costs and benefits and making choices which maximize his utility based on perfect information – are fatally contradicted by most caring decisions which rely upon altruism and sacrifice of personal interests to the interests of another . . . The economy of care which underpins the economy of paid work and production has its own laws and circulations, but its guiding principles contradict the founding assumptions of neoclassical economics: rational man who maximizes his private utility. Carers make decisions that shape labor market participation, production and consumption – indeed which shape the official economy – based on motivations where costs are a minor player. These decisions are instead related to love, reciprocity and a complex economy of relationships, community and family where 'gain' derives not narrowly from individual utility but also from obligations, love and responsibility that can not be measured in dollars or individually, and often cannot be predicted. Perfect knowledge about effects, events, costs and benefits rarely accompanies care decisions. (Pocock, 2003: 16–17)

Pocock argues that the relationship between work and care has changed in recent decades as a result of a large increase in the participation of women in the workforce, and a significant, if smaller, decline in the participation of men. The result is a shrinkage of the family's capacity to undertake unpaid work, particularly for children. This must be met by the 'intensification' of work undertaken by traditional unpaid family workers, by a 'contraction' in the amount of caring work that is done, or by what she terms a 'redistribution' of the work of care to others outside the family (Pocock, 2003: 19).

Concerns about demographic growth are not a cause of the need for care here, but a consequence. The simplest way for individual women to reduce the effects of this clash between work and care is to limit, postpone or reduce the number of children to which they give birth (Gray and Stanton, 2002). Rather than being forced to build a life dedicated to others by sacrificing their career to the uneconomic activity of child-rearing, women are increasingly choosing to use citizenship rights and other opportunities to achieve personal goals such as autonomy and achievement (Beck-Gernsheim, 2002). While technology and changed social conventions now enable women to chose the timing of giving birth or having a family, the development of care arrangements outside the home that can support these choices have kept pace in only a select few countries, most notably those of Scandinavia.

What we are experiencing is an incomplete social revolution (Hochschild and Machung, 1989; Hochschild, 2003; Pocock, 2003). The feminist goal of the entry of women into public life through engaging in paid work outside the home has been realized, at least in part. But it has not been accompanied by the attainment of related changes in the responsibility for care, either in the home or in the community and public life. The failure of the institutions of families, markets, workplaces and government to work towards the achievement of a redistribution of caring work causes the collision between work and care.

Catherine Hakim's approach to the question of what she calls 'work–lifestyle preferences' largely confirms this picture of family care being caught in a clash between the changing requirements of the workplace and the home (Hakim, 2000, 2001). Hakim, however, emphasizes the importance of the attitudes and personal preferences of individual women in shaping what she calls 'lifestyle choices of prosperous, liberal, modern societies' (Hakim, 2000: 3). On the basis of data from a range of empirical surveys, she argues that these lifestyle choices fall into three main clusters:

1. A rather traditional, 'home-centred' lifestyle, focused on care for the children and support of the husband and household, is an option chosen by around 20 per cent of women.
2. A work-centred lifestyle is also chosen by around 20 per cent of women. This is the one in which childless women are most concentrated.
3. A somewhat diverse cluster, mainly composed of women who wish to combine employment and family but including also those whom Hakim calls 'drifters' and those with 'unplanned careers'.

In total, this group includes around 60 per cent of women. The women in this group are likely to be most responsive to policy incentives concerning both family and employment options, according to Hakim.

Hakim's perspective was first spelt out in a controversial article confronting what she called 'five feminist myths' (Hakim, 1995, 2000). She argued that it is not the discriminatory practices of employers, but the preferences of individual women to combine work and family responsibilities or to give priority to family by choosing to stay at home that have held women back in the labour market and prevented them from attaining full parity with men in the workplace. She elaborated this argument in subsequent texts, developing what she calls the new perspective of 'preference theory':

> Preference theory is concerned primarily with women's choices between family and market work: a genuine choice in affluent modern societies. This choice does not, yet, arise for men in anything like the same way, although it may do so in the future, if men demand equality with women. (Hakim, 2000: 1)

Her approach angered many feminists, not just because it broke with the feminist argument that women are oppressed in advanced liberal capitalist societies, but also because she asserted that social arrangements could be understood as the result of deliberate choices made by ordinary women. Women, in this view, were not the victims of an unjust and patriarchal social order but had become instead the orchestrators, managers and benefactors of these arrangements. By emphasizing the importance of women's preferences and ignoring those of men, she effectively wrote men out of the equation. Similarly, as Lewis observed, her approach 'ignores the part played by government policies in constructing the work/welfare relationship' (Lewis, 2003: 183).

Yet attention to women's preferences should not be dismissed out of hand. As Ann Oakley, drawing on the work of Barbara Ehrenreich, has recently argued, the irony is that men have also effectively voted with their feet, retreating from never-ending responsibility for 'the Family' in the twentieth century just as women began to do in increasing numbers in the final decades of the century (Oakley, 2002: 117). In doing so, men and women may have much more in common in this debate than is often acknowledged. The policy challenge, Oakley points out, is 'to improve family life'. This includes 'improving the experiences of children and parents of both genders' (Oakley, 2002: 120).

Post-Industrial Welfare Regimes

Social policies both shape and respond to changing patterns of family and personal relationships. Welfare state systems established in the immediate post-war period (1945–75) were based broadly around the employment patterns characteristic of industrial society and were designed to support male breadwinner families. In the move towards service-based, post-industrial, globalized economies in the final decades of the twentieth century, a complex process of restructuring and redesign has been evident which has seen greater emphasis given to an 'adult worker' model of the family (Williams, 2004). To adapt to an economy in which both men and women are wage-earners, policy changes have included the reformulation of laws on marriage, divorce and family responsibilities, the introduction and expansion of care allowances, care payments and changing eligibility conditions for income support policies, the introduction of child-care services, child-care payments and policies for the provision and access to child care and other care services (Daly, 2002), as well as policies for the regulation (or deregulation) of working life and employment. Work/life balance issues have been a motif in the process of this restructuring, but, in the English-speaking countries at least, it has been an issue honoured more in rhetoric than in action. This contrasts quite markedly with the way it has been dealt with in a number of West European nations (Duncan, 2002; Ackers, 2003; Kay, 2003).

The processes by which policy is developed and implemented, however, is not a smooth functional process of translation of demographic, economic and social changes. Policy is an inherently political process, and its development shaped by economic considerations, reflecting the conflict between competing interests and social forces. Esping-Andersen's (1999) analysis of welfare regimes provides a valuable approach with which to understand the transition from social policy systems designed for male-breadwinner families. The core of Esping-Andersen's approach is summed up in the concept of 'welfare regimes' (Esping-Andersen, 1990). This is a term he originally used in 1990 as a way of distinguishing three broadly distinct societal patterns, or more correctly 'regimes' or 'worlds', of welfare capitalism: the social democratic approach encountered in Scandinavia; the conservative or corporatist approach evident in most Western European nations; and the liberal approach, most clearly expressed in the English-speaking countries. The approach was intended to draw out both the distinctiveness of particular national approaches to welfare and the similarities evident amongst clusters of nations with comparable approaches to issues of welfare. Esping-Andersen (1999) later revised the concept to analyse better the forms that social policy is assuming in the new 'post-industrial' societies of the twenty-first century, in which the household economy must be recognized as the 'alpha and omega to any resolution of the main post-industrial dilemmas' (1999: 6).

Building on Titmuss's account of the social division of welfare (Titmuss, 1958), the term 'welfare regimes' refers to the characteristic patterns of interaction between the major institutional sectors of advanced societies – the state, the market and the family (or household). Each of these institutional forms is an important source of welfare for individuals, forming what is often referred to as 'the welfare triad'. (The term welfare should be read here as meaning 'well-being', not the impoverished and often stigmatized transfers suggested by the use of the term 'welfare' in much contemporary political discourse. As Esping-Anderson points out in a footnote (Esping-Andersen, 1999: 36), some contemporary advocates of voluntary organizations insist on recognition also of non-government, civil responses, forming a fourth point of reference, so creating a 'welfare diamond'. He notes, however, that 'in practice it may make little empirical difference', because when the role of the 'third sector' is major, it is typically because it is subsidized by the state. Historical evidence shows that the forms taken by the third sector are determined by the interaction of the state, the market and the family, so to posit a form of relative autonomy is to undermine the analytic capacity of the model.) For Esping-Andersen, these institutional elements are brought together in national and multination constellations, or welfare regimes. Because these regimes also present a form of consistent logic, characteristic patterns of response or practice, they can be thought of as national political–economic cultures. Each of the regimes exhibits what Esping-Andersen terms 'institutional path dependency', setting out a characteristic response pattern for the management of social risks, such as those posed by the inability of families in post-industrial societies to sustain full responsibility for the care of dependants.

In capitalist societies, the market is the key means of generating income and wealth and is therefore an important determinant of the level of welfare enjoyed by the population. The workings of the market, in turn, dictate much of the character of the operation of the family and community life. Markets are governed by the logic of competition and distribution by cash, which depends on the commodification of goods, services and the labour that is involved in their production. As the evidence of the work/life collision discussed above shows, the effects of the commodification of labour on the household are profound, impacting directly on the capacity of the family to provide care, just as it frames the policy responses that are induced. The effects of the workings of markets are particularly evident in liberal welfare regimes, in which a relatively deregulated economy has been encouraged to promote economic growth. Market responses are also important in the development of the means for family substitution through the provision of various kinds of human services, products and as a source of labour. The system of market-based employment, in turn, limits the capacity of the family to provide its own care solutions.

Just as markets are the chief source of production in capitalist societies, the family has been the social form most responsible for social reproduction, providing the means for the conception and rearing of children, the support of the elderly and the sharing of risks between members of all ages. The dominant approach to redistribution within the family, notes Esping-Andersen, is that of 'reciprocity' (Esping-Andersen, 1999: 35). While the family is clearly an important locus of decision-making in post-industrial societies, the non-market actions of families and of individual family members, especially women, have long been ignored by economics and political economy. A model of welfare in post-industrial societies is now required in which families are both taken more seriously in the analysis and become more supported by policy. In recognition of the problem of defining 'the family' and the increasing diversity of domestic forms evident in post-industrial societies (Bittman and Pixley, 1997; Cheal, 2002), the term 'household' may, at times, be more accurate.

The third pillar of welfare regimes, the state, provides political and legal authority for the organization of contemporary societies and has become the means for the expression of collective political aspirations in democracies. The state, importantly, provides a key mechanism for mediating between the market and the family, with considerable (although clearly limited) capacity to regulate and manage markets, as well as the judicial authority to intervene in most domestic issues. There is not, however, a uniform template spelling out the way in which the state must interact with the market of families/households. Rather, argues Esping-Andersen, the characteristic ways these processes of intervention and mediation occur in post-industrial societies is neither uniform nor arbitrary, but is shaped by processes of 'institutional path dependency' (Esping-Andersen, 1999: 170 ff.), through which, as Mahon explains, regimes tend to respond to the challenges facing contemporary societies, such as the changing character of families/households, globalization and the shift to post-industrial economies, through largely incremental policy responses. This is because there are many beneficiaries of existing regimes who seek to defend what they perceive as their own interests. Further, each welfare-regime type tends to produce its own constituency, so extending the process (Mahon, 2002b: 11).

The welfare state, according to Esping-Andersen (1999), can be thought of as a form of national political management of social risks. The post-industrial challenge to welfare states is to manage the new risks arising from the fragility of the family and from the impact of globalization and the increasingly insecure patterns of employment associated with the service economy. A key new task, according to this analysis, is that of ensuring that the family will not be left alone to provide its members with the care and support they require. This task, termed rather awkwardly 'defamilialization', can be seen as the state acting in ways that are 'family friendly', providing specialized forms of social support that lessen the most intense caring burdens imposed on families (Lister, 1994; Esping-Andersen, 1999: 45; Knijn, 2004). The provision of quality child care and reliable community care services are good examples of the approach. Each of these programmes enables the family to care for children or for frail, older people or disabled members whilst ensuring that adult members, especially women in the family, can continue in employment outside the home. Paid maternity leave, in contrast, works by reinforcing the concept of the primacy of familial (maternal) care. When implemented without safeguards, it may undermine the right of the mother to continuity in paid employment, disrupting and perhaps even undermining progression in her career. Similarly, carer (or care-giver) payments to the relatives of older people, may serve to reinforce familialism. Each of these strategies has labour market consequences: defamilialization care policies maximize workforce participation rates, while policies premised on reinforcing familial responsibilities prevent a high proportion of the potential mature-age workforce from participating in paid employment.

Child Care and Employment

For Rianne Mahon, the reconfiguration of public and private responsibility for the financing and provision of child care is 'an important component of an effective post-industrial employment strategy' and therefore central to the redesign of the welfare state in the twenty-first century (Mahon, 2002a: 345). The link between employment and the need for child care is crucial. Mothers, like fathers, need to be freed from unremitting domestic responsibility for care in order to be able to seek employment outside the home, while children need to be prepared to take their place in the knowledge-based workplaces of the future. The benefits accrue to the broader economy as well as the mothers, their parental partners and children, in part through sustaining fertility. But while families need child care, Mahon continues, they can not rely on markets to provide it at a level of quality and in sufficient quantity to ensure ready access to it. Public support in some form is necessary. The need for child care is thus seen as a question of economic options for women and a political–economic question for governments. While the demography of fertility decisions is implicated, the importance of public support for child care is not one that can be reduced to demographic calculations (Mahon, 2002a). Similar analyses of the political characteristic of the development of child-care provisions apply to the development (or lack of development) of publicly supported child care in North America and Europe (Lewis and Lewis, 1996; Lewis, 1998; Rostgaard and Fridberg, 1998; Michel and Mahon, 2002; Anttonen, Baldock and Sipila, 2003).

As shown in Table 6.4, the development of formal child-care services varies significantly between countries. A broad system of patterning of service use is evident between welfare regimes, as Esping-Andersen's typology would predict. The varied levels of service use and the characteristics assumed by child-care provisions in each country can not be understood simply as reflections of cultural or familial differences between the different countries. Rather, there is an interaction between family-level behaviours and the political processes, institutional structures and labour markets involved. Important differences between countries considered as having the same type of welfare regime are also evident. These differences can only be understood by careful attention to the importance of political organizing at the national level, as well as the differences between those belonging to different regimes.

Amongst the English-speaking countries which Esping-Andersen has termed liberal welfare regimes, considerable variation in the levels of use of child-care services is evident. This can only be understood by considering political developments at the national and subnational level. Public support for child care in Canada, for example, has been the result of organized advocacy, with the most successful advocacy targeted at the provincial level. As a result, achievements have been

Table 6.4   Proportion of young children who use day-care facilities up to mandatory schooling age, 1998

	0–3-year-olds	3–mandatory school age
Australia	15	60
Canada	45	50
England (UK)	34	60
Ireland	38	40
New Zealand	45	90
United States	54	70
Austria	4	68
Belgium	30	97
Finland	22	66
France	29	99
Germany	8	40
Italy	6	95
Japan	13	34
Netherlands	6	98
Portugal	3–5	75
Spain	5	84
Denmark	64	91
Norway	40	80
Sweden	48	80

Source: OECD General Social Indicators and Tables, 2002. *SS15.2* Original *source:* DEELSA/ELSA /WP1(2000)6, Family-friendly policies: The reconciliation of work and family life, OECD, Paris. http://www.oecd.org/dataoecd/

incremental, leading to a fragmented and varied set of services and entitlements within but especially across the nation (Prentice, 2001). The most extensive provincial programme, the 'five-dollars-per-day' policy of affordable, publicly supported child care introduced in Quebec in 1997, came about as the result of decades-long campaigns in which feminists, together with provincial 'femocrats', trade-unionists and educationalists worked through a series of provincial government enquiries, promoting child care as a way to counter poverty and promote gender equality. Child care was also seen as a way of improving educational outcomes across the province, providing a means of addressing the demands of women to seek work and allow-ing provincial authorities to enforce new employment requirements imposed on low-income mothers (Jenson, 2001). By making the case for child care part of a broader picture for the redesign of provincial social policy, advocacy was successful in this instance in expanding public support. This contrasts with the experience in other provinces, such as British Columbia, Ontario and Saskatchewan, where linking advocacy of child-care policies to particular political parties led to advances that have not always been sustained after a change in govern-ment (Collier, 2001; Martin, 2001; Mahon and Phillips, 2002).

Activism by feminists for accessible, publicly supported child care have not been so successful in the USA, according to Sonya Michel (1999). Strong conservative traditions of 'family values' accompany long-held policies of allowing the market to operate relatively free of government intervention (O'Connor, Orloff and Shaver, 1999; Mahon, 2002a; Heffernan, 2003). Low market-based wage rates and the acceptance of a high degree of economic inequality has enabled the market to provide some form of child care (often provided by migrant, Hispanic or Afro-American staff) to a relatively large group of working women. Successful child-care campaigns led by education-alists have focused largely on the benefit of 'early intervention' in low-income, single-parent families, with the result that there is no national publicly supported programme of child care, but a series of state-based initiatives typically linked to educational rationales (Hobson, 1993; Michel, 1999; O'Connor, Orloff and Shaver, 1999). Market-based, private child care (day centres and private nannies in particu-lar) is used by those families that can afford them, although even advocates report significant problems with this approach. One inten-sive study of 400 day-care centres in four states found most centres to be 'poor to mediocre', noting that 'only one in seven centres provides a level of quality that promotes healthy development' (Helburn, 1995, cited in Blau, 2001: 66–7). David Blau, a conservative economist, suggests that this is owing to the need for the private sector to keep costs low enough for at least some families, forced to pay the full costs, to be able to afford to use them. The low rates of remuneration for child-care staff lead to high staff turnover, he argues, while the lack of information available to consumers concerning quality and care outcomes ensures 'market failure' (Blau, 2001).

Deborah Brennan notes that over the course of the twentieth century, child care in Australia moved from being a peripheral matter during times of relatively high birth-rates, to become a 'high profile, vigorously debated political and public policy issue' in the final decades of the century, a time marked by strongly reduced fertility. The shift in the construction of child care from a marginal philan- thropic issue to one in 'the mainstream agenda of Australian politics' (Brennan, 1998: 1) was the result of a long process of political strug- gle, dominated by campaigns mounted by feminists, with support over time from trade unions, some employers and national government, based on advocacy around the rights of women with children to employment (Brennan, 1998; O'Connor, Orloff and Shaver, 1999). These campaigns were successful in the 1970s and 1980s in ensuring the introduction and rapid expansion of a system of subsidized, community-based, non-profit child-care centres that was at the time the most extensive in the English-speaking world. However, from the early 1990s policy reforms saw increasing emphasis placed on the participation of private, for-profit providers in the subsidy programme. After 1996 and the election of a conservative government with an agenda favouring the expansion of market solutions to welfare and the traditional male breadwinner family, a massive expansion of private child care has taken place, leading to the stock-market listing of a number of large child-care corporations. There has been a move away from the payment of operational subsidies to child-care providers and significant changes in the payment of financial assistance to parents for the use of child care. While the total numbers of children using child care has increased somewhat, the new fee and subsidy system based on taxation rebates has made it more difficult to obtain child care for children under the age of two (Brennan, 1998; AIHW, 2003, pp. 215–74).

Government was also unwilling to intervene effectively in the issue of child care in Britain until the early 1990s. Until that time, only a small number of registered day nurseries, playgroups, and 'registered childminders' were made available, intended mainly for small numbers of parents with demonstrated needs for child care. As Land and Lewis (1998: 66) note, the official view was that the health and well-being of young children was best safeguarded if their mothers stayed at home to look after them. Other parents who needed child care were reliant on the private market, using nannies and au pair girls, relatives, friends or neighbours, where they could. A subsidized private-market approach came close to being tried in Britain in the latter years of the Conservative government, with a system of vouchers sufficient to pay for the cost of part-time day-care services in the private sector foreshadowed by the Major government before it lost power. A more ambitious programme, the National Childcare Strategy, was introduced by Tony Blair's Labour Government in 1998. This went a long way to reversing the long-held attitude opposing the employment of the mothers of young children outside the home (Land and Lewis, 1998; Lewis, 1998; Randall, 2002). The approach expanded private child-care services for infants, as well as 'nursery education' which was to become available to all children from the age of four. Other components involved the improved regulation of services and training for child-care staff, and a system of working families tax credits and child-care tax credits to subsidize access to services by low-income earners. According to Baldock, the new policy was intended to ensure that child care outside the home would be available for all children aged 14 or under, based on the principle that 'all parents of young children should be enabled to work if they choose so' (Baldock, 2003: 118).

While there are clearly differences in child-care policy between the different English-speaking countries, there is also a degree of commonality that, according to Esping-Andersen, reflects the patterning of welfare regimes in the liberal model of social policy in which an emphasis is given to the priorities of the market over the state or the family (Esping-Andersen, 1990, 1999; O'Connor, Orloff and Shaver, 1999; Mahon, 2002a). Policy in most countries in continental Europe has followed a more familialistic or conservative approach, in which governments have emphasized the preservation of the 'traditional' breadwinner family rather than increasing the labour-force participation of mothers (Dean, 2002). This approach has resulted in extensive differences in the take-up of child care, with low levels of use before the age of three and much higher levels for the pre-school (or early childhood) education programmes provided to older infants, as can be seen in Table 6.4. The approach is most starkly recognizable in southern European nations such as Portugal, Italy and Spain (Dean, 2002), and in Japan (Peng, 2002; Heffernan, 2003; Takahashi, 2003). In these countries, the absence of formal, publicly supported child-care services forces those who come from families that can not afford to buy in family help to refrain from giving birth or to give up paid work and shoulder the burdens of family care unaided. In the southern European countries, affordable child-care services are not widely available. While some families use private domestic workers of immigrant origin, this is not affordable for many families with women of child-bearing age (Bettio, Simonazzi and Villa, 2004). This is combined with the familialist tendencies of social policies that continue to reserve prime employment for male breadwinners, and enforce the continued dependence of the relatively large numbers of unemployed young women (and men) on their families of origin. Viewed in this way, the drop in fertility rate in these countries should not be surprising, but understood as a rational response to the care penalty that women who bear children must confront.

More interventionist and supportive familial policies are found in a number of northern European countries, in particular France, Germany, Belgium, the Netherlands (Esping-Andersen, 1999) and Finland (Mahon, 2002a). The emphasis here is on the provision of support for the 'family' through the extended paid maternity leave and other family benefits that enable mothers to withdraw from the labour market for a prolonged period after the birth of each child (Morgan and Zippel, 2003). By providing direct financial support for women who take on domestic responsibility for the care of young children, policies embody a traditional approach to the family that is translated into measures that provide incentives to women to assume the duties of a full-time care-giver and mother. Because it promotes unpaid maternal care over labour-market participation, there is also far less attention given to the development of viable formal services as an alternative or complement to family care.

A third alternative is that termed the 'social democratic' (Esping-Andersen, 1990; 1999) 'egalitarian' (Mahon, 2002a) or 'gender equality' (Duncan, 2002; Mahon, 2002a) model. This is encountered primarily in Scandinavia, where extensive, high-quality child-care services are made available in order that women are not forced to choose between motherhood and employment, but are enabled to engage in both (Rostgaard and Fridberg, 1998; Mahon, 2002a; Anttonen, Baldock and Sipila, 2003). There remain deficiencies and problems in the system of services in each country, yet it is clear that the principles underlying and inspiring the development of child care in each country have differed from those elsewhere in Europe for several decades. Here, policy has been used to pursue gender and social equity while also promoting high levels of labour-market participation. This has been achieved primarily through high levels of tax, thus avoiding the pressures to minimize social spending. However, recent budgetary constraints in Sweden and Denmark in particular appear to have put pressure on the model, although it is not clear whether this is substantial enough to raise doubts about its long-term sustainability. In the latter years of the twentieth century, the levels of public child-care provision in these societies were deliberately lifted considerably, with the intention of enabling women to both work and have children. As the figures on the use of child care for young children show (Table 6.4), the availability of child care in these countries is matched by their comparatively high levels of use, especially notable for those children aged under three. Child care, which also functions as a form of education, is regarded as a right for children. Considerable effort has also been made to ensure the democratic, civic character of such services, to ensure that families have a voice in their operation.

Although generalized and abstract, the welfare-regimes approach of Esping-Andersen provides a valuable analytic tool that encourages reflection on the ways in which state policies mediate and shape family interaction with the labour market. The approach is based on the categorization of countries with broadly comparable welfare mixes, rather than on the impact of policies on women and families. In turn it has also stimulated a significant effort in comparative research in recent years that has focused more on the outcomes for women and family care, based on detailed analyses of empirical data (Knijn and Ungerson, 1997; Lewis, 1998; Anttonen, Baldock and Sipila, 2003; Stark, 2005). Perhaps the most detailed and important of these accounts is the analysis of European 'care regimes' that draws together an extraordinary amount of detail specifically related to the way in which care was provided in different Western European countries in the late 1990s (Bettio and Plantenga, 2004). By combining detailed time-budget data from the European Community Household Panel (ECHP) with information on national policies, the two authors carefully compare the mix of formal and informal care provisions evident in both child care and aged care across a wide spectrum of measures. At the household level, the data enable the authors to compare countries on the basis of the extent of the reliance on informal care for children and aged people, the extent of intergenerational care of young children, and the share of domestic care tasks undertaken by women. These measures were then combined with data on legal entitlements and the availability of formal services, including entitlements to maternity and parental leave for children, child-related tax allowances and family allowances, use of child-care services, care leave for older family members, community and residential services for the aged, and public financial support (pensions) available to the elderly. This approach lead to the identification of five care-regime clusters in Europe, as set out in Table 6.5.

The key feature distinguishing between each cluster is the extent and character of family responsibility for care. At one end of the spectrum of European regimes are the Mediterranean countries of Italy, Greece, Spain and Portugal, together with Ireland. Bettio and Plantenga (2004) report that each of these countries shares a strong emphasis on care as primarily the responsibility of the family. At the other end of the spectrum, the Nordic countries in the study, Denmark, Finland and Sweden, provide extensive support to families and a range of services, benefits and leave provisions that mean that women are not forced to withdraw from paid employment to ensure that their children or aged parents receive care. The six countries between these two poles, argue Bettio and Plantenga, share significant details of family policy with one other country, hence producing three additional clusters. With the exception of the UK, which Esping-Andersen groups together with the USA and other English-speaking lands, each of these countries belongs to the welfare-regime type originally identified as 'corporatist'.

It is important not to get lost in the details of classificatory schemes, although this happens all too often in academic debate. The key point to keep in mind here is not where and how many boundaries should be drawn between groups of countries on the basis of particular details of policy at a particular point in time. Rather, it is the larger issue of the challenges that traditional approaches to care, based upon the male breadwinner family, face in the globalized, post-industrial societies of the twenty-first century.

Table 6.5 Care regimes in Europe: strategies for care of children and elders

	Informal care	Women f/t home carers(a) (%)	Level of provisions for child care		Level of provisions for care of the elderly	
			Index of parental leave provisions	Public Services for children 0–3	Residential care	Community care
Italy	high	37.0	medium	low	low	low
Greece	high	39.0	low	low	low	low
Spain	high	37.7	low	low	low	low
Portugal	low	14.8	low	low	low	low
Ireland	medium	41.7	low	low	medium	medium
UK	high	16.0	low	medium(b)	high	n.a.(c)
Netherlands	high	15.3	low	low/medium	high	medium
Austria	medium	20.5	medium	low	medium	low
Germany	medium	17.8	medium	low	medium	low
Belgium	medium	19.9	medium	medium	high	low
France	low	11.3	medium	medium	high	low
Denmark	low	2.9	high	high	medium	high
Finland	low	8.3	high	medium	n.a.	medium
Sweden	n.a.	n.a.	high	high	n.a.	high

Notes: (a) Share of female population aged 25–59 with full-time responsibilities for unpaid care (1996).
(b) Entry adjusted by MF in line with Table 6.4.
(c) Data not available in comparable form for Bettio and Plantenga.

Source. Adapted from Bettio and Plantenga (2004: 100, 103). Downloaded from http://www.tandf.co.uk/journals

In the debates that have arisen about child care and work/life conflict, the concept of care is defined broadly as family support. Care, in this context, is understood in the broad sense of responsibility for family. This contrasts with the narrower definitions of care typically invoked in discussion about carers and responsibility for the primary care for older adults. The demand for child care and for other family-friendly policies such as care leave in turn reflect the conflict evident between time for paid work and unpaid time with family. This conflict arises from the demands of employers, from an increasingly competitive and globalized market and from the limited capacity of private households to respond to the needs for personal support without assistance. Rather than being demographically driven, as is the case with reforms to aged-care services, child care and other family policies thus serve as a way of resolving the tensions affecting families as they operate within the market.

A collective social response to these tensions is required because the earnings of most women will not otherwise be sufficient to do more than offset the cost of quality child care, removing any economic incentive they may have to work. Such a social response, in which there is a public entitlement of access to care services and family leave for males as well as females, is also called for because individual women and their families facing global competition for family-friendly work conditions are not able to bargain with employers. Demands for child care are framed in this context as a product of the changed family system and are indicative of the need to forge new sets of relations between the market, the family and the state.

To understand how these relationships are changing in the increasingly individualized world of the twenty-first century, and how the increasing awareness of risk and the new organizational logic of globalized market economies affects the way we need to think about providing care, I turn in the final part of this book to consider critically the contribution that contemporary social theory might make.

PART 3

Care and Social Theory

Social research, and the discipline of sociology in particular, strives to understand the complexity and changing patterns of social life, the way that people live collectively and as individuals. Social theory should, then, have a lot to say about care. The concept of care and research into the practices of caring are likely to be encountered in writing and in sociology courses on gender, the family and social support, and in the field of social policy or health sociology. Yet at its most ambitious and general level, that of major macrosociological theories of contemporary social life, there are few if any direct references to care.

In this respect social theory is no better than economics, which, as Nancy Folbre argues, has long ignored care in both theory and practice (Folbre, 2001b). Economics serves as the guide to what is important in the economy. The fact that care work is omitted from the national accounts and any expenditure on care is considered to be unproductive is likely to shape economic decisions and fiscal policy. The omission of care from social theory similarly serves to maintain its invisibility. At best, its treatment as a marginal or specialist topic in the major works of theory can only encourage the response from policy-makers and other key decision-makers that it is an issue that has only passing importance, or that it might be important, but only for small interest groups.

There is a strong parallel here with other social concepts, such as gender. Mainstream social science in the 1950s sustained the Parsonian ideals that family and sex roles were normative and functional, that women should adhere to their roles as mothers and home-makers, and that those who sought to act differently were deviants and their families dysfunctional. It was in the writing of feminist social theorists, such as Simone de Beauvoir, Betty Friedan and Kate Millet, that an alternative approach was first articulated. The introduction of the concept of gender into feminism and subsequently into main-stream social theory enabled experts to make a distinction between a person's biologically determined sex and their engagement in the social world (Eisenstein, 1984; Tong, 1998). Similarly, if the importance of care is to be recognized in the twenty-first century, its importance to social life must be emphasized in the social sciences – in social theory as well as economics – and not treated as just another specialized or marginal topic. This must be a two-way process. The body of recent work in sociology and other social science disciplines has much to offer anyone who wants to try and understand changing patterns of caring and the apparently contradictory developments in care and human services that characterize our age. It is in the interests of both practical politics and social research to build on the existing dialogue and for sociological theory to develop general accounts of social life in which care is central.

In Part 3, to indicate the direction that I believe the dialogue should take, I address a number of key themes to have emerged from contemporary sociology that relate to the topic of care. The discussion commences with a consideration of the microsociological themes of the body, individualization and personal life in Chapter 7. The attention given to each of these themes in recent years signals an important new direction in sociological perspectives, opening new possibilities for an imaginative understanding of how people can live together that has considerable importance for understanding developments in care. The global transformation of social structures in post-industrial societies in recent decades also indicates the continuing importance of developments at the macrosociological level. In Chapter 8, therefore, I focus on the concepts of risk and the new organizational logic. These developments are increasingly shaping the way that the social institutions associated with the state and the market respond to the challenges of ensuring appropriate care solutions will be available for those who need personal support.

In the twenty-first century, opportunities for both individual growth and collective effort are considerable. The challenge to social theory and to those of us living in ageing, low-fertility societies is this: to ensure that care moves from a taken-for-granted element of social life to be recognized as an essential and foundational practice which defines the character and quality of the humanity we inevitably must share with others, in much the same way as do the practices and institutional structures of work and employment, politics and systems of exchange.

CHAPTER 7

The Body, Individualization and the Transformation of Personal Life

In a now famous formulation, C. Wright Mills (1959) saw sociology's subject matter as the 'intersection of history and biography'. Yet most research until recently placed the emphasis on questions of history, or social structure, with relatively little attention being given to the issues that might be considered biographical. The rise of feminism, the recognition of the importance of sexuality for social life and the dramatic transformation of personal and domestic life in the closing stages of the twentieth century have forced social analysts to pay greater attention to issues linked to self, identity and the significance of the actions of individuals. Attention to these more biographical issues has had a very significant impact on contemporary social theory, opening up new ways of thinking about social life that are of direct relevance to any attempt to understand care. In this chapter, therefore, I focus on three of the main themes to emerge from this new work – the themes of the body, individualization and the transformation of personal life.

As well as enhancing our understanding of the dilemmas to be faced in care in high modernity, recognition of the body and the precarious vulnerability of physical life provides a powerful conceptual tool with which to explore the central place that issues of care occupy in human societies. The sociology of the body, I argue, also provides a basis on which care can be seen as central to the development of social theory. The thesis in this chapter, following the work of Turner and Rojek (2001), is that social theory can and should recognize the bodily foundations of our existence as individual, sentient beings. From that basis flows the need for social theory to recognize the fundamental importance of care as a social response to the vulnerability that arises from our embodied human existence. Acknowledgement of the body and its link to social life, in turn, helps make sense of the related process of individualization, at a time in which personal life and the social institutions with which it is most closely linked, households and the family, are undergoing such radical transformations.

The Rise of the Body in Sociological Theory

Although sociological interest in the body is relatively new, it can be traced back through the founders of the discipline of sociology in the nineteenth and early twentieth centuries (Williams and Bendelow, 1998), through Marx, Weber and Durkheim, who referred to the body extensively as a metaphor for social life. This interest continued through writers such as Simmel and, more recently, Goffman and Elias. With the more recent work of French philosopher Merleau-Ponty (1962, 1968) and Michel Foucault (1978, 1980), who was concerned with the social significance of bodily discipline, new conceptual approaches became possible. Mary Douglas, for example, wrote about the body as a source of pollution (Douglas, 1966), while more recently Brian Turner (1984, 1996) fostered the development of the sociology of the body.

According to Chris Shilling (1995), the 'rise of the body' in recent sociological theory can be understood as a response to at least four phenomena:

1. the arrival of second-wave feminism, with its concern for bodily issues such as sex and gender, the beauty myth, advertising imagery, work and the supposed natural inability of women to perform certain tasks;
2. the ageing population of Western societies, which required attention to the body so that distinctions might be made between physical processes and the social construction of ageing;
3. the expansion of consumer culture, with its emphasis on the physical self through the rise of exercise, diet and fashion regimes and though its focus on the body beautiful;
4. bio-technical developments such as organ transplants, genetic engineering and the expansion of cyberspace, each of which

extends the concept of life, blurring the boundaries between what is real, what is mechanical and what is virtual.

Many embodiment theorists find death, the end of the living body, to be of particular sociological interest (Shilling, 1995). Death is frequently preceded by a period of extended care, just as birth, the appearance of the body, is followed by a prolonged period of care and dependence. Care, and particularly the extended personal care required by children or those nearing death, no less than the events of birth or death themselves, I argue, needs to be understood as a social response to the needs for personal support arising from the vulnerability and inadequacies of the body.

While sociological argument since the 1960s has tended to stress the 'social construction' of social life (Berger and Luckman, 1967), Turner and Rojek (2001) speak out against the extreme extension of this proposition. They argue that it is wrong to assume that the physical existence of the body can be understood as being similar, ontologically, to social events and processes. Life events, including birth and death, are shaped by social expectations, enacted as rituals and given symbolic meanings. But the body can not be reduced to a social construction in the same way. The body has a materiality, a visceral and physical presence absent in symbolic social phenomena. Most importantly, the body is part of a living, conscious being that, in the nature of its existence, participates in, but is distinct from, the social relationships and cultural forms that shape social life.

Social conditions are significant at each point in an individual's life. The facts of conception and birth, for example, are shaped by social, cultural, religious, ethical, legal and economic conditions. From birth, a child must first survive and then learn to become a competent adult. Care is central to this process. Since it is a necessary condition if infants are to survive, we can think of care as an elementary social form. In this way, recognition of the body in social theory provides an important step towards an acknowledgement of the fundamental importance of care as a primary building block for social life. I return to this issue in the final section of this chapter.

Care Work as Body Work

Providing what in nursing is referred to as 'personal care' inevitably involves physical contact between a care-giver while she (or he) attends to the support of the bodily functions of another (Twigg, 2000). It can, indeed, be argued that, at the final point of delivery, care is necessarily concerned with practices that require the tending of the body of another. Care, at this level, is an active social relationship in which sustaining a person's bodily existence is the most basic priority. It is a bodily engagement in two senses: first, personal care involves attending to the body and bodily needs of the recipient; second, the act of providing care also involves direct physical engagement and bodily exertion from the care-giver.

The level of bodily involvement is arguably most extensive in the breast-feeding and cuddling of infants, as the care recipient's incapacity is physical, not just emotional, and the care-giver's body becomes a direct instrument of care. Physical contact is also essential for other forms of care, such as attending to the needs of frail, older people and disabled people and the sick, where it is necessary to provide support to assist such people directly in tasks that they are physically unable to complete without assistance. In providing care, tending to the well-being of others, it is not just muscle power which is involved; touch is a fundamental rather than an incidental feature. The physical dexterity, strength and skill of the care-giver is crucial in determining the viability of particular acts of care-giving.

Some of the potential for recognizing the links between the body and the social response of care is captured in the following brief extract from Julie Godyer's moving account of caring for patients with Alzheimer's disease:

> I had never been so conscious of people's bodies as when I began working in nursing homes. Patients, especially those with dementias like Alzheimer's Disease, were often handled without any awareness or consideration of their 'selfness', handled as if they were only bodies and nothing else. Often they were wrenched from slumber in the very early hours, pulled forcibly out of bed, placed firmly on commode chairs and wheeled to the shower. Here they were stripped, washed, dried and dressed again – often without a word of explanation, because of a belief that they didn't understand what was going on anyway. The daily routines pivoted around getting food into the patients and ensuring the subsequent, and required daily bowel motion . . . The intimacy of physical contact necessary for these routines between nurse and patient was something over

which patients had no control. They were touched, handled, repositioned, toileted and so on constantly throughout the day and had no choice over when or where they were touched. Many became limp, immobilized, refusing to move themselves or help in any way even if they could. Refusing also to speak, these patients began to seem like heavy lumps of flesh, nothing else – all body. This treatment of people with Alzheimer's Disease was not (in my nursing experience) seen to be either unfair or unusual in an institution where the control of bodies is sanctioned by a medical discourse, and, subsequently, a society, which has already abjected those with dementias such as Alzheimer's Disease. This was simply called 'care'. (Goyder, 2001: 123–4)

By enclosing the term 'care' in inverted commas, Godyer signals her scepticism, as a direct care-giver, about the character and nature of support provided to those who are no longer able to act as conscious, intelligent people. Unable to express personal preferences or exercise choice in a way that usually signals the personhood of individuals in high modernity, staff working in facilities for the care of those suffering advanced dementia or a range of other comparable conditions are confronted with the task of sustaining a body in life while many of the other signs of personhood (such as awareness of the immediate situation) may be absent. Is it possible to recognize a person as an individual if they are physically dependent on care and unable to direct the care-giver?

Body Work as Dirty Work

Norbert Elias (1994) argued that the 'civilizing process' that led to the development of modern mass societies has been accompanied by a general sanitizing and depersonalization of social interaction, in which cultural codes of interaction between strangers enforce a respect for personal space and an avoidance of intimate personal contact except in situations involving sexual behaviour. Bodies are regarded as private and intimate, bodily fluids and other excretions experienced as dirty and polluting, and (sexual partners aside) close bodily contact avoided between strangers, colleagues, friends and even family members (Hall, 1969). However, as Julia Twigg's ethnographic study of community care in the UK carefully documents, the act of providing personal care inevitably involves touching, cleaning, massaging, comforting, dressing and undressing the recipient (Twigg, 2000). When care staff attend to clients, much of their work involves transgressing these unspoken cultural and personal boundaries. This is clearly an enormous obstacle for those who first receive care as well as an issue for those providing it. Fear of intimacy and of acknowledging dependency and handing control to a stranger may help explain the reluctance commonly encountered amongst older people to accept personal assistance when self-care still appears a possibility (Fine and Thomson, 1997).

Providing personal care is typically a responsibility assigned to female staff. In the process, a range of strategies are deployed to manage the mutual embarrassment involved. Humour may be used, or awkward silences endured when difficult moments are encountered. Many of the accounts given to Twigg by care-worker informants concern how they manage in these very intimate bodily moments. One snippet helps capture the feeling of delicacy and awkwardness particularly graphically: 'We joke – I joke, specially if you're actually washing them and they start having a motion and, you know, you say: "Oh, we've just got a surprise here – one minute!" You know, but you just, you can't do it any other way really' (Twigg, 2000: 148).

The way in which the two parties to the care interaction manage to deal with the care of the body also tells us much about the way in which the experience of care, as a deeply personal, intimate form of sociality, is understood as shaping an individual's sense of self. By maintaining a humorous but warm and accepting form of interaction with the care recipient, the careworker cited above is attempting to affirm her esteem for the person. It is also possible to use the interactions involved in care to humiliate the recipient, or to patronize or infantilize them, as accounts of less desirable forms of care have frequently shown (Goffman, 1968; Penglase, 2005).

Despite the sensitivity with which careworkers documented by Twigg undertook their work, care staff typically reported being denied the social recognition that might be thought of as their due. Twigg attributes this wider ambivalence about care work to broader social attitudes towards the body and body work. Taking her cue from Lawler's account of the body in nursing (Lawler, 1991), Twigg notes that body work is associated with low-status, low-paid occupations, often in poor conditions. In the field of care work, managers, senior nursing staff and other health professionals tend to be distanced from the necessity of this polluting contact as their responsibilities for care become a matter of procedures, policies, communication and concern. The ambivalence about body work is one of the main barriers encountered in nursing, too, as nurses seeking to provide care of the close and personal kind face a continual struggle for recognition as true health professionals as a result (see also Chapter 2). Those whose work involves washing the patients and cleaning the bedpans are seen as doing the work that others avoid, but rather than being rewarded for it, they face an occupational and financial penalty, the predominantly female practitioners receiving low levels of social recognition and poor remuneration (Baines, 1998; Franzway, 2001; England, Budig and Folbre, 2002).

Drawing on the theme of the avoidance of bodily functions, Twigg's analysis points to an even more sinister aspect of care work, as she argues,

> Fundamentally, carework is 'dirty work' because it deals with aspects of life that society, especially modern secular society with its ethic of material success and its emphasis on youth and glamour, does not want to think about: decay, dirt, death, decline, failure. Careworkers manage these aspects of life on behalf of wider society, ensuring they remain hidden, tidied away into the obscurities of institutions or private homes. (Twigg, 2000: 145)

This approach echoes Giddens's comments on the sequestration of experience (Giddens, 1991). Yet, while it is possible to recognize that care involves 'dirty work', the question must be asked – is care/body work exceptional in the occupational system? Can the low status of providing physical care be compared with that of other workers, such as manual workers, where physical effort by the worker receives little or no recognition in pay or the occupational status hierarchy? Are Twigg and Lawler correct in focusing just on the body of the care recipient? What is the significance of the physical nature of much of the careworker's work?

One way in which the careworker's body has received attention from researchers is in relation to the question of gender. There were, for example, few men in Twigg's sample of domestic careworkers – reflecting the low numbers of males working in the occupation. Those who were encountered spoke of having ended up doing the work almost accidentally, as very few males deliberately chose to enter this occupational field. This, Twigg suggests, reflects common attitudes of care being seen as women's work, and therefore demeaning and unsuitable for men. Those who do seek employment in this field soon discover the mistrust of males undertaking work that involves intimate contact with bodies. Men who undertake this work, for example, are routinely portrayed as being gay – a suggestion that their masculinity is somehow compromised or incomplete. In community-based care, the proportion of males is typically even lower than in residential settings. The intimacy of dealing with the body in the privacy of the home, suggest Twigg and her informants, makes this an even more difficult sphere in which to manage expectations.

This suggests that the issue of the body in care is considerably more complex than a focus on the body of the care recipient alone might at first indicate. Comparisons of aspects of behaviour towards the body and care amongst different client groups (children, HIV/AIDS patients, clients from different cultural groups and social backgrounds) appear to be just one possible direction that this research could take.

Individualization in Contemporary Social Theory

Moves towards the recognition of the body in recent sociological theory parallel the reawakening of another long-standing theme in sociology – that of the importance of the individual and of the social process of individualization. The process, whereby individuals have increasingly come to be seen and to be held accountable as social beings in their own right rather than as members of some predefined social group, class or category, has long been recognized as a central dynamic of modernization (Lukes, 1973; Durkheim, 1984; Elias, 1991). Given this long-run recognition of the process of individualization, it is somewhat surprising to realize that for most of the history of sociological thought, emphasis has been placed on social structure, rather at the expense of recognizing the importance of human agency. Individual human beings came to be seen as the product of systems over which they had no control, a condition that Denis Wrong famously criticized as 'oversocialized' (Wrong, 1961). In recent decades sociological theory has increasingly rejected the oversocialized approach, embracing the concepts of 'identity' and the 'subjectivity' and 'agency' of individuals. This change in theoretical stance has accompanied a broader process of social change in advanced societies that has intensified and extended the process of individualization.

Individualization, Identity and the Self

Two sociologists from the modern German tradition, Norbert Elias and Ulrich Beck, have been particularly important in addressing the shift away from solidaristic social formations such as family, community and social class, towards a more ego-focused individual identity in late modernity. Their concern for how this has been shaped by the institutions of the welfare state, as well as by broader economic and cultural processes, help make their accounts of seminal interest to the study of care.

Like Simmel before him, Elias is deeply concerned with the fundamental question of, as he puts it, 'the problem of the single person within the plurality of people' that is termed society (Elias, 1991: ix). Through his historical 'process sociology' approach, he identifies individualization as a process that is not unique to modern industrial or post-industrial society, but one which has also occurred earlier, albeit on a more limited scale. One such occurrence can be traced to the dissolution of tribal communities into Germanic feudal society; another to the time of the Renaissance, which saw the emergence of a small, secular-bourgeois class freed from the tight social ties and constraints of the rigid feudal social order (Elias, 1994: 63, 232 ff.). These historical moments represent points in the process of social integration where smaller, relatively tightly knit social units are absorbed into a larger social unit, causing a shift in the position of people in relation to the social unit to which they belonged. Such a shift came to be designated by Elias as a change in the 'We–I balance', as people are detached from traditional groupings, placing greater emphasis on the I-identity of the individual person (Elias, 1991: 165 ff.).

Elias (1991: 180–1) also points insightfully to what he terms a 'quite peculiar double function' of the modern welfare state in relation to the individual citizen in our own era. The state, seeking to use social policy to integrate people into the larger social whole, strives to treat all people equally, ironing out differences between individuals. But, he argues, while

the state apparatus . . . embeds the individual in a network of rules
which is by and large the same for all citizens, the modern state
organisation does not relate to people as sisters or uncles, as
members of a family group or one or other of the pre-state forms
integration. (Elias, 1991: 180–1)

Citizens of modern states are not treated differently according to their
affiliation to a particular community or even social class, but as individuals. In this way, Elias argues, the welfare state has made its own
contribution to the new advance of what he terms 'mass individualization'. Key concepts here, then, are those of the loosening of existing ties with the incorporation of people into new and larger social
formations, and the impact of administrative law, with its injunction to
impersonal equality of individuals before the law.

Beck's (1992) account of the historical significance and social
processes underlying individualization has much in common with that of
Elias. He is, however, more strident in his assertion that the individualization evident in advanced modernity represents a new type of social
order. Individualization, for Beck, is the key dynamic by which social
relations are presently being reconfigured. Not to be confused with selfish, self-centred withdrawal from social life, the term is a translation
from the original German term *Individualiserung*, which, he claimed
recently, may be best translated by the term 'institutionalized individualism' (Beck and Beck-Gernsheim, 2002: xxi). Individualization, in
Beck's sense, is thus not the same as individualism, or individuation. Nor
can it be reduced to the notion, advocated by liberals and neo-liberals,
of market individualism based on competition between self-interested
individuals as workers and consumers. Rather, Beck claims, the concept
of individualization refers to the structural transformation of social institutions and of the relationship of individuals to society. It represents the
process whereby 'modernity has freed people from historically inscribed
roles [and] . . . simultaneously created new forms of social commitment'
(Beck and Beck-Gernsheim, 2002: 202). Individualization, in this sense,
is a process that involves liberation or disembedding from traditional
roles and social constraints on the one hand, while creating new forms
of social commitment based on individualized identity and personal
commitment on the other:

The individual, not his or her class, becomes the unit for the reproduction of the social in his or her own lifeworld. Individuals have to

develop their own biography and organize it in relation to others. If you take as an example family life under conditions of individualization, there is no given set of obligations and opportunities, no way of organizing everyday work, the relationship between men and women, and between parents and children, which can just be copied. (Beck and Beck-Gernsheim, 2002: 203)

Beck's identification of the labour market as the 'motor' of individualization (Beck, 1992: 92) is central to his approach. While he argues that individualization in the eighteenth and nineteenth centuries was derived essentially from the ownership and accumulation of capital, in late modernity individualization is seen as a by-product of the labour market, made apparent through the processes of workers acquiring work skills, offering them for sale and applying them. There are three main dimensions of this process, according to Beck (1992: 94):

1. education, with its emphasis on individual achievement;
2. the mobility of labour in the search for jobs, careers and better rewards;
3. competition between individuals, which undermines the equality of equals, causing the isolation of individuals within homogeneous social groups.

These components, he argues, supplement and reinforce each other, while other developments also play an important role. Chief among these are what we might loosely term affluence and consumerism, as expressed by increasing standards of living and higher incomes which have led to a process of 'collective upward mobility' and the democratization of formerly exclusive types of consumption and styles of living. By emphasizing the responsibility of individuals for their actions as well as using the law to adjudicate labour relations, the legal system has also served to strengthen the trend towards individualization (Beck, 1992: 95–6).

Beck posits a link between individualization, institutionalization and standardization. Individuation is not a process of unending social differentiation and division. Rather, he argues, the means for the achievement of individualization also institutionalize and standardize relations between people. Comparing the process to Simmel's account of how money, as a means of exchange between people, both individualizes and standardizes, Beck (1992: 131) asserts that there is an 'institution-dependent control structure of individual situations. Individualization becomes the most advanced form of societalization, dependent on the market, law, education and so on.'

Importantly, Beck does not claim that all of social life is comprehensively individualized, nor does he claim that there are simple, linear effects or outcomes of the process. Rather, he suggests, there is a complex and rather messy triple process of individualization involved (Beck, 1992: 125–38):

1. *Liberation.* Individuals are set free from traditional constraints and obligations (such as strict gender roles) that had dictated how they led their lives.
2. *Disenchantment.* This represents a reaction to the loss of stability that arises as the consequence of the disembedding of relationships from their previously stable and predictable foundations.
3. *Reintegration.* The third stage, an ongoing, incomplete and still elusive process, involves the development of new forms of social commitment and integration. This final step represents the search for a re-embedding of relationships based on the outcomes of individualization.

Beck further distinguishes subjective, mental components of the individualization process from objective, behavioural components. As an objective life situation, he argues, individualization has been only incompletely achieved for the bulk of the population of advanced societies. However, as a subjective ideal it has increasingly become the standard to which people in late modernity refer in making any decision concerning life matters.

Life Politics and the Transformation of Intimacy

The advancement of structuration theory in the 1980s (Giddens, 1984) contributed conceptually to breaking down the duality between structure and agency that had long characterized much sociological thought. Subsequently, in the early 1990s, Giddens, like Beck, came to emphasize the increased pressures of individual responsibility and risk that accompany the 'disembedding' of individuals from the relatively stable social institutions of industrial society and the concern in late modernity with personal self-actualization as the goal of life. In his most extensive and well-known analysis of life politics, Giddens (1991, 1993) examined what he terms 'the transformation of intimacy'. He proposed that the ideal of the 'pure relationship' has emerged as the prototype, the ideal social form for the achievement of self-identity in high modernity. Once a privileged indulgence of a small leisured elite, this has now become the universal modern ideal, encountered across all social classes. In contrast to traditional systems of social relationships which are reliant on external constraints (typically manifest in legally codified form), a pure relationship, he argued, is one that exists solely for the rewards that it can provide to each participant.

A relatively neglected element of Giddens's discussion that is important from the perspective of understanding developments in care concerns the 'sequestration of experience'. This term refers to the way that experiences and events linked with issues that disturb us are sequestered or kept separate from daily experience so as not to disturb our sense of ontological security. This is achieved as a result of abstract systems and other institutional arrangements which remove the modern citizen from needing to have direct or personal confrontation with most troubling matters. This leads, according to Giddens (1991: 146–7), to the development of an incapacity for moral engagement with such issues, although under certain circumstances an almost primitive demand for action, for something to be done, may result. Disputing Giddens's claims, Carol Smith argues that rather than the result being a retreat from morals, the sequestration of experience has led to the development of the 'rights talk' which she claims characterizes late modernity (Smith, 2002).

Individualization, Women and Family Care

Both the democratic and emancipatory potential of individualization and the confusion and uncertainty that accompany the disembedding of people from secure social institutions are illustrated in the link that is the title of an important paper by Elizabeth Beck-Gernsheim (2002), *From 'Living for Others' to 'A Life of One's Own'. Individualization and Women.* Beck-Gernsheim argues that while full 'liberation' may not yet have been achieved, women are increasingly able to choose to extricate themselves from the socially constructed fate of lifelong wife and housekeeper in which their only choice was living for others – their husband, children and family. In the patriarchal breadwinner family which preceded the current period of individualization, the main identity open to women was that ascribed through marriage. The social position that resulted was one based on the economic and legal state of dependence on their husbands, their life choices based on the principle of self-sacrifice for others.

Rather than the result of a single moment of revolutionary change, the process has been one Beck-Gernsheim characterizes as many small steps over a long period of modernity. The expansion of democracy with its suffragette campaigns for changes to the franchise further fostered this realization in the early twentieth century, as did the increasing opportunities for employment outside the home that developed from the 1960s. Greater sexual freedom and opportunities to develop personal relationships outside the family gradually accrued, slowly enabling women in advanced societies to be able to assert their democratic 'rights' as individuals to develop a life of their own. Individualization, seen in this way, involved the extension of democracy into the family, providing women, in particular, with choices denied in earlier times.

For Beck and Beck-Gernsheim, individualization has thus been central to changes in the family. Writing together, they argue that new opportunities for women have combined with the search for personal meaning and happiness in life to undermine the patriarchal form of the nuclear family, leading to a search for new and more flexible forms of love and domesticity:

> The nuclear family, built around gender status, is falling apart on the issues of emancipation and equal rights, which no longer conveniently come to a halt outside our private lives. The result is the quite normal chaos called love.

> If this diagnosis is right, what will take over from the family, that haven of domestic bliss? The family, of course! Only different, more, better: the negotiated family, the alternating family, the multiple family, new arrangements after divorce, remarriage, divorce again, new assortments from your, my, our children, our past and present families. It will be an expansion of the nuclear family and its extension in time; it will be an alliance between individuals as it has always been, and it will be glorified because it represents a sort of refuge in the chilly environment of our affluent, impersonal,

uncertain society, stripped of its traditions and scarred by all kinds of risk. Love will become more important than ever and equally impossible. (Beck and Beck-Gernsheim, 1995: 2)

In this vein, the emergence of new types of family can be understood as one of the ways in which individuals are reintegrated or re-embedded into social life. In the case of the family, some of the contours that this transformation are forming have already become clear. In most Western countries, divorce law reforms introduced in the latter part of the twentieth century have gone hand in hand with individualization and increased emphasis on women's rights, with quite dramatic consequences for family forms. The normative nuclear family continues to be a reality for many, but is no longer the sole form of recognized family (Stacey, 1990; Bittman, 2000; Cheal, 2002). Single-parent families, mixed or blended families formed through remarriage, extended families, domestic groupings that call themselves families without the legal foundation of marriage, these are just some of the main forms that family living has taken. Together, these represent a shift from the patriarchal, authoritarian style of family that once characterized industrial society to what Giddens (1998: 89–98) has termed 'the democratic family'.

What holds families together now, according to contemporary social theory, is 'love' and personal affinity, rather than duty, convention or legal compulsion. As recent empirical research by Fiona Williams and colleagues associated with the Care, Values and the Future of Welfare Programme (CAVA) at the University of Leeds has convincingly shown, affinity, friendship and the search for meaningful personal relationships are also increasingly important for the development of new forms of personal relationships (Williams, 2004). Yet conservative and neo-conservative commentators have anguished over the impact of feminism and changes to the family, arguing that the weakening of the 'traditional' breadwinner form of the nuclear family leads to weak families and a lack of commitment (Cheal, 2002; Wilson, 2003; McLanahan, 2004). The suggestion is that with the development of alternative forms of family and domestic relations, the family capacity to provide reliable and consistent care has been undermined. Research by Williams and her colleagues directly addressed this through a programme of qualitative studies. These studied personal support in a range of non-conventional family and household forms, including sole-parent families, families following divorce (including blended and step families), and unions between same-sex couples. A common feature to emerge from the data was the importance of friendship, and the blurring of friendship and lover relationships. As Williams notes,

> This evidence of the importance of friendship would seem to support one of the tenets of the individualization thesis: that changes in intimacy have seen a move away from the significance of *fixed, given* or *ascribed* relationships towards ones which are more *fluid, chosen* or *floating*. (Williams, 2004: 49)

However, Williams continues, adding an important caveat and clarification:

> The blurring of friends and family, according to Pahl, and of friends and lovers, according to Roseneil and Budgeon, is what marks many people's communities and their connection to the social world. This may seem an obvious point when we think about who our loved ones are, but the empirical details above show the limitations of arguments which see social change mainly taking place through the transformation of intimacy in the adult couple sexual relationship. This neglects the significance of other, lateral, relationships, as well as generational attachments and commitments between parents and children which . . . play as important a role in defining people's sense of themselves and belonging. These studies of friendship reinforce the point that diversity in the shape of people's commitments does not lead to a weakening of commitment or connectedness. (Williams, 2004: 49–50)

Problems with the Individualization Thesis

While there are many plaudits, the accounts of both Beck and Giddens have been widely criticized for being overly theoretical, for generalizing from limited personal experience rather than sound empirical studies and for being overly optimistic about the democratic and emancipatory capacity of such changes in personal relations. Castells suggests that the accounts ignore the continuing importance of social inequality and the denial of opportunity for individualized and flexible life planning for most of the world's population. He therefore proposes some important qualifications. The unequal and dislocating effects of globalization and the disjunctures of power and experience, he argues, mean that

> reflexive life planning becomes impossible, except for the elite inhabiting the timeless space of flows of global networks and their ancillary locales. And the building of intimacy on the basis of trust requires a redefinition of identity fully autonomous *vis a vis* the networking logic of dominant institutions and organizations. (Castells, 1997: 11)

This reminder that social inequality has not ceased, that new kinds of socially induced precariousness and vulnerability limit people's capacity to act reflexively at all times and that many, perhaps most, people will continue to feel that their lives are out of control is important.

Another troubling issue for these approaches concerns the increasing emphasis being placed on the issue of the independence of human agency and the treatment of gender in social policy (Hoggett, 2001; Shaver, 2002). Paul Hoggett (2001), for example, argues that Giddens's approach involves a 'lopsided' model of agency. He argues that Giddens too readily assumes that human subjects are in a position rationally to know and calculate the different possibilities of their actions, and that he gives too little attention to the problem of the powerlessness and 'psychic injury' of individuals who have experienced or face injustice and oppression. An understanding of human agency must also deal more effectively with the question of choice, a key term in popular and neo-liberal discourse. As Deacon and Mann have argued, social policy must increasingly be concerned with 'enabling people to make responsible choices' (Deacon and Mann, 1999: 433). Although this is a capacity that Giddens appears to assume for all people, his apparent optimism is far from convincing for those who experience ongoing social inequality or significant cognitive deficits.

In a political climate involving globalization and the economic restructuring of the welfare state and social services, promoting individualization as involving choice is often a code for reducing citizenship rights and promoting an agenda of self-sufficiency. Market ideology readily assimilates, indeed promotes, the idea of individualization. Consumerism is bolstered by the promotion of the idea of individual choice and the promotion of competition between commercial suppliers to meet the demands of individual consumers. Reconstructing industrial relations to reduce the influence of trade unions is similarly commonly portrayed as promoting a more direct relationship between employers and individual workers (Edgar, 2005). Reducing social protection and increasing the need for individuals to manage their own affairs by exercising personal choice and individual responsibility in their dealings with powerful corporate powers serves to emphasize the positive potential of recognizing a capacity for individual agency, but at the cost of ignoring the very real inequalities of power and opportunity which exist and which effectively deny real choices to those most likely to need assistance.

In short, there is a danger in universalizing the experience of particular actors and privileged social groups, as well as problems that arise from the political co-option of the concept of individualization. Many of the ambiguities and dangers entailed in using the concept are obscured in the work of Beck and Giddens. Acknowledging this does not, however, negate the sociological value of the concept. To explore the potential of this concept, the final section of this chapter therefore considers the implications of the individualization thesis for understanding a number of developments and the dilemmas of care in formal settings.

Individualization and Care

Individualization can be understood as a process involving the deinstitutionalization of traditional social relations and the subsequent emergence of a more fluid system in which individuals are increasingly recognized as the chief agents of social life. The weakening of relatively long-standing but inflexible social forms and stable institutions mirrors the well-recognized policy of the deinstitutionalization of human services that has been implemented over the same period.

Central to this development has been the shift away from institutional forms of providing long-term care. In some jurisdictions and fields of policy, this has been accompanied by an unprecedented period of service innovation. In others, such as occurred with the programmes of deinstitutionalized mental health services in a number of countries, the approach has been at best a benign neglect accompanied by the assignment of personal responsibility to those most in need of support (Dear and Wolch, 1987; AIHW, 2001). While institutions such as mental asylums, nursing homes, long-stay facilities, orphanages and care homes of various kinds had long been the public face of 'care' in Western societies (Penglase, 2005), the 1960s saw the unleashing of a powerful broadside of social criticism directed at the inhuman treatment entailed in rigid programmes of institutional care, with writers such as Barton and Townsend in the UK, Foucault in France, and Jules Henry in the USA providing powerful, well-researched documentation of the impersonal, dehumanizing effects of such rigid social regimes (Jones and Fowles, 1984). Goffman's powerful sociological critique of 'total institutions', perhaps more than any other account, made clear that the result of such mass management programmes was that inmates were forced to conform to a totalitarian regime of rules and supervision that deprived them entirely of individual identity (Goffman, 1968). It is no coincidence that Goffman's 'chief concern [was] to develop a sociological version of the structure of the self' (Goffman, 1968: 11). Each person in a total institution, argued Goffman, was required to carry out his/her daily activity in the immediate company of a large number of others. Each was 'treated alike and required to do the same thing together', as they were managed according to a single plan imposed from above, which denied opportunities for any inmate to express an individual identity (Goffman, 1968). The result, he noted, was the 'mortification of the self'. Institutionalization, in other words, represents the antithesis of individualization.

The alternative that has emerged – non-institutional community and home-based care – in contrast holds the promise of enabling those who require ongoing assistance or supervision to remain in their own homes and to maintain their possessions and daily routines, offering them a degree of choice and control. Contemporary developments, such as case management, the tailoring of care to fit the individual, individualized care plans and the introduction of legal safeguards including complaints and appeals procedures and charters of patients' rights incorporate the logic of the individualization of care. This is not to say that all forms of institutional or congregate care have been, or can be, abolished. But where congregate forms of care continue, the importance of adapting care provision to individual needs has increasingly become the standard by which service adequacy can be assessed.

Child-care centres, for example, continue to be one of the preferred means for delivering child care, in part because the social experience of bringing children together in groups is considered valuable for education and childhood socialization. However, a history of reports over the past thirty years suggests that the effects on the individual children cared for in centres has become the key measure of the appropriateness of the administration and staffing of different centres (Hill, Waldfogel and Brooks-Gunn, 2002; Brennan and Kinnear, 2002; Wise, 2002). In contrast, there is a widespread acceptance of other forms of social intervention, such as paid maternity leave, family-based day care and such like which enable the care regime to be adjusted to the individual child. The continuing dilemmas of child care can in this way be seen as reflecting a tension between the recognition of the rights of mothers to paid employment outside the home and the rights of children to appropriate individual attention and care.

Formal and Informal Care

It is not just in the form in which services are provided that individualization is significant. By laying the foundations for a new relationship between human service providers and care recipients, individualization and the related changes in intimate relations and domestic life also hold the potential to constitute a new social demography of formal and informal care. The demographic changes resulting from the gradual transformation of the lives of individuals and domestic units suggest a revision of the analyses which located caring as a distinctively female activity, closely associated with the intimate relations in 'private places' of the home and family and with the social and psychological construction of femininity – the boundary between 'female' and 'male'. Individualization means that care-giving relationships have the potential to be structured less by gender and more by the patterns of reciprocity and obligation (which may themselves have gender dimensions, of course) which build up over a lifetime.

The domestic relationships within which the overwhelming amount of care-giving takes place have the potential to be structured more by the patterns of reciprocity and intimacy than was the case when responsibility for care was ascribed solely on the basis of gender. This development will not simply evolve of its own accord, but will require support both in policy and, perhaps more importantly, in employment contracts through the enforcement of male-carer-leave provisions. Although the available data suggest that men are taking only marginally greater responsibility for child care or domestic labour (Bittman and Pixley, 1997; Bittman, 2004), it is clear that the amount of care provided by men in the domestic setting has frequently been underestimated (Arber and Gilbert 1989). Research examining patterns of care for older people has shown that the resilience of familial support of older people in the latter decades of the twentieth century in Australia and Britain owes much to the assistance provided by co-resident partners (Arber and Gilbert, 1989; Arber and Ginn, 1990; Hirst, 2001; AIHW, 2003). Somewhat surprisingly for many, the proportion of older men (aged over 65) who report providing personal care for their female partner equals or exceeds that of women caring for a male partner, although the greater number of women living beyond retirement age means that, overall, women carers continue to predominate in old age. Similarly, the rapid emergence of formal and informal support networks amongst the gay community in response to HIV/AIDS demonstrates the viability of care relationships based on very different foundations of intimacy and gender (Layzell and McCarthy, 1992). In each case the availability of informal care is more closely predicted by the individualization thesis than by a projection of traditional gender roles, indicating that the scope for policy based on this approach is far from exhausted.

Individualization also underpins the current rethinking of the carer–dependant paradigm. As discussed in Chapter 5, a rethinking of the more traditional carer–dependant paradigm is already well under way, affecting both informal and formal forms of care (see also Fine and Glendinning, 2005). In place of the hierarchical pattern of the assumption of responsibility and control by the carer and passivity and gratitude on the part of the care recipient, a role pattern theorized by Talcott Parsons as 'the sick role' (Parsons, 1951; Gerhardt, 1987), a more engaged, active relationship is required between care-givers and recipients, based on the recognition of the rights of the care recipient as an individual. Care, in this sense, needs to be seen not simply as a one-directional service undertaken by the care-giver, but as the outcome of a relationship between the different parties in which mutual respect and the fostering of the capabilities and sense of autonomy of the recipient are foremost. The emergence of concepts such as 'self-care' and the 'co-production of care' which need to be respected and fostered (Wilson, 1994) are suggestive of the sorts of changes required.

A further set of issues arises in relation to policies within human

services. Individualization has already had a major impact on the way
services are delivered in most jurisdictions. This is reflected in the form
of the greater social recognition accorded to individual clients or
service users, in at least three different dimensions:

1. the legal protections afforded service users;
2. the restructuring of service organization along such lines as
   patient- or person-centred care, case or care management and
   personalized programmes;
3. the opportunities for people to exercise both 'choice' and 'voice'
   (Hirschman, 1970) in their dealings with services.

Recognition of the individual humanity of care recipients is increasingly evident to even the most casual of observers through the basic
terminology used to refer to those who receive care. Rather than the
passive term 'patient', many services have attempted to use more
neutral terms such as 'client', 'consumer' or 'service user' to suggest a
more active engagement. The term 'consumer', however, has clearly
come to be favoured, partly, no doubt, because of the increasing
market orientation of services, with the granting of direct financial
power to service users held by some to be the key to the empowerment
of individual recipients (Feinberg and Ellano, 2000; Glendinning et
al., 2000). But the appeal of the term goes beyond that of the market,
perhaps because it extends the possibility (if not always the reality) of
personal choice, a normalized identity and a recognition of the individuality of the recipient (Baldock and Ungerson, 1994; Thomas,
2000; Francis, Colson and Mizzi, 2002).
    Beyond this, individualization has also had an impact on the inter-
action between staff and care recipients, and on the way that services
operate. Nurses and other human service professionals, for example,
increasingly seek to ensure a more holistic form of interpersonal
support. In this they are acknowledging the reality of embodied individuals before them, breaking free from the traditions of medicine that
saw bodies in mechanistic Cartesian terms (Benner, 2000). The recognition of the individual recipient as the chief beneficiary of human
service delivery implies not only an attempt to tailor the service to fit
the preferences and circumstances of the individual recipient but also
the provision of opportunities for the recipient to take part in the
decision-making relating to the planning, organization and delivery of
the particular service concerned. Services are increasingly being urged

to offer greater recognition to individuals than in the past, with the restructuring of service organization along such lines as patient- or person-centred care, an expansion of case or care management and the introduction of a variety of personalized programmes in evidence (Clark, 1998; Feinberg and Ellano, 2000; Glendinning et al., 2000; Fisher and Fine, 2002). These developments have been accompanied by moves for the improved legal protection of consumers through advocacy and user-rights provisions. The extent to which these goals move beyond rhetoric and policy to be realized in practice, however, remains a challenge to service providers and policy-makers (Shaddock and Bramston, 1991; Waters and Easton, 1999; Hoggett, 2001). A key force in shifting the approach of service providers has been the emergence of consumer activists and broader social movements concerned with the legal rights, quality of life and general empowerment of those dependent on care (Thomas, 2000).

I have emphasized here the positive potential that acknowledging the importance of individualization can have because the development is so often ignored, glossed over or misrepresented in the literature on care. But it is equally important to identify the potential for ideologies of individual responsibility to be used in more negative ways. Individualization and the promotion of choice have been used, for example, as a justification for enforcing unrealistic levels of responsibility for self-support. They are also cited as justifications by conservative governments for winding back programmes of social support and enforcing user-pays systems, and blaming the victims for the misfortune that they may face. The undesirable consequences of this approach are already evident in the homelessness, personal despair and rise in criminality and drug offences that arose in the wake of the deinstitutionalization of mental health services where alternative provisions were not made available (Dear and Wolch, 1987), and appear in other forms as alternative services to disabled people have been impeded by lack of funds, opposition by neighbourhood groups, and financial barriers to services arising from the enforcement of user-pays provisions (Gleeson, 1997).

There is also evidence, as Julia Twigg (2000) reminds us, that care remains hidden from public view. The sequestration of experience, of which Giddens (1991) writes, evident in the way that care in the nineteenth and twentieth centuries typically required the warehousing of inmates in closed institutions, continues under policies of community care. With most citizens shielded from direct experience of the shortcomings of systems of long-term care, it is relatively easy for abusive or neglectful care arrangements to continue in the midst of otherwise affluent welfare societies of high modernity.

Care as a Social Response to Bodily Need

I argued earlier in this chapter that it is not possible to conceive of care without recognition of the body, and that care involves precisely the intersection between physical/biological foundations and social construction that makes the study of culture and social life so engrossing, and so tricky. This intersection of bodily vulnerability and social conditions gives care both its fundamental importance to human social life and continues to produce complex responses that have profound social significance. More specifically, the need for care can be understood as arising primarily from the physical incapacities of the recipient. In contrast, the response to provide care, which involves a vast range of possibilities, involves culturally shaped, socially constructed action.

This is not to suggest that the need for care is reducible, in some simple sense, to biological imperatives, nor to claim that the way that care is provided is dictated by physiology. Physiological need and social form interact while having their origins in the biology of our species; physical needs are also shaped by our upbringing and by social conditions. Neither is this an attempt to introduce sociobiological determinism into the field. Rather, the approach is an appeal for a recognition that the need for care is not simply another example of arbitrary cultural symbolism. It is not just another cultural code that can be read into particular situations in a subjective and arbitrary fashion by any onlooker. Instead, at its base, the need for care is a physical incapacity of the recipient to undertake basic tasks of living in an autonomous way, and this has social consequences.

This approach has much in common with, and is informed by, that of the feminist philosopher Eva Kittay, discussed in Chapter 4. Kittay argues that what she calls the 'paradigm model' of care may be thought of as 'dependency work', arising in response to the bodily dependency of the recipient as a result of the physical vulnerability evident in infancy, frail old age, disability and sickness (Kittay, 1999). The social arrangements implemented as part of this process, in turn, typically foster and extend dependency in other, secondary forms.

Care-givers (and women in general) have been made socially and economically dependent through social arrangements that impose a form of referred social dependency on carers as a result of their reliance on the support of those she calls 'the provider' (Kittay, 1999). As her analysis demonstrates, there is much to be gained by sustaining an awareness that many of the social forms and consequences of care are social rather than biological in origin. But to extend this logic and assume that the very need for care can be reduced to arbitrary social convention would be to ignore the prior ontology of physiological vulnerability that underlay the need for care in the first instance.

The need for care, in the ideal-type sense in which I wish to consider it here, is typically manifested as physical incapacity. But for this to result in the provision of care involves both an acknowledgment of the link between the body and mind of the recipient and also a recognition that the identification of the need is itself a social process. In certain instances, such as the need for care of a new-born infant, physical frailty is obvious and is closely linked, indeed inseparable from, cognitive or mental incapacity. In other cases, of which dementia in old age provides a clear example, the physical capacity of the person requiring care may be quite comprehensive, but the sufferer's inability to direct this capacity ensures that some form of 'care' will be required if the sufferer is not to perish, possibly placing others in danger in the process.

We might still ask at what point the sufferer's need for care is recognized? Isn't the diagnosis ('dementia', for example) itself a medical and, ultimately, social label that is simply one way amongst many of understanding and explaining behaviour? Usually, by the time an underlying disease such as dementia has been diagnosed, there have already been numerous little incidents that suggest, either to the person affected or to a significant other, that something is wrong (Levin, Sinclair and Gorbach, 1989; Fine and Thomson, 1995). Even the establishment of the diagnosis itself is quite a fraught expert medical task that is by no means always accurate and does not mark the commencement of the biological pathology that causes the demented behaviour and cognition. Here the distinction made in medical sociology between disease (the physical pathology) and illness (the social label and role assigned to its bearer) (Parsons, 1957; Morgan, Calnan and Manning, 1985) is useful, as it enables us to distinguish between physical and social aspects of the same condition.

Since it is also clear that the disease may exist for quite some time before it manifests itself in any way (indeed, one medical hypothesis is that dementia may even lay dormant in our genes from conception), it could be argued that it is not the disease, the biological cause, that is the basis of the need for care, but the diagnosis. There is, indeed, much in this argument. But to assert that the condition of dementia is produced only as a result of the capacity of medical experts to provide a diagnosis is to mistake the semantic label for the condition itself and, in so doing, to undermine the case for a social response to the need.

An example of the overgeneralization of the social construction argument can be found in the application of the social model of disability, in which a sharp distinction is drawn between impairment, which is seen as essentially involving physical differences between individuals, and disability, viewed as arising from the social treatment of these differences (Barnes, 1998; Oliver and Barnes, 1998; Gordon and Rosenblum, 2001). As Twigg (2002: 430) points out, this identifies the topic of the body with a 'reactionary and oppressive discourse, one that individualizes and demeans disabled people'. However, as Hughes and Patterson (1997, cited in Twigg, 2002: 430) argue, this leaves the issue of impairment undescribed and untheorized, as if the only difficulties experienced are social labels and stigmas, the only needs to be met those concerning social identity.

Acknowledgment of the body, therefore, is an important development in sociological theory that can do much to help us understand the central importance of the need for care. Embodiment is also strongly linked to the response to provide assistance. As Maurice Hamington (2004) argues, the empathic understanding of need that arises from our experience of our own bodily functioning provides the basis for a caring response to the needs of others. The interconnectedness that is care begins with a recognition of shared embodiment. As he succinctly puts it, 'my body knows an array of feelings that can help me empathize not only with the positions concerning an issue but with the affections and relations that accompany the position . . . My body captures an implicit understanding of the other' (Hamington, 2004: 126).

If the need for care at important transitional points in life, and the evocation of empathy in a concerned other is recognized as a foundational or axiomatic condition arising from the existence of the body, the action of providing care is, just as certainly, a social response. This can be seen, for example, in care for the new-born. The response to the basic bodily fact of life of the infant's frailty, however 'natural' it is believed to be, is already and inevitably a social act. Through sustained nurturance – which involves not only the provision of fluids, food and shelter but also human warmth, touch, speech, song and companion-ship – social interaction is established. At the core of this interaction is the infant–carer(s) relationship, typically seen as that of the mother and child, although variations are both possible and reasonably widely documented. This is held from a number of theoretical perspectives to be a basic template or model for care, one that is capable of being modified and transferred but that, in one guise or another, forms the basis of the social response to frailty and vulnerability that is care (Ruddick, 1989; Bowden, 1997). What form this pattern of interaction can and should take, the impact of sex and gender differences that might dispose women to adopt the role of care-givers or to be disposed towards an ethic of care for others, and how social resources should be organized and distributed to support those responsible for responding to frailty are important questions for social theory that can not be addressed while care is treated as an issue of marginal interest to theory. The ability to breast-feed might be considered a bodily capa-bility that advantages mothers over fathers and other males in the care of young infants. But this physical characteristic is not necessary for other forms of care and can not be invoked as a universal explanation for assigning responsibility for all forms of care to women.

Here it is sufficient to note that the infant–carer relationship, like other care relationships, does not exist in isolation from other social arrangements. Care relations may be thought of as a key set of rela-tionships, embedded within broader social arrangements which sustain them and to which they, in turn, contribute. Care, in this way, is an elemental form of both intimacy and sociality, a foundation not just for the young child's developing life or the support of others who need care, but for the patterns of social solidarity that underlie all human societies. The patterns of interconnectedness and mutual interdependencies that form the basis of social life thus can be seen as arising in response to the ontological insecurities of bodily frailty and vulnerability. But for all the warmth and emotion that the concept of care can elicit, it would be unwise to adopt a sentimental or idealized picture of these arrangements. As Turner and Rojek remind us, all social relationships and institutions are precarious. Fragmentation, risk and rapid social change are today endemic; as in other periods of human history, conflict, injustice and exploitation are ever-present obstacles to achieving the potential of love, interdependency and solidarity on a global scale which appears these days to remain tantalizingly outside our reach.

Acknowledging the importance of the body and the significance of individualization in sociological theory provides an important conceptual tool for understanding the dilemmas posed by the need for care in the twenty-first century. These concepts do not, however, provide a set of ready-made answers to the dilemmas that need to be faced. Instead, they help us pose new questions about the dilemmas and challenges we face.

CHAPTER 8

Risk, Care and the New Logic of Global Capitalism

For most of the twentieth century, including the period in which the welfare state was developing, care was primarily a private matter, a responsibility of the family with or without help purchased through the market. The state intervened only in critical cases such as child protection or long-term institutional care of the aged, assuming responsibility in cases in which the alternatives were demonstrably inadequate or were held to have failed (Fine, 1999a). In consequence, informal and formal care operated in a more or less self-contained fashion, as alternatives, with care recipients who were unable to rely on informal support at home typically being forced to accept complete reliance on formal provisions. Families who wished to continue responsibility for care after it was assumed by the state, or by a self-contained private organization such as a nursing home or orphanage, were considered as interfering and their involvement typically discouraged. A simplified overview of different forms or modes of care is provided in Figure 8.1.

At home, care was part of the domestic division of labour and was typically gendered work, informal and unqualified. However, it was otherwise not broken down into a specific category and was typically undifferentiated from a range of other domestic activities such as cooking, cleaning, washing, shopping, financial management and transportation, and was provided to particular, known individuals – a child, partner, needy parent, relative or friend. Generally, such care at home was unpaid, although paid domestic assistants, nannies and other forms of private care staff were available to wealthier families in some countries.

Formal care, in contrast, was subject to registration and regulation,

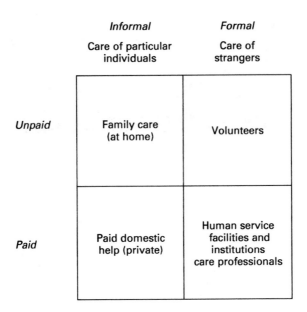

Figure 8.1   Modes of care provision: A basic schema.

and was systematic, planned and extensive in its availability. Whether assigned to unpaid volunteers or provided by professionally qualified staff, it was formalized and legally regulated, commonly requiring evidence of expertise on behalf of the staff responsible. The introduction of risk management practices in recent years, as we have seen, has typically added to the rigidity of bureaucratically based standardization and formalized procedures. Where informal care was inherently particularistic, provided to specific, known individuals, formal care was provided to strangers, those whose claim to support arose not from their long-standing personal relationship with the care-givers, but from impersonal characteristics such as the recipients' capacity to pay for services rendered or their entitlement to support based on an assessment of their eligibility and need.

These different modes are no longer self-contained. Nor do they operate as alternatives. The search for innovative solutions to meet the real and potential care deficit has led to the forging of hybrid or 'partnership' solutions which use public, publicly subsidized or privately purchased formal services to supplement the unpaid care provided in the context of the home and family (see Figure 8.2).

	Informal	Hybrid forms of care	Formal
Unpaid	Family care Informal care networks	Care shared by family and formal services (paid and unpaid)	Human service volunteers
Paid	Domestic employees nannies	Care allowances tax credits and cash payments Use of private domestic help	Paid care workers Professionals

Figure 8.2 Simplified model of hybrid forms of shared care

The processes of reform, restructuring and innovation in the field of human services and care appear not to be slowing. Care is assuming ever more hybrid forms as these different modes are found in combination, or can no longer be considered analytically distinct, as is the case when the increasingly prevalent payments for care go to family members (Glendinning et al., 2000; Daly, 2002). While these important and fundamental changes that occurred gradually over the final quarter of the twentieth century now appear clear in hindsight, their development has been largely eclipsed by the political controversies and economic disputes that have accompanied the restructuring of formal services which had been closely linked to the development of the welfare state in the period following World War II. There are at least five main forms that the restructuring of such formal services has taken.

First is the phenomenon of *the contracting state*, characterized by a reduction in the direct provision of services by the state and the increased reliance on market and market-like mechanisms. Some of the main approaches encountered have been the privatization of former public services, the increased provision by private-for-profit providers, the introduction of compulsory competitive tendering and the increased use of user payments, quasi-vouchers and individualized, service-linked funding. Evidence from both aged care and child care shows, however, that public funding of privately controlled provisions, particularly where the funding is open-ended (ie not capped) and linked to the individual use of services, has been a very powerful source of private-sector growth in a number of countries.

Secondly, there has been *a search for new government administrative arrangements*, with the introduction of a range of performance-monitoring surveillance techniques in place of other, more direct, bureaucratic control mechanisms. These developments include the introduction of 'funder–provider splits' within government and between government and non-government agencies; the increased reliance on contractual relations between government departments and non-government agencies; and the adoption of output-based funding models.

A third type of change concerns the search for ways to enhance efficiency by *overcoming the fragmentation of service provision and improving coordination* between services, as well as by developing better links between community-based services and other types of provision. Perhaps the most widely recognized approach is that of case management (or, as it is sometimes known, care coordination) which aims to tailor the care available from a range of different agencies into a package that is closely matched to the needs of individual consumers. A range of other approaches have also been used to improve coordination. These include: the networking of services; the introduction of common protocols governing referrals between agencies; the application of information technology to facilitate the exchange of information between agencies; co-location strategies through which different services are provided with adjacent accommodation; and the use of common points of assessment and referral (Leutz, 1999; Fine, 1999b). Increasingly, the system of funding and administration is being identified as a blockage to coordination, and a variety of different approaches are being trialled to deal with this, including the pooling of funding from different services and programmes. Larger-scale administrative changes, such as the creation of megahealth and community services departments and portfolios, have also been prominent.

Closely related to the issue of service coordination is *the promotion of substitution policies*, intended to encourage the use of less intensive and cheaper forms of support in place of the inappropriate use of more intensive care services.

A fifth type of change is concerned with attempts to enhance or constrain access to support by *improving the targeting of services*, a highly controversial approach, as attempts to provide some individuals with extra amounts of support usually entail a reduction in the amount of assistance made available for a large number of potential recipients of relatively low levels of support.

Why are these sorts of developments occurring? In this chapter I explore how social theory can help us understand how changes of this nature have come to dominate policy development in the field of care. Drawing on the approaches developed by contemporary sociological theorists, in particular by Castells and Beck, I explore the applicability of two key developments in contemporary social theory to understanding developments in human service – the newly emerging organizational logic in an increasingly globalized world and the appearance of a new discourse on risk and risk management. The way we understand developments that have been responsible for a political–economic transformation of the market and of public life has profound implications for the way we think about, and need to plan for, the provision of care in the twenty-first century.

The Bureaucratic Iron Cage

In the early twentieth century Max Weber famously predicted a future for modern societies in which bureaucracy would dominate. Weber saw that bureaucracy was the most effective form of organization known, providing an unrivalled tool for the administration of human affairs:

> The decisive reason for the advance of bureaucratic organization has always been its purely technical superiority over any other form of organization. The fully developed bureaucratic apparatus compares with other organizations exactly as does the machine with the non-mechanical modes of production. Precision, speed, unambiguity, knowledge of the files, continuity, discretion, unity, strict subordination, reduction of friction and of material and personal costs – these are raised to the optimum point in the strictly bureaucratic administration, and especially in its monocratic form. (Weber, 1978L 973)

Weber's confident prediction about the advance of bureaucracy was largely fulfilled over the twentieth century. Just as it did in industry, commerce and government, the bureaucratic form provided an organizational blueprint that shaped the formal institutions through which care was provided – hospitals, nursing homes, schools and care centres of various kinds, charitable and civic organizations, government departments, private corporations. From the total institutions that Goffman and others studied (Goffman, 1968; Jones and Fowles, 1984), to the administrative means for policy development and administration, bureaucracy became in practice the 'iron cage' that Weberian theory had forecast. It was at once a ubiquitous, enabling and stable institutional means for the generic administration of human affairs, and a controlling, rationalistic and impersonal framework of control. The very term came to be used as a shorthand for rigidity and inflexibility.

As the twentieth century came to an end, the organizational logic of the iron cage of bureaucracy began to give way and a new organizational form began to emerge – the network. It ushered in what Manuel Castells has called the 'new organizational logic of global societies'. Together with the new understandings of risk and risk management, the new organizational logic and the increasingly marketized and corporate economy that accompanies it has deep implications for the future of care and human services.

Informational Capitalism and the New Economy

Central to Castells's account of globalized social change is the rise of what he terms 'the new economy'. His analysis is based on the intertwining of three core propositions: the new economy is increasingly *informational*, dependent on the capacity to generate, process and apply knowledge-based information; it is *global*, rather than locally based, with the core activities of production, consumption and distribution increasingly organized on a global scale; and it is *networked*, its productivity increasingly dependent on global networks of interaction rather than locally based hierarchies of command (Castells, 2000: 77).

The new globalized economy, Castells claims, originated mainly in the USA. Following the economic and fiscal crisis of the 1970s, economic restructuring shifted the balance in favour of employers and increased corporate power, leading to a revitalized market system based on the globalized growth of capital. Subsequent growth was strong through the 1980s and more so in the 1990s, spreading fast into Europe and the Asian Pacific. The most significant aspect of its expansion, for Castells, lies in the 'development of a new organizational logic', that is at once global but not uniform, manifested in different forms in various institutional and cultural contexts. In making this claim, Castells draws on Nicole Biggart's concept of 'organizational logic': 'By organizational logics I mean a legitimating principle that is elaborated in an array of derivative social practices. In other words, organizational logics are the ideational bases for institutionalized authority relations' (Biggart, 1992; cited in Castells, 2000: 164).

In place of the rational, bureaucratic logic identified by Max Weber, the organizational logic which Castells identifies as characteristic of the informational society is that of the network. This is a logic that promotes flexibility, innovation and access to multiple sources of information in place of the bureaucracy, hierarchy and authority of tradition and precedent that have previously dominated.

Network logic encompasses a number of specific trends. One of the most important is the shift from mass production to flexible production, a development often described as the transition from 'Fordism' to 'post-Fordism' (Amin, 1995). This has seen a decreased reliance on large, vertically integrated corporations and organizations, a reduction in the task-specific division of labour referred to as Taylorism, the 'scientific management' of work. The new organizational logic also involves an increased openness towards more flexible, innovative forms of organization. Other important developments in the new economy include the adoption of new methods of management which stress such features as multifunctional labour, total quality control, interfirm networking through licensed subcontracting and umbrella corporations, and the rise of the model of the 'horizontal corporation' (Castells, 2000: 163–210). Rather than security and stability, flexibility has become the watchword for the management of labour.

Drawing on a comparison with Weber's account of the Protestant ethic as the spirit of capitalism (Weber, 1976), Castells argues that the spirit of informationalism, its ethical force, is the corporate ethos of accumulation and the renewed appeal of consumerism. Within the enterprise, he argues, there is no fixed or stable system of culture of corporate values. Rather, there is a culture of the ephemeral, of strategic decisions and the promotion of the values of consumption over those of production and hard work. This is given expression as a patchwork of experiences and interests that can never be crystallized lest it become too rigid for the rapidly changing challenges thrown up by informationalism.

The shift from a society built on the values associated with industrial production to one built on the values of consumerism has also been an important theme in the work of a number of high-profile sociologists in recent years. George Ritzer's approach, summarized in his concept of 'the McDonaldization of society', for example, suggests that the increased rationalization of employment and the development of franchising and marketing, has seen a shift in modern lifestyles, from a production-based regime to a consumption-based, leisure-centred regime (Ritzer, 1993, 1999). At the heart of Ritzer's analysis is Weber's concept of rationality. McDonaldization, for Ritzer, represents a continued refinement of the application of rationality, one that is manifest as consumerism, increasingly built on the foundations of a system of low-cost, casualized employment. Zygmunt Bauman (1998), developing and extending the argument about the importance of consumerism, argues that 'ours is a consumer society' in which the 'work ethic' has been replaced by the 'aesthetic of consumption' (Bauman, 1998: 23). The values of hard work, thrift, deferred gratification and lifelong duty and commitment that lay at the heart of the Protestant ethic are no longer what is valued. Instead, the capacity to consume and the values of consumerism dominate global culture, replacing the discipline and drill of industrial society. While Bauman is insightful in pointing to the strong cultural emphasis on consumption evident in contemporary capitalist societies, he is surely wrong in thinking that this has come about as the result of a reduction in the importance of employment or work for social structure. Work and consumption are increasingly locked together, not separated as alternatives. As the feminist and disability movements have long realized, work and maintaining income through employment has not just continued but become increasingly important, as discussed earlier. The implications of this are that it remains essential to analyse and understand the new forms that work has assumed and how this affects other aspects of our lives.

In contrast to the position taken by Bauman, Castells (2000: 216) argues, correctly in my opinion, that 'the process of work is at the core of social structure'. The transformation of work and of production relationships that flow from its restructuring under informational capitalism and the network society, he maintains, are the 'main lever by which the informational paradigm and the process of globalization affect society at large'.

The Rise of the Service Economy

Using current and historical data, Castells traces the shift in employment in countries belonging to the G7, the 'Group of Seven' nations that have shaped international monetary policy since 1945. The results chart a common direction among advanced societies, although considerable differences remain. Two main transformations are revealed.

1. *A shift in the structure of the economy over the course of the twentieth century, first towards then away from manufacturing to service-based employment.* The shift in economic structure began in the early twentieth century as a continuation of the previous century's shift from agricultural and primary production towards employment in transformative industries (manufacturing and construction), distributive services (which includes transport, communication, wholesale and retail) and social services. Subsequently, from about 1970, there was a fall in the manufacturing workforce, and a marked growth in service employment, which included a modest increase in work in the producer services (banking, insurance, property) and a much more pronounced rise in employment in the social services. By the 1990s, the final period for which data is presented, employment in the social services included over a quarter of all employees, exceeding employment in the transformative industries in the UK, the USA and Canada. These countries are evidence of a pattern of employment which Castells terms 'the service economy model'. In Japan and Germany, and to a certain extent in France and Italy, similar broad trends are evident. However, the continued importance of employment in manufacturing (and, at a lower level, in primary industries) and a more restricted pattern of growth in social services in these countries means that employment in the social services remains below that of manufacturing and other transformative industries. Castells terms this model the 'industrial production model' (Castells, 2000: 245).

2. *A transformation of the labour process and employment patterns.* The second transformation concerns the labour process and employment patterns. Rather than increased productivity leading to the 'end of work' or the 'deskilling of labour' as some writers had predicted, what has emerged is a dynamic but unstable and segmented labour market that is increasingly globalized. At the core of the informational economy are the information managers and professionals, the 'symbolic analysts' and knowledge workers who enjoy relatively high pay and

secure employment prospects, although not necessarily secure employment conditions. The demands on this segment of the workforce to work longer hours, display their dedication to the corporate goals and adopt a competitive, productive approach to their work are strong. Many others are either unable to sustain the effort or are displaced in the process of restructuring.

Alongside this core of relatively privileged professional/managerial knowledge workers, works what Castells calls the 'disposable labor force'. Disposable workers endure poor working conditions and are easily laid off when labour market conditions are unfavourable. This group, which includes most unskilled workers, has a disproportionate number of workers born overseas and women, a great many of whom typically work in part-time or casual positions and enjoy little or no control over their work lives. For Castells, the global dimension to this means that there are now always others, somewhere on the globe, willing to work harder, cheaper and for longer hours. In a global economy, work and life for those reliant on disposable employment is insecure, with choice constrained by limited local opportunities.

Care and the Segmented Labour Market

Employment in care work is discussed by Castells only in passing. It is clear, however, that such work constitutes a significant and increasing proportion of employment in the expanded social service sector of modern societies. The growth of the social services in general represents both a key area of increased employment for women and a major source of alternative forms of support that have enabled women to seek paid employment as a way to leave the home. The labour market for care work, in turn, exemplifies the dual structure of core and disposable workers that Castells identifies.

The professional/managerial core of experts working in fields involving care work – doctors, social workers, registered nurses, paramedical professionals and, perhaps most important now, managers, accountants and administrators of various kinds – enjoy a relatively privileged position in this system. Their importance, based on their command of knowledge and of key strategic administrative positions, is bolstered by professional systems of registration and codes of conduct. In various forms of care service the occupants of such positions include both men and women. Experience, performance and above all qualifications, generally university-based or their equivalent, are more important than ascribed characteristics such as gender or race. Other staff, in particular the majority of the direct care staff in most systems, are assigned work conditions indicative of their more marginal position in the labour market. Predominantly female and often of ethnic minority, immigrant or temporary-worker status, such workers are prone to low rates of pay and insecure employment with limited or no promotional prospects, in many cases receiving little or no recognition of their knowledge and experience. There are typically few opportunities for advanced training in these fields (Nelson, 1990; Wallace, 1990; Neysmith, 1999; Franzway, 2001; Meagher, 2003). It is no exaggeration to identify casual and part-time employment in care as constituting the disposable labour force to which Castells refers.

Women, especially those from ethnic minorities, including a disproportionate number of immigrants and workers with temporary or no citizenship rights, rely on such employment as a growing alternative to the declining employment in manufacturing. By supplementing the supply of locally born women seeking work in the field of care, the international patterns of migration and labour exchange that underlie globalization have supported the growth of care services based on the economics of low-paid front-line work (Parrenas, 2001; Ehrenreich and Hochschild, 2002; Hu-Dehart, 2003). As if to emphasize the precariousness of their foothold in the labour market, volunteer programmes, in which work is undertaken entirely without pay (Baldock, 1990; Neysmith and Reitsma-Street, 2000), often see unpaid workers alongside paid staff in these positions.

The division between core and marginal segments of the care labour force can be seen as representing two alternative futures for human services. On the one hand, professional experts enjoy respect and relatively high rates of pay, and suggest a legitimacy for formal interventions based on their command of expert knowledge and their capacity to provide a quality professional service that is simply not available in the ordinary household. On the other, a workforce of low-paid care staff suggests a future of McDonaldized care, workers undertaking standardized tasks for which qualifications are not required, providing cheap, affordable and replaceable care labour, available at short-term notice, wherever and for however long assistance is required.

The industrial welfare states of the mid-twentieth century treated these two approaches not as alternatives but as interdependent social classes, brought together in bureaucratically ordered organizations, forming a single system in which low-paid care workers performed work under the direction of their professional and managerial supervisors. In a globalized world, corporate managerial power has increased. Meanwhile, professional power, long sustained by state legislation, is threatened by the extension of market logic to all spheres of life, including the governance and administration of care work (Freidson, 1990) and by the availability of detailed information through the internet. Under such conditions, the work of the more highly paid professional staff may become progressively more marginal, relegated to the role of consultants who design expert systems used by managers to order and organize the work of their less-well-off colleagues. Divisions within the professional managerial group are also likely to increase, with discord between senior staff as those whose interest is in care as a professional concern for their charges are increasingly likely to find themselves in conflict with those whose interest is principally financial and managerial. With the intention of ensuring flexibility for employers and reducing costs for consumers, governments and other funding bodies, pressures to extend systems of casualized, low-pay work that are standardized and predictable are likely to increase. Similarly, the provision of care payments (Ungerson, 2003, 2004) and the relatively high incomes of professional and managerial knowledge workers has helped develop a black market in private domestic employment in many countries (Meagher, 2003; Bettio, Simonazzi and Villa, 2004).

An important recent study that replicated the results of other research around the world found that those undertaking care work in the USA were paid less than those in other occupational fields (England, Budig and Folbre, 2002). Care work was defined broadly in terms of social and educational services including such occupations as teaching, counselling, providing health services and supervising children. Even after allowing for such factors as the education and employment experience of the workers and a range of occupational and industry characteristics, the findings remained strong. The 'wage penalty' for working in care occupations was found to affect both the men and the women employed. But as women predominate in the field, the authors argue that gender is clearly the primary factor implicated. In economic terms, what this means is that these are jobs to which women are particularly (although not exclusively) attracted, in sufficient numbers compared to demand that it sustains a relative downward pressure on wages in comparison to other fields of employment. A significant proportion of employees, particularly those in the lower-paid and more insecure segments of the labour market, see themselves as involved not in building a career over time, but in engaging in meaningful work that is fitted into home life. This adds to the difficulties of organizing trade unions and other forms of industrial representation in these fields. The so-called 'compassion trap' is also often invoked in explaining these lower wages accepted by women working in care-based occupations. Because the work itself is seen as intrinsically rewarding, there is less of a need to pay the high wages that less attractive work (such as coal-mining or transport) might involve.

Other factors also need to be considered in understanding the way that care labour is being organized and deployed as part of the globalized economy. The status of workers as immigrants and ethnic minorities, referred to above, is a closely related feature of the workforce that should not be conflated with gender. Similarly, the characteristics of the labour process involved must also be considered crucial. A central characteristic of care work is that it involves a personal service, a form of body work performed by one person for another that is not readily mechanized or made more productive in the ways that other forms of production have been.

The problem of achieving productivity gains in the human service field is a feature that the economist William Baumol noted when comparing the economics of service industries to those of the production of goods (physical commodities). In services, production occurs at the point of consumption. In the production of goods, in contrast, production and consumption are clearly distinct. Drawing on this observation, Baumol's Law, as it is known, states that while productivity growth in manufacturing is readily achievable through mechanization, standardization and increased revenues obtained through efficient marketing, productivity growth in services is not (Baumol, 1967, 1993). The 'cost disease' that results is particularly evident in the delivery of personal social services (Esping-Andersen, 1990).

Child care, for example, requires someone to attend to the child's physical needs, as well as to provide emotional support and assistance with personal and social development, which requires attention, engagement, interaction, cuddling, and so forth. These tasks can not, in general, be mechanized or automated without significant reductions in the quality of care provided. In human services, the amount of care it is possible to produce per worker is thus severely constrained in a way that the production of goods is not. As a result, the cost of goods is falling, while in comparison the cost of services is increasing. Service production, therefore, assumes a greater proportion of national budgets, presenting problems for governments and the future of the welfare state and making strategies such as the McDonaldization of the labour process attractive to corporate, domestic and public employers alike. Care work faces ongoing cost pressures that are expressed in terms of the wages paid to care staff. Ongoing structural reforms (restructuring) are also required, as discussed later in this chapter. As Kittay (1999, see also Chapter 4) has shown, workers in this field are also dependent on providers and economic conditions that are beyond their direct control.

Public Policy, Employment and Human Services

The organization of care work in the new economy has been shaped by the historically close link between human services and public policy. Cut-backs and constraints on government spending over the past twenty years mean that occupations closely linked to the public sector have typically seen wages set at lower levels than those in many other sectors of the economy. The pressures on public expenditure have been manifest both in the pressures on public wages, and in the attempts to constrain spending by the restructuring of public programmes through privatizations, the contracting-out of services and a range of other reforms. The introduction of risk principles and risk management practices suggests that formal care services are ceasing to operate like large public service bureaucracies and are increasingly being run like businesses. This development is particularly in evidence in countries such as the UK, that have seen extensive levels of public-sector restructuring. Instead of attempting, with the assistance of waiting lists and other forms of bureaucratic demand management, to provide some assistance on a universal basis to all who meet the basic eligibility criteria, services are increasingly adopting risk-profiling, user payments and fees, and other performance management techniques from business to ensure that operations remain within budget.

In their decisions, governments in the twenty-first century face the financial and economic constraints of what Iversen and Wren have termed the 'trilemma' of service economies (Iversen and Wren, 1998). This 'three-way-dilemma' arises, they argue, because economic growth and employment in post-industrial societies is generated more by the expansion of the service economy than by the expansion of manufacturing. Manufacturing industry was the motor for the growth of the welfare state in the post-war period, but industrial employment has been shrinking for decades, while productivity has increased. Those industries that have not seen production moved offshore typically achieve productivity increases without creating lifetime jobs. Growth in employment, instead, has been in the service industry, where increased production equals increased jobs. Accordingly, governments in post-industrial nations face an invidious choice between achieving budgetary restraint, income equality and employment growth. Reliant on the increasing provision of services to generate employment, governments can attempt to achieve two of these goals, but it is not possible to achieve all three simultaneously. Attempting to steer a course that involves a trade-off between these goals presents governments with the macroeconomic trilemma that shapes policy options, forcing the continual restructuring of the welfare state, including, most importantly, funding for human services.

Hartley Dean argues that family policy faces a similar trilemma in the post-industrial economy: 'how is it possible to sustain functional families, while maximizing labor force participation, yet minimize social spending?' (Dean, 2002: 5–6). In Britain, he claims, the principle thrust of the New Labour government has been to seek a 'third way' solution to the problems facing the welfare state, which involves promoting the ideal of all parents being able to combine work and family life. The logic of this broad strategy – 'from welfare to work' – is at once both moral and economic, intended to minimize welfare-state dependency by maximizing labour-force participation, with government, employers and community working together in partnership. The system works favourably to some extent for the employment for those in 'core', skilled, professional and reasonably secure employment, according to Dean, as the higher incomes these professionals enjoy enables them to employ lower-paid substitute care-givers in their place. Although the take-up rate is typically low (especially for males), opportunities also exist to enable such staff to negotiate occasional family-friendly breaks. Problems emerge, however, in the secondary labour market, where peripheral workers are forced to accept 'flexible' (typically casual and part-time) employment, as they are not otherwise in a strong position to negotiate family care responsibilities with their employers. In the families and households of both sets of workers, however, arrangements for care are increasingly problematic; the core group are likely to be short of time, while for those in 'flexible' employment, insecurity makes forward planning, in the short term, difficult and often impossible. There is a need to go beyond promoting work through paid employment at any cost, a need to view care at home and outside the home not simply as the responsibility of the individual but as a social responsibility. Within the constraints set by the economic trilemma, these sorts of adjustments are not easy.

Risk and Modernization

The new organizational logic of which Castells writes may be thought of as ushering in a transformation in managerial and administrative principles for corporate affairs in the twenty-first century. A closely related development of modern global culture is the emergence of a pervasive sense of insecurity, risk and uncertainty, and the spread of risk management strategies into nearly all elements of public and private life. Risk is increasingly seen as a characteristic of modern life and this new understanding is helping to reshape the way that care work is understood and provided.

The key to the link between the new modernity and risk, as it is understood by Beck, is to grasp the idea that life is no longer understood just to happen, to be beyond our control or comprehension or to be determined by social structure, as sociologists once liked to say. For every aspect of life, at every level, there is an attempt to hold someone responsible for the decisions made. At the level of our own personal lives, we are increasingly required to take on that role of decision-maker and to accept the consequences of the decisions we are supposed to have made.

Of course, neither risk nor the idea of risk is new. Throughout history, people have had to confront issues of uncertainty and danger in the knowledge that life, in Hobbes's famous phrase, is 'brutish and short'. For those of us living in the affluent post-industrial world, daily life in the twenty-first century is objectively more certain, rational and predictable than at any point in the past. What differs is how we understand and respond to risk. As Giddens (1991: 109–43) explains, in earlier times the concepts of fate, fortune, and religious belief operated to account for the tribulations and opportunities understood as beyond human control. Today, these sorts of explanations, although not banished outright, are no longer considered adequate. Instead, rational, scientific explanations are sought for every hazard faced.

Risk has also emerged on a new, global scale, so that what Beck has called 'risks of modernization' differ, both in their global reach and our understanding of the nature of their causes, from those faced in previous eras. Risk in today's world, according to Beck, may therefore be defined as 'a systematic way of dealing with hazards and insecurities induced and introduced by modernization itself' (Beck, 1992: 21).

For Beck, the sense of risk arises from a growing awareness of the hazardous side effects of the production of wealth, particularly the potential for nuclear and ecological catastrophes with the likelihood of irreversible loss of life and damage to the environment. These risks represent some of the costs of the prosperity which affluent industrialized countries have enjoyed. Increasingly, such risks extend beyond a specific geographic locus and exceed the capacity of existing risk management mechanisms, such as private insurance, to deal with them. The risks associated with nuclear power plants, the effects of climate change, and terrorism in the post-September 11 world, for example, present a new scale of human-induced threats to life that are global and omnipresent, threatening all people regardless of their personal circumstances, social class or even locality of residence. As Beck comments, 'In advanced modernity the latter have disembodied and reshaped the inner social structure of industrial society and its grounded and basic certainties of life conduct – social classes, familial forms, gender status, marriage, parenthood and occupations' (Beck, 1992: 87).

The inner lives and personal relationships of modern individuals, at home and at work, thus seem increasingly insecure, just as the social ties that once bound us to others have become insecure and uncertain. Modern society, for Beck, is thus a *Risk Society* or, more precisely, is becoming a risk society because, as he argues, we are moving towards a collective social self-consciousness governed by ideas of risk. Life has become conditional, uncertain and risk-filled in the sense that all domains are now subject to deliberate decision-making. Today nothing can be assumed to be simply beyond our control.

Individuals, argues Beck, can no longer expect to live out a socially inscribed 'fate', a standard biography determined by the facts of their birth. Instead, we face a situation in which our lives, our employment, our communities and our marriages and families are subject to ongoing and deliberate decisions, subject to processes of 'rational' calculation. Despite the general reliability of most features of modern life, risk thus brings with it uncertain outcomes. Individuals, communities and nations are now exposed to risk; indeed, the whole world is facing unknown consequences and uncertain outcomes at every level. Everything, even the vagaries of the climate in this time of global warming with its episodes of 'wild weather', are seen as precarious and increasingly understood to be a consequence of human actions.

Beck's approach defines and conceptualizes risk as a social creation, as well as identifying how risk management opens up a new social dynamic based on the legal, political and economic consequences of the awareness of risk. It thus opens the way for a new understanding of social causality in high modernity. A number of other writers have also developed important analyses (Douglas, 1986, 1992; Luhmann, 1993; Lupton, 1999). Surveying the literature, Deborah Lupton (1999) points to the divergent assumptions and conclusions behind cognitive science approaches to risk on the one hand and sociocultural critiques on the other. Cognitive science approaches, she affirms, are based on assumptions about rationally calculating individuals. Socio-cultural theories, instead, consider risk to be a discourse or dominant cultural force that is increasingly important in shaping post-industrial societies. She reports marked areas of disagreement between the cultural and symbolic approach advocated by Mary Douglas, those of the governmentality school inspired by Foucault's stance on power (Dean, 1999), and Beck's risk-society approach. Other work has also sought to apply the concept to the analysis of specific policies and social conditions. The debate about risk in the fields of health and social policy and welfare has had particular relevance for understanding developments in care and human services (Culpitt, 1999; Taylor-Gooby, 2000; Edwards and Glover, 2001; Kemshall, 2002).

Although they receive little attention from Beck and other sociocultural theorists, corporate financial calculations represent another key element of the contemporary awareness of risk. Acknowledging risk has long been a key element in business, economics and entrepreneurship (Bealey, 1999). In conditions of perfect competition, risk is understood as borne by producers and distributors, not consumers, so that the risk of investment is considered one of the main justifications for profit and shareholder sovereignty. Techniques for managing the uncertainty of investment through the calculation of financial risk, planned risk-taking, the use of risk capital, the management and hedging of risk, identifying the risk-averse behaviour of consumers, and so forth are vital for the successful management of capital and enterprises. When we speak about the social consequences of risk and note the profusion of risk management strategies, we are inevitably acknowledging the extent to which the market and business management practices have infiltrated every aspect of contemporary social life. By acknowledging and embracing the language of risk, sociology is also developing an awareness that social life, like the economic sphere, is not, and can not be, determined. To acknowledge risk is to acknowledge a level of calculated uncertainty about human affairs and the link between means and outcomes.

Risk and Welfare

Hazel Kemshall contends that the discourse of risk has now become central to social policy. The welfare state, as it developed in the UK in the decades following World War II, was intended to provide welfare on a *universal* basis to those with a *demonstrable need for support*. Expressed in terms of risk, the key objectives of Beveridge's original design for a universal system of social entitlements involved pooling risks 'to protect everyone from shared vulnerability to the contingencies of industrial society, and to establish common standards in the provision of universal needs' (Jordan, 1998: 100, cited in Kemshall, 2002: 27).

Assistance was to be provided as a right, on the basis of citizenship, regardless of previous income or occupation. As Carol Pateman (1989) has pointed out, such a conception of citizenship included a recognition that men's path to citizenship was based on their paid work, that of women on their work as mothers and family care-givers.

Changes to universal entitlement and shared patterns of social need were introduced in Britain (and most other comparable countries) during the 1980s and 1990s, cutting back entitlements and changing the system of welfare to a more targeted system. In the process, argues Kemshall, the concept of risk replaced that of need:

> The contention is that social policy is no longer about the allevia-
> tion of the needs of the individual or the pursuit of the collective

good. Instead, it is about the prevention of risk and the displacement of risk management responsibilities onto the 'entrepreneurial self' who must exercise informed choice and self-care to avoid risks. (Kemshall 2002: 22)

Kemshall's discussion of the shift from need to risk in the field of welfare attributes the shift in approach to the impact of new right cutbacks and the recasting of welfare from a universalist public system to a residualized, private and charity-based approach. But is there more to the concept of risk? Giddens, who might agree with much of Kemshall's analysis, also stresses a more positive prospect: 'Risk is not just a negative phenomenon – something to be avoided or minimized. It is at the same time the energizing principle of a society that has broken away from tradition and nature' (Giddens, 1998: 241).

Risk, he argues, can not be defined purely in negative terms. Opportunity and innovation are positive features of risk-taking and need to be encouraged through what he calls the 'active exploration of risk environments'. Risks need to be identified, acknowledged and managed, but it is not possible or desirable always to attempt to avoid them. Enabling welfare clients to accept and manage risks on their own, for example, can be a way of avoiding fostering welfare dependency.

The search for ways of caring that recognize the right of recipients to take risks can be a form of emancipation and democratization, representing a welcome departure from the rigid, bureaucratic form of rule-based provision. But it may also be a strategy to mask cost-cutting. These are not questions that should be decided in the abstract. The details and context of each particular case need to be carefully considered. Enabling children in child care to take risks, for example, need not be something to be avoided on principle. Responsible risk-taking through play or by providing opportunities for the children to exercise responsibility or initiative, is important if child care and child protection are not to be simply sites for custody and supervision. Similarly, providing applicants for aged-care services with a choice between regular but intermittent care at home and admission to a residential facility in which round-the-clock supervision is available brings with it an acknowledgement of the risk involved. Accepting the risk can be liberating for the individual concerned, although this clearly brings with it a degree of uncertainty and insecurity that may affect family carers and others.

A degree of ambivalence about the use of risk-management approaches is evident in much research into contemporary dilemmas of social care, as Kathryn Ellis and Ann Davis's analysis of changes to British community care policy adopted in the 1980s (Ellis and Davis, 2001) demonstrates. Drawing on data from an empirical study, they report that risk-management approaches based on the development of client-prioritization criteria were used for assessing applicants and their carers. The intention, they report, was to minimize cost to the services. The result was that many applicants in need of assistance were refused as being too great a risk. In this case, the adoption of risk-management procedures served to narrow, rather than to broaden, the choices available to applicants. Ellis and Davis argue, however, that 'oppositional discourses of risk' continue to survive. The activities of a specialized disability team, for example, enabled clients to gain a degree of independence, assuming a certain 'dignity of risk' by remaining in their own homes, that might otherwise not have been possible if they had been placed in a more restrictive residential care setting.

Restructuring Care Provision

If Beck and the other risk theorists are correct, there can be no turning back to a world in which risk is seen in terms of chance or divine intervention, beyond the ability of humankind to affect. The general question that acknowledging risk poses for modern societies in the twenty-first century is how the risks identified are to be managed. How might concerns about risk intersect with the advancement of the new organizational logic of the globalized network society? In the fields involving social care and other human services, this question can be put as how an awareness of risk, and the adoption of risk-management practices might affect the way that services are provided?

Drawing on her work with colleagues (Kemshall et al., 1997), Kemshall argues that in the fields of child protection and aged care, the increasing preoccupation with assessment and the management of risk has contributed significantly to the form taken by services. This is evidenced by:

1. *Increased accountability procedures for service delivery and care workers.* Increased accountability and monitoring of care staff is a forensic

resource, in Mary Douglas's terms, making sure that someone is held accountable in a world where every death has become chargeable, every accident treated suspiciously as 'caused by someone's negligence, every sickness a threatened prosecution' (Douglas, 1992: 27, cited in Kemshall, 2002: 83). The approach is also a response to the movement of care away from systems of direct supervision, as occurs in a residential facility, to one that involves indirect supervision and control though standardized pathways and procedures. By setting out clear guidelines for the performance of duties, it is possible for senior management to direct the actions of subordinate, lower-level staff, even when personal supervision is not possible. This approach can therefore be considered a part of the procedures for what, following Ritzler (1993), might be termed the McDonaldization of care.

2. *The requirement to ration services achieved using enhanced targeting and assessment.* The increased targeting of services identifies those 'at risk' as having the highest priority for service, while those not at risk or assessed as able to provide for themselves have lower priority, possibly relegated to a waiting list or left to their own devices. Targeting on the basis of risk may therefore be understood as a rationing procedure, with two key aims – achieving a degree of economic efficiency by ensuring limited resources are put to their most efficient use (Davies and Knapp, 1994), and identifying those for whom not intervening could lead to charges of negligence or a breach of duty of care.

3. *The introduction of strategies for harm reduction and risk management as a balance to the requirement to ensure clients' freedom and choice* (Kemshall, 2002: 67–89). Harm minimization and risk-management strategies are typically reliant on paperwork-based exercises and are often required as part of audit procedures (Gregoire, Rapp and Poertner, 1995). They, too, serve to manage risk by setting limits on the autonomy of care staff and clients.

The insecure and less centralist character of the state that Castells (Castells, 1997) describes as emerging in informational economies is evident in the reforms and restructuring of the public sector, in the rise of corporate finance and in the increased reliance on competition between private for-profit and voluntary non-profit providers in the delivery of human services. With historical hindsight, the moves towards deinstitutionalization (Dear and Wolch, 1987) might be considered a first step towards the replacement of direct provision by large, public sector departments with a range of different approaches, many of them adopted from, and sometimes imposed by, the corporate world. As Alan Walker's account of changes to European aged-care services shows, subsequent reforms include the following:

• a reduction in the reliance on professional staff, and the increased use of generic management and performance management techniques;
• increased reliance on the outsourcing of work (especially for specialized, costly or difficult-to-staff activities such as out-of-hours weekend work) from large-scale services to small-scale specialist providers;
• the development and deployment of new organizational technologies such as case management;
• the development of systems of service networks and partnerships;
• the increased permeability of the formal system of human services and civil society, including family labour provided by unpaid caregivers. (Walker, 1993)

Other developments concern enhancements of the efficiency and effectiveness of service provision through large-scale public sector reforms, including privatization and contracting arrangements, and through case management and other means for improving the coordination and integration of services (Fine, 1998; Glendinning, 1998; Glendinning, Powell and Rummery, 2002). An important dimension of these sorts of changes is that portrayed by Paul Hoggett as reforms of modernization (Hoggett, 1990, 1994). Many of these use new organizational and information technologies to provide what he terms 'remote control mechanisms'. These managerial reforms allow slimmed-down central command systems to monitor performance in the field and exert ever greater control over service delivery, despite significant reductions in what might be thought of as supervisory, middle-management positions.

Conclusion: Work and the Future of Care

Castells (2000: 216) argues that 'the process of work is at the core of social structure' of informational economies. The challenge, for social theorists and those concerned with care and the achievement of a caring society, is to ensure that care in the twenty-first century is understood to be no less important. Reading contemporary sociological theory and surveying the social landscape with which we are confronted in the early twenty-first century, it is difficult to be convinced that anything more than gestures in this direction have been made. Yet a wealth of research exists that documents the importance of care. Nor is there a shortage of powerful and imaginative ways of theorizing the topic, with major contributions produced by feminists, moral philosophers, social policy analysts and other social scientists demonstrating the exciting potential that acknowledging care has for reimagining social life in the twenty-first century.

Insofar as care has been acknowledged, for most of the twentieth century these two foundations of social life, work and care, production and reproduction, were given expression as hierarchically ordered but separate social spheres. Care was practised as if it were a complementary activity, the opposite of work, but it remained a private issue, with little recognition of its importance in public life or social theory. Men worked in the public world and bore authority; women cared at home, in private, and offered support and encouragement. The task of tending bodies and providing emotional support effectively became the residual domestic work that industrial progress had not yet managed to conquer. Economic, demographic, political, democratic and social developments that can not be reversed have changed that equation for the twenty-first century.

For many, the ideals of care, including empathy, connection, concern and altruism, continue to present an alternative to the hegemonic values of the market, in which a sense of aggressive competition between individuals dominates, producing winners and losers. The emphasis placed on the single-minded pursuit of the work ethic is evidence of the dominant place that these activities have in the public culture of most Western nations. But, as many have argued, work and care can no longer be regarded as mutually exclusive (Standing, 2001; Edgar, 2005). Much care is, of course, already undertaken as paid work and this is likely to continue to increase in the coming decades. Whether paid or unpaid, caring inevitably involves physical and mental labour. Recognition of the opportunity costs of undertaking unpaid care have effectively made the activity functionally equivalent to paid employment. The cashing-out of entitlements to services through care payments and financial assistance to care-givers serves as a further recognition that care is already a form of work.

Although each of these reasons would, in itself, be sufficient, none is as decisive as the convergence of the demographic, economic and democratic pressures that we must live with in the twenty-first century. Simply, the demographic and economic imperatives that need to be faced in post-industrial societies increasingly require women to work in paid employment. The democratic recognition of women as individuals with citizenship rights equal to those of men also means that, barring the unpredictable, such as the return to a theocratic state as a result of war or ecological disaster, it is no longer possible to deny the right of women as citizens to realize their ability to participate in social life through paid employment as well as other means. The consequences of these developments mean that care will increasingly need to be undertaken and recognized as paid employment. Unpaid care at home will also inevitably be subject to the same pressures, as time at home will effectively be time away from paid employment. As a result, the artificial distinction that has been drawn between work and care in the twentieth century will cease to be of relevance.

How might this occur? The path by which care might be recognized and translated into policy is less obvious than many writers and advocates on the topic seem aware. Because the concept of care is capable of being interpreted in apparently contradictory ways, a generalized, abstract concept of care does not provide a clear political or moral programme with which to confront the one-sided emphasis placed on work, the economy and self-interest in the post-industrial societies of the twenty-first century. While the concept of 'care' clearly has broad appeal as a normative social value, it is necessary to go beyond general assertions about its importance. Careful analyses of the changing needs for care, and the problems faced by care-givers under different circumstances must continue to be undertaken. But a mountain of empirical data on its own is not enough. Care must also be acknowledged in social and economic theory and its importance spelt out in a programme of social rights based on a recognition of its collective or social dimensions. The approach implicit in the work of a number of contemporary writers on care is articulated by Knijn and Kremers' (1997) proposal for inclusive citizenship, which calls for every individual to be assured of the right both to give and to receive care. It is developed further in the approaches advocated by Morris (2001) and Williams (2001), which see care as a human right and a substantial economic activity. The right to care for others, as well as to care for ourselves, must accompany a right of access to care services when required.

A key requirement for such a project is the continuation of high levels of female participation in the labour market. This condition already exists in most post-industrial societies and, as argued throughout this book, is a key reason for the emergence of care as a public issue and the subsequent debate about the importance of care for social life and the responsibility for its provision. Despite conservative attempts to take back the right of women to employment outside the home, to return to a system based on 'traditional' family values in which women are the unpaid carers and men the family breadwinners, would be disastrous for the global economy. Equally threatening is the promotion of care solutions as low-cost services to be paid for directly by consumers. Such an approach, with its promise that care can be made affordable and accessible for future generations, is based on capturing the concept of care and repackaging it as a commodity to be provided by care corporations and labour-hire firms. A necessary condition for this is the exploitation of careworkers, based on the premise that remuneration for care work should be kept as low as possible.

Other theorists and social policy experts may argue more programmatically about the future of care. Esping-Andersen's model of welfare regimes, for example, suggests the importance of 'institutional path dependency' (Esping-Andersen, 1999). Historically shaped patterns of interaction between the state, the market and families in each country are likely to continue to be decisive for the way that care is conceptualized and structured. As Chamberlayne and King's study of carers in Britain, and the former East Germany and West Germany has shown, different 'cultures of care' develop over time in response to the different welfare regimes (Chamberlayne and King, 2000). Changes to the systems of care in each of these countries over the past decade, however, reminds us how precarious any set of social institutions is, just as they emphasize the importance of continuing public debate over social, economic and political goals.

At both the general theoretical or conceptual level and in the more substantive empirical work that has been undertaken, new ground has been broken over the past 25 years that has done much to heighten awareness of the importance of care and has indicated the directions that further social research on the topic must continue to follow. To sustain this effort, what is required is not the development of a new specialized discipline in which discussion takes place between experts, but interdisciplinary work which draws together practitioners, theorists and empirical researchers from diverse professional backgrounds. One of the key tasks is to identify the gaps and silences in the theories of sociology and the other social sciences, and in the policy and professional literature, in order that they might be remedied. In doing so, it is important not to be daunted by the apparent dominance of current social and economic doctrines that privilege the values of work, employment and consumer lifestyle, while marginalizing those that promote social connection.

Guy Standing reminds us that it was not until the twentieth century that the performance of work as employment was elevated to a social right (Standing, 2001: 17). Work was, of course, important before that time, but the idea that citizens would be seen as having a right to work, or to financial support if that was not achievable, would have seemed peculiar to most social observers in the nineteenth century. The challenges of care in the twenty-first century present the prospect of building on the nested dependencies that human vulnerability represents. Demographic, political and economic developments make the search for different sources of care and the development of new social solidarities imperative. The challenge, for those who seek to see a more caring society in future, is to work towards the realization of this ideal, not through personal sacrifice but through the promotion of care as a foundational principle of citizenship and social solidarity.

References

Abrams, P. (1978), *Neighbourhood Care and Social Policy*, Berkhamstead, Volunteer Centre (repub. 1989, London, HMSO).

ABS (1990), *Carers of the Handicapped at Home, Australia, 1988*. Canberra, Australian Bureau of Statistics, Cat. No. 4122.0.

ABS (1999a), *Caring in the Community, Australia, 1998* Canberra, Australian Bureau of Statistics, ABS Cat. No. 4436.0.

ABS (1999b), *Disability, Ageing and Carers: Summary of Findings Australia, 1998*, Cat. No. 4430.0, Canberra, Australian Bureau of Statistics.

Ackers, P. (2003), 'The Work–Life Balance from the Perspective of Economic Policy Actors', *Social Policy & Society*, 2 (3): 221–9.

Adams, G. and M. Rohacek (2002), 'More than a Work Support? Issues around Integrating Child Development Goals into the Child Care Subsidy System', *Early Childhood Research Quarterly*, 17 (2002): 418–40.

AIHW (2000), *Disability and Ageing: Australian Population Patterns and Implications*, AIHW Cat. No. DIS 19, Canberra, Australian Institute of Health and Welfare.

AIHW (2001), 'Deinstitutionalisation', *Australia's Welfare, 2001*, Australian Institute of Health and Welfare, Canberra: 96–139.

AIHW (2002), *Older Australia at a Glance* (3rd edn), Australian Institute of Health and Welfare, AIH Cat. No. AGE 25, Canberra.

AIHW (2003), *Australia's Welfare 2003*, Australian Institute of Health and Welfare, AusInfo: Canberra.

Amin, A. (ed.) (1995), *Post-Fordism: A Reader*, Oxford and Cambridge, MA, Blackwell.

Anderson, G. F. and P. S. Hussey (1999), *Health and Population Aging: A Multinational Perspective*, New York, The Commonwealth Fund.

Anstie, R. K. (1988). Government Spending on Work-Related Child Care: Some Economic Issues, Canberra, Centre for Economic Policy Research, Australian National University: Discussion Paper 191.

Anttonen, A., J. Baldock and J. Sipila (eds) (2003), *The Young, the Old and the State: Social Care Systems in Five Industrial Nations*. Globalization and Welfare Series, Cheltenham, and Northampton, MA, Edward Elgar.

Arber, S. and N. Gilbert (1989). 'Men: The Forgotten Carers.' *Sociology*, 23(1): 111–18.

Arber, S. and J. Ginn (1990), 'The Meaning of Informal Care: Gender and the Contribution of Elderly People', *Ageing & Society*, 10 (4): 429–54.

Aronson, J. (1992), 'Women's Sense of Responsibility for Care of Old People: 'But Who Else is Going to Do It?', *Gender & Society*, 6 (1): 8–29.

Aronson, J. and S. Neysmith (1996), 'You're Not Just There to Do the Work', Depersonalizing Policies and the Exploitation of Home Care Workers' Labor', *Gender & Society*, 10 (1): 59–77.

Baines, C. T. (1998), 'Women's Professions and an Ethic of Care', in C. T. Baines, P. M. Evans and S. M. Neysmith (eds) *Women's Caring. Feminist Perspectives on Social Welfare*, Oxford University Press, Toronto: 23–46.

Baines, C. T., P. M. Evans and S. M. Neysmith (eds) (1998), *Women's Caring. Feminist Perspectives on Social Welfare*, Oxford University Press, Toronto.

Baldock, C. V. (1990), *Volunteers in Welfare*, Sydney, Allen and Unwin.

Baldock, J. (2003), 'Social Care in the United Kingdom: A Pattern of Discretionary Social Administration', in A. Anttonen, J. Baldock and J. Sipila (eds) *The Young, the Old and the State: Social Care Systems in Five Industrial Nations*, Cheltenham, Northhampton, MA, Edward Elgar: 109–41.

Baldock, J. and A. Evers (1992), 'Innovations in Care for the Elderly: The Cutting-Edge of Change for Social Welfare Systems. Examples from Sweden, the Netherlands and the United Kingdom', *Ageing and Society*, 12(3): 289–312.

Baldock, J. and C. Ungerson (1994). Becoming Consumers of Community Care: Households within the Mixed Economy of Welfare, York, Joseph Rowntree Foundation: 1–56.

Baldock, J. and C. Ungerson (1996), 'Money, Care and Consumption: Families in the New Mixed Economy of Social Care', in H. Jones and J. Millar (eds) *The Politics of the Family*, Aldershot, Avebury: 167–87.

Baldwin, S. (1985), *The Costs of Caring*, London, Routledge and Kegan Paul.

Barnes, C. (1998), 'The Social Model of Disability: A Sociological Phenomenon Ignored by Sociologists?', in T. Shakespeare (ed.) *The Disability Reader: Social Science Perspectives*, London and New York, Cassell: 65–78.

Barnes, M. (1997), *Care, Communities and Citizens*, Harlow, Addison, Wesley Longman.

Barnes, M. (2001), 'From Private Carer to Public Actor: The Carers Movement in England', in M. Daly (ed.) *Care Work: The Quest for Security*, Geneva, International Labour Office (ILO): 195–210.

Barrett, M. and M. McIntosh (1982) *The Anti-Social Family*, London, Verso.

Barton, R. (1959), *Institutional Neurosis*, Bristol, John Wright and Sons.

Bauman, Z. (1995), *Postmodern Ethics*, Oxford, Blackwell.

Bauman, Z. (1998), *Work, Consumerism and the New Poor*, Buckingham, Open University Press.

Bauman, Z. (2001), *Community. Seeking Safety in an Insecure World*, Cambridge, Polity.

Baumol, W. J. (1967), 'Macroeconomics of Unbalanced Growth: The Anatomy of Urban Crisis', *American Economic Review*, 62: 415–26.

Baumol, W. J. (1993), 'Health Care, Education and the Cost Disease: A Looming Crisis for Public Choice', *Public Choice*, 77: 17–28.

Bealey, F. W. (1999), *The Blackwell Dictionary of Political Science*, Blackwell Publishers, Cambridge, Entry on 'Risk', downloaded June 2005, http://www.xreferplus.com/entry/725756

Beaujot, R. (2000), *Earning and Caring in Canadian Families*, Peterborough, Broadview Press.

Beck, U. (1992), *Risk Society. Towards a New Modernity*, (first pub. in German 1986), London, Sage.

Beck, U. and E. Beck-Gernsheim (1995), *The Normal Chaos of Love*, Cambridge, Polity (first pub. in German 1990).

Beck, U. and E. Beck-Gernsheim (2002), *Individualization*, London, Sage.

Beck-Gernsheim, E. (2002), 'From "Living for Others" to "A Life of One's Own". Individualization and Women' (first pub. in German 1983)', in U. Beck and E. Beck-Gernsheim (eds) *Individualization*, London, Sage: 54–84.

Bell, C. and H. Newby (1971), *Community Studies*, London, George Allen and Unwin.

Bellah, R. N. (1994). 'Understanding Caring in Contemporary America', in S. S. Phillips and P. Benner (eds) *The Crisis of Care. Affirming and Restoring Caring Practices in the Helping Professions*, Washington DC, Georgetown University Press: 21–35.

Bellah, R. N., R. Madsen, W. Sullivan, A. Swidler and S. Tipton (1985), *Habits of the Heart. Individualism and Commitment in American Life*, London, University of California Press.

Bellah, R. N., R. Madsen, W. Sullivan, A. Swidler and S. Tipton (1991), *The Good Society*, New York, Random House.

Benhabib, S. (1995), 'The Debate Over Women and Moral Theory Revisited', in J. Mechan (ed.) *Feminists Read Habermas. Gendering the Subject of Discourse*. New York, Routledge.

Benner, P. (1984), *From Novice to Expert: Excellence and Power in Clinical Nursing*, Menlo Park, CA, Addison-Wesley.

Benner, P. (1994a), 'Caring as a Way of Knowing and Not Knowing', in S. S. Phillips and P. Benner (eds) *The Crisis of Care. Affirming and Restoring Caring Practices in the Helping Professions*, Washington DC, Georgetown University Press: 42–62.

Benner, P. (1994b), *Interpretive Phenomenology: Embodiment, Caring, and Ethics in Health and Illness*, Thousand Oaks, CA, Sage.

Benner, P. (2000), 'The Roles of Embodiment, Emotion and Lifeworld for Rationality and Agency in Nursing Practice', *Nursing Philosophy*, 1: 5–19.

Benner, P. and J. Wrubel (1989), *The Primacy of Caring. Stress and Coping in Health and Illness*, Menlo Park, CA, Addison-Wesley.

Berger, P. and T. Luckman (1967), *The Social Construction of Reality*, Garden City, NY, Doubleday.

Bertone, C. (2003), 'Claims for Child Care as Struggles over Needs: Comparing Italian and Danish Women's Organizations', *Social Politics*, 10 (2): 229–55.

Bettio, F. and J. Plantenga (2004), 'Comparing Care Regimes in Europe', *Feminist Economics*, 10 (1): 85–113.

Bettio, F., A. Simonazzi and P. Villa (2004), 'The 'Care Drain' in the Mediterranean: Notes on the Italian Experience', in *Conference of the International Working Party on Labour Market Segmentation*, Brisbane, http://www.gu.edu.au/school/gbs/irl/working_party/papers.html

Biggart, N. (1992), 'Institutional Logic and Economic Explanation', in J. Marceau (ed.) *Reworking the World: Organizations, Technologies and Cultures in Comparative Perspective*, Berlin, Walter de Gruyter: 29–54.

Bittman, M. (2000), 'The Nuclear Family in the Twentieth-Century', in J. M. Najman and J. S. Western (eds) *A Sociology of Australian Society: Introductory Readings* (3rd edn), Melbourne, MacMillan: 301–28.

Bittman, M. (2004), 'Parenting and Employment. What Time Use Surveys Show', in N. Folbre and M. Bittman (eds) *Family Time. The Social Organization of Care*, London, Routledge: 152–70.

Bittman, M., L. Craig and N. Folbre (2004), 'Packaging Care. What Happens when Children Receive Nonparental Care?', in M. Bittman (ed.) *Family Time. The Social Organization of Care*, London, Routledge: 133–51.

Bittman, M., P. England, L. Sayer, N. Folbre and G. Matheson (2003), 'When Does Gender Trump Money?: Bargaining and Time in Household Work', *American Journal of Sociology*, 109: 186–214.

Bittman, M. and J. Pixley (1997), *The Double Life of the Family. Myth, Hope and Experience*, St Leonards, Allen and Unwin.

Bittman, M. and C. Thomson (2000), 'Invisible Support: The Determinants of Time Spent in Informal Care', in J. Warburton and M. Oppenheimer (eds) *Volunteers and Volunteering*, Sydney, Federation Press: 98–112.

Blau, D. (2001), 'Rethinking US Child Care Policy', *Issues in Science and Technology*, Winter 2001–2: 66–72.

Bourdieu, P. (1986), 'The Forms of Capital', in J. Richardson (eds) *Handbook of Theory and Research for the Sociology of Education*, New York, Greenwood Press: 241–58.

Bowden, P. (1997), *Caring. Gender-Sensitive Ethics*, London, Routledge.

Boykin, A. and S. O. Schoenhofer (2001), *Nursing as Caring: A Model for Transforming Practice*, Sudsbury, MA, Jones and Bartlett, National League for Nursing Press.

Bradley, J. C. and M. A. Edinberg (1986), *Communication in the Nursing Context* (2nd edn), Norwalk, CT, Appleton-Century-Crofts.

Brennan, D. (1998), *The Politics of Australian Child Care: Philanthropy to Feminism and Beyond* (2nd edn), Cambridge, Cambridge University Press.

Brennan, D. and P. Kinnear (2002), 'Childcare: Good or Bad for Kids?', *The Australia Institute Newsletter*, 31 (June 2002): 10–11.

Briar, C., R. Munford and M. Nash (eds) (1992), *Superwoman, Where are You? Social Policy and Women's Experiences*, Palmerston North, Dunmore Press.

Brody, E. (1981), 'Women in the Middle and Family Help to Older People', *The Gerontologist*, 26: 373–81.

Bubeck, D. (1995), *Care, Gender, and Justice*, Oxford, Clarendon.

Bubeck, D. G. (2002), 'Justice and the Labor of Care', in E. F. Kittay and E. K. Feder (eds) *The Subject of Care. Feminist Perspectives on Dependency*, Lanham, Rowman and Littlefield: 160–85.

Bytheway, B. and J. Johnson (1998), 'The Social Construction of Carers', in A. Symonds and A. Kelly (eds) *The Social Construction of Community Care*, London, MacMillan: 241–53.

Campbell, M. (1999), 'Knowledge, Gendered Subjectivity, and the Restructuring of Health Care: The Case of the Disappearing Nurse', in S. Neysmith (ed.) *Restructuring Caring Labour. Discourse, State Practice and Everyday Life*, Ontario, Oxford University Press: 186–208.

Cancian, F. M. (2000), 'Paid Emotional Care. Organizational Forms that Encourage Nurturance', in M. Harrington-Meyer (ed.) *Care Work: Gender, Labor and the Welfare State*, New York, Routledge: 136–48.

Cantor, M. (1979), 'Neighbours and Friends: An Overlooked Resource in the Informal Support System', *Research in Aging* 1(4): 434–63.

Cantor, M. (1989), 'Social Care: Family and Community Support Systems', *Annals of the American Academy of Political and Social Science*, 503 (May): 99–112.

Cantor, M. and V. Little (1985), 'Aging and Social Care', in R. H. Binstock and E. Shanas (eds) *Handbook of Aging and the Social Sciences*, New York, Van Nostrand Reinhold: 745–81.

Castells, M. (1997), *The Power of Identity, The Information Age: Economy, Society and Culture*, Oxford: Blackwell.

Chamberlayne, P. and A. King (2000), *Cultures of Care. Biographies of Carers in Britain and the Two Germanies*, Bristol, Policy Press.

Chappell, N. and A. Blandford (1991), 'Informal and Formal Care: Exploring the Complementarity.' *Ageing and Society*, 11: 229–317.

Chappell, N. L. (1985). 'Social Support and the Receipt of Home Care Services', *The Gerontologist* 25(1): 47–54.

Chappell, N. L. (1991), 'Living Arrangements and Sources of Caregiving', *Journal of Gerontology: Social Sciences* 46(1): 1–8.

Cheal, D. (2002), *Sociology of Family Life*, Houndmills, Palgrave.

Chesterman, J., D. Challis and B. Davies (1987), 'Long-Term Care at Home for the Elderly: A Four-Year Follow-Up.' *British Journal of Social Work*, 18: 43–53.

Clark, C. (1998), 'Self-determination and Paternalism in Community Care: Practice and Prospects', *British Journal of Social Work*, 28: 387–402.

Clement, G. (1996), *Care, Autonomy and Justice*, Boulder, CO, Westview.

Clifford, R. (1992), *The Social Costs and Rewards of Caring*, Aldershot, Avebury.

Coleman, J. (1988), 'Social Capital in the Creation of Human Capital', *American Journal of Sociology*, 94: S95–120.

Collier, C. (2001), 'Working with Parties: Success and Failure of Child Care Advocates in British Columbia and Ontario in the 1990s', in S. Prentice (ed.) *Changing Child Care. Five Decades of Child Care Advocacy and Policy in Canada*, Halifax, Fernwood Publishing: 117–32.

Corker, M. and T. Shakespeare (2002), 'Mapping the Terrain', in M. Corker and T. Shakespeare (eds) *Disability/Postmodernity. Embodying Disability Theory*. London, Continuum: 1–17.

Costa, D. L. (2000), 'Understanding the Twentieth-Century Decline in Chronic Conditions among Older Men', *Demography*, 37 (1): 53–73.

Costa, D. L. (2002), 'Changing Chronic Disease Rates and Long-Term Declines in Functional Limitation among Older Men', *Demography*, 39 (1): 119–38.

Crittenden, C. (2001), 'The Principles of Care', *Women and Politics* 22(2): 81–105.

Crow, L. (1996), 'Including All Our Lives: Renewing the Social Model of Disability', in J. Morris (ed.) *Encounters with Strangers: Feminism and Disability*. London, Women's Press: 206–26.

Culpitt, I. (1999), *Social Policy and Risk*, London, Sage.

Dalley, G. (1988, 2nd edn 1996), *Ideologies of Caring: Rethinking Community and Collectivism*, Houndmills and London, Macmillan.

Daly, M. (2002), 'Care as a Good for Social Policy', *Journal of Social Policy*, 31 (2): 251–70.

Daly, M. and J. Lewis (2000), 'The Concept of Social Care and the Analysis of Contemporary Welfare States', *British Journal of Sociology* 51(2): 281–98.

Davies, B. (1994), 'British Home and Community Care: Research-Based Critiques and the Challenge of New Policy', *Social Science and Medicine*, 38 (7): 883–903.

Davies, B., A. Bebbington, H. Charnley, B. Baines, E. Ferlie, M. Hughes and J. Twigg (1990), *Resources, Needs and Outcomes in Community-Based Care. A Comparative Study of the Production of Welfare for Elderly People in Ten Local Authorities in England and Wales*, Aldershot, Avebury.

Davies, B. and D. Challis (1986), *Matching Resources to Needs in Community Care*, Aldershot, Gower.

Davies, B. and M. Knapp (1980), *Old People's Homes and the Production of Welfare*. London, Routledge and Kegan Paul.

Davies, B. and M. Knapp (1994), 'Improving Equity and Efficiency in British Community Care', *Social Policy and Administration*, 28 (3): 263–85.

Deacon, A. and K. Mann (1999), 'Agency, Modernity and Social Policy', *Journal of Social Policy*, 28 (3): 413–35.

Deakin, N. (2001), *In Search of Civil Society*, Houndmills, Palgrave.

Dean, H. (2002), 'Business versus Families: Whose Side is New Labor on?' *Social Policy & Society*, 1 (1): 3–10.

Dean, M. (1999), 'Risk, Calculable and Incalculable', in D. Lupton (ed.) *Risk and Sociocultural Theory: New Directions and Perspectives*, Cambridge, Cambridge University Press.

Dear, M. J. and J. R. Wolch (1987), *Landscapes of Despair. From Deinstitutionalization to Homelessness*, Princeton, NJ, Princeton University Press.

Douglas, M. (1966), *Purity and Danger: An Analysis of the Concepts of Pollution and Taboo*, London, Routledge and Kegan Paul.

Douglas, M. (1986), *Risk Acceptability According to the Social Sciences*, London, Routledge.

Douglas, M. (1992), *Risk and Blame: Essays in Cultural Theory*, London, Routledge.

Dudeley, V. (1994), 'Feminist Perspectives on the Ethic of Care', in *Bibliography number 69 in the series 'Wisconsin Bibliographies in Women's Studies'*, Madison, WI, University of Wisconsin, downloaded from www.library.wisc.edu/libraries/WomensStudies/bibliogs/ethicbib.html May 2003.

Duncan, S. (2002), 'Policy Discourses on "Reconciling Work and Life" in the EU', *Social Policy & Society*, 1 (4): 305–14.

Dunlop, M. J. (1994), 'Is a Science of Caring Possible?', in P. Benner (ed.) *Interpretive Phenomenology: Embodiment, Caring, and Ethics in Health and Illness*, Thousand Oaks, CA, Sage: 27–42.

Durkheim, E. (1984), *The Division of Labor in Society* (trans. by W. D. Halls) New York, Free Press.

Economist (2002), 'Special Report: Half a Billion Americans? – Demography and the West', *The Economist*, 364 (8287): 22–4.

Edgar, D. (2005), *The War Over Work. The Future of Work and Family*, Carlton, Melbourne University Press.

Edwards, R. and J. Glover (ed.) (2001), *Risk and Citizenship: Key Issues in Welfare*, London, Routledge.

Ehrenreich, B. and A. Hochschild (eds) (2002), *Global Women. Nannies, Maids and Sex Workers in the New Economy*, New York, Metropolitan Books.

Eisenstein, H. (1984), *Contemporary Feminist Thought*, London, Unwin.

Elias, N. (1991), *The Society of Individuals*, Oxford (ed. by Michael Schroter, trans. by E. Jephcott), Blackwell.

Elias, N. (1994), *The Civilizing Process* (revised edn), Oxford (trans. by Edmund Jephcott), Blackwell.

Ellis, K. and A. Davis (2001), 'Managing the Body: Competing Approaches to Risk Assessment in Community Care', in R. Edwards and J. Glover (eds) *Risk and Citizenship. Key Issues in Welfare*, London, Routledge.

England, P., M. Budig and N. Folbre (2002), 'Wages of Virtue: The Relative Pay of Care Work', *Social Problems. Berkeley*, 49 (4): 455–73.

England, P. and N. Folbre (1999), 'The Cost of Caring', *The ANNALS of the American Academy of Political and Social Science*, 561 (1): 39–51.

Esping-Andersen, G. (1990), *The Three Worlds of Welfare Capitalism*, Cambridge, Polity.

Esping-Andersen, G. (1999), *Social Foundations of Postindustrial Economies*, Oxford, Oxford University Press.

Esping-Andersen, G. with D. Gallie, A. Hemerijk and J. Myles (2002), *Why We Need a New Welfare State*, Oxford, Oxford University Press.

European Commission (1999), *Towards a Europe for All Ages – Promoting Prosperity and Intergenerational Solidarity*, KOM (1999) 221, Brussels, Ministry for Health and Social Affairs.

Evans, R. G., K. M. McGrail, S. G. Morgan, M. L. Barer and C. Hertzman (2001), 'APOCALYPSE NO: Population Aging and the Future of Health Care Systems', *Canadian Journal on Aging*, 20 (Supplement 1): 160–91.

Evers, A. (1994), 'Payments for Care: A Small but Significant Part of a Wider Debate', in C. Ungerson (ed.) *Payments for Care: A Comparative Overview*, Aldershot, European Centre Vienna/Avebury: 19–42.

Fagermoen, M. S. (1999), 'Humanism in Nursing Theory: A Focus on Caring', in H. S. Kim and I. Kollak (eds) *Nursing Theories. Conceptual and Philosophical Foundations*, New York, Springer.

Feinberg, L. F. and C. Ellano (2000), 'Promoting Consumer Direction for Family Caregiver Support: An Agency-Driven Model', *Generations*, 24 (3): 47–53.

Finch, J. (1989), *Family Obligations and Social Change*, Cambridge, Polity.

Finch, J. and D. Groves (1980), 'Community Care and the Family: A Case for Equal Opportunities', *Journal of Social Policy*, 9: 487–511.

Finch, J. and D. Groves (eds) (1983), *A Labour of Love: Women, Work, and Caring*, London and Boston, Routledge & Kegan Paul.

Finch, J. and J. Mason (1990), 'Filial Obligations and Kin Support for Elderly People', *Ageing and Society* 10: 151–75.

Finch, J. and J. Mason (1993), *Negotiating Family Responsibilities*, London, Routledge.

Fine, M. (1994), 'Supporting, Exploiting or Displacing the Family? Community Support for Disabled and Frail Older People', in J. Inglis and L. Rogan (eds) *Flexible Families. New Directions for Australian Communities*, Sydney, Pluto Press.

Fine, M. (1998), 'Acute and Continuing Care for Older People in Australia: Contesting New Balances of Care', in C. Glendinning (ed.) *Rights and Realities. Comparing New Developments in Long-Term Care for Older People*, Bristol, Policy Press: 105–26.

Fine, M. (1999a), 'Ageing and the Balance of Responsibilities between the Various Providers of Child and Aged Care: Shaping Policies for the

Future', in Fine (ed.) *Policy Implications of the Ageing of Australia's Population: Conference Proceedings Melbourne, 18–19 March 1999*, Melbourne, Productivity Commission and Melbourne Institute of Applied Economic and Social Research: 263–92.

Fine, M. (1999b), 'Coordinating Health, Extended Care and Community Support Services. Reforming Aged Care in Australia', *Journal of Aging and Social Policy*, 11 (1): 67–90.

Fine, M. (2004), 'Care: Renewing the Social Vision', *Australian Journal of Social Issues*, 39 (3): 217–32.

Fine, M. (2005a), 'Dependency Work. A Critical Exploration of Kittay's Perspective on Care as a Relationship of Power', *Health Sociology Review*, 14 (2): 146–60.

Fine, M. (2005b), 'Individualisation, Risk and the Body. Sociology and Care', *Journal of Sociology*, 41 (3): 249–68.

Fine, M. and C. Glendinning (2005), 'Dependence, Independence or Interdependence? Revisiting the Concepts of "Care" and "Dependency" ', *Ageing and Society*, 25 (4): 601–21.

Fine, M. and C. Thomson (1995), *Three Years at Home: The Final Report of a Longitudinal Study of Community Support Services and Their Users*, Sydney, Reports and Proceeding No. 121, Social Policy Research Centre, University of New South Wales.

Fine, M. and C. Thomson (1997), 'Beyond Caring: Informal Care and the Use of Community Support Services by Home and Community Care Clients', in V. Minichiello, N. Chappell, H. Kendig and A. Walker (eds) *Sociology of Aging: International Perspectives*, London and Melbourne, International Sociological Association: 207–25.

Fisher, B. and J. Tronto (1990), 'Towards a Feminist Theory of Care', in E. Abel and M. Nelson (eds) *Circles of Care. Work and Identity in Women's Lives*, Albany, NY, State University of New York Press.

Fisher, K. and M. Fine (2002), 'Care Coordination, Case Management Theory and the Coordinated Care Trials. Reconsidering the Fundamentals', in Fisher and Fine (eds) *The Australian Coordinated Care Trials: Reflections on the Evaluation* (Vol. 2), Canberra, Department of Health and Ageing: 23–39.

Fjelland, R. and E. Gjengedal (1994), 'A Theoretical Foundation for Nursing as a Science', in P. Benner (ed.) *Interpretive Phenomenology: Embodiment, Caring, and Ethics in Health and Illness*. Thousand Oaks, CA, Sage.

Folbre, N. (2001a), 'Accounting for Care in the United States', in M. Daly (ed.) *Care Work: The Quest for Security*, Geneva, International Labour Office: 175–91.

Folbre, N. (2001b), *The Invisible Heart: Economics and Family Values*, New York, The New Press.

Folbre, N. and M. Bittman (eds) (2004), *Family Time: The Social Organization of Care*, New York, Routledge.

Foucault, M. (1965), *Madness and Civilisation* (orig. *Histoire de la Folie, 1961,* trans. by Richard Howard), New York, Pantheon.

Foucault, M. (1978), *Discipline and Punish: The Birth of the Prison,* trans. by Alan Sheriden, New York, Vintage Books.

Foucault, M. (1980), *The History of Sexuality. Vol. 1: An Introduction,* trans. by Robert Hurley, New York, Vintage Books.

Foucault, M. (1988a), *The Care of the Self,* (trans. by R. Hurey), New York, Vintage Books.

Foucault, M. (1988b), 'The Ethic of Care for the Self as a Practice of Freedom', in D. Rasmussen (ed.) *The Final Foucault,* Cambridge, MA, MIT Press.

Fox Harding, L. (1991), *Perspectives in Child Care Policy,* London and New York, Longman.

Francis, L. E., P. W. Colson and P. Mizzi (2002), 'Ethics in Community Mental Health Care: Beneficence vs. Obligation: Challenges of the Americans with Disabilities Act for Consumer Employment in Mental Health Services', *Community Mental Health Journal,* 38 (2): 95–110.

Franzway, S. (2001), *Sexual Politics and Greedy Institutions,* Annandale, NSW, Pluto Press Australia.

Fraser, N. and L. Gordon (1994), 'A Genealogy of Dependency: Tracing a Keyword of the US Welfare State', *Signs,* 19 (2): 309–34.

Freedman, V., L. G. Martin and R. F. Schoeni (2002), 'Recent Trends in Disability and Functioning among Older Adults in the United States', *Journal of the American Medical Association,* 288(24): 3137–46.

Freedman, V. A., E. Crimmins, R. F. Schoeni, B. C. Spillman, H. Aykan, E. Kramarow, K. Land, J. Lubitz, K. G. Manton, L. G. Martin, D. Shinberg and T. Waidmann (2004), 'Resolving Inconsistencies in Trends in Old-Age Disability: Report from a Technical Working Group', *Demography,* 41 (3): 417–41.

Freidson, E. (1990), 'The Centrality of Professionalism to Health Care', *Jurimetrics Journal,* 30 (4): 431–46.

Friedan, B. (1993), *The Fountain of Age,* London, Vintage.

Fries, J. F. (1980), 'Aging, Natural Death, and the Compression of Morbidity', *New England Journal of Medicine,* 3 (2): 130–35.

Fries, J. F., L. W. Green and S. Levine (1989), 'Health Promotion and the Compression of Morbidity', *The Lancet,* 1989: 481–3.

Galvin, R. (2004), 'Challenging the Need for Gratitude. Comparisons Between Paid and Unpaid Care for Disabled People', *Journal of Sociology,* 40 (2): 137–55.

Gardiner, J. (1997), *Gender, Care and Economics,* Houndmills, MacMillan.

Gaut, D. A. (ed.) (1993), *A Global Agenda for Caring,* New York, National League for Nursing Press.

Gerhardt, U. (1987), 'Parsons, Role Theory, and Health Interaction', in

G. Scrambler (ed.) *Sociological Theory and Medical Sociology*, London, Tavistock.

Giddens, A. (1984), *The Constitution of Society: Outline of the Theory of Structuration*, Cambridge, Polity.

Giddens, A. (1991), *Modernity and Self-Identity. Self and Society in the Late Modern Age*, Cambridge, Polity.

Giddens, A. (1993), *The Transformation of Intimacy: Sexuality, Love and Eroticism in Modern Societies*, Cambridge, Polity.

Giddens, A. (1998), *The Third Way. The Renewal of Social Democracy*, Cambridge, Polity.

Gilligan, C. (1977), 'In a Different Voice: Women's Conceptions of Self and of Morality', *Harvard Educational Review* 47(4): 481–505.

Gilligan, C. (1982), *In a Different Voice*, Cambridge, MA, Harvard University Press.

Gilligan, C. (1986), 'Remapping the Moral Domain: New Images of the Self in Relationship', in T. Heller (ed.) *Reconstructing Individualism: Autonomy, Individuality and the Self in Western Thought*, Stanford, CA, Stanford University Press: 237–52.

Glazer, N.Y. (1990), 'The Home as Workshop: Women as Amateur Nurses and Medical Care Providers', *Gender and Society*, 4 (4): 479–99.

Gleeson, B. (1997), 'Community Care and Disability: The Limits to Justice', *Progress in Human Geography*, 21 (2): 199–224.

Glendinning, C. (1983), *Unshared Care: Parents and their Disabled Children*. London, Routledge and Kegan Paul.

Glendinning, C. (1989), *The Costs of Informal Care: Looking Inside the Household*, London, HMSO.

Glendinning, C. (ed.) (1998), *Rights and Realities. Comparing New Developments in Long-Term Care for Older People*, Bristol, Policy Press.

Glendinning, C., S. Halliwell, S. Jacobs, K. Rummery and J. Tyrer (2000), 'New Kinds of Care, New Kinds of Relationships: How Purchasing Services Affects Relationships in Giving and Receiving Personal Assistance', *Health and Social Care in the Community*, 8 (3): 201–11.

Glendinning, C., M. Powell and K. Rummery, (eds) (2002), *Partnerships, New Labour and the Governance of Welfare*, Bristol, Policy Press.

Goffman, E. (1968), *Asylums*, Harmondsworth, Pelican.

Golini, A. (1997), 'Demographic Trends and Ageing in Europe. Prospects, Problems and Policies', *Genus*, 53 (3–4): 33–74.

Gordon, B. O. and K. E. Rosenblum (2001), 'Bringing Disability into the Sociological Frame: A Comparison of Disability with Race, Sex, and Sexual Orientation Statuses', *Disability and Society*, 16 (1): 5–19.

Goyder, J. (2001), *We'll Be Married in Fremantle*, Fremantle, Fremantle Arts Centre Press.

Graham, H. (1983), 'Caring; a Labor of Love', in J. Finch and D. Groves (eds)

A Labor of Love: Women, Work and Caring, London, Routledge and Kegan Paul.

Graham, H. (1991), 'The Concept of Caring in Feminist Research: The Case of Domestic Service', *Sociology* 25(1): 61–78.

Gray, M. and D. Stanton (2002), 'Work and Family Life: Our Workplaces, Families and Futures', *Family Matters*, 61 (Autumn): 4–11.

Gregoire, T., C. Rapp and J. Poertner (1995), 'The New Management: Assessing the Fit of Total Quality Management and Social Agencies', in R. L. Edwards and B. Gummer (eds) *Total Quality Management in the Social Services: Theory and Practice*, New York, Research Foundation, State University of New York: 3–32.

Gruenberg, E. M. (1977), 'The Failures of Success', *Milbank Memorial Foundation Quarterly / Health and Society*, 55 (1): 3–24.

Hakim, C. (1995), 'Five Feminist Myths about Women's Employment', *British Journal of Sociology*, 46 (3): 429–55.

Hakim, C. (2000), *Work–Lifestyle Choices in the 21st Century: Preference Theory*, Oxford, Oxford University Press.

Hakim, C. (2001), 'Taking Women Seriously', *People and Place*, 9 (4): 1–6.

Hall, E. T. (1969), *The Hidden Dimension: Man's Use of Space in Public and Private*, London, Bodley Head.

Hamington, M. (2004), *Embodied Care. Jane Addams, Maurice Merleau-Ponty, and Feminist Ethics*, Urbana and Chicago, University of Illinois Press.

Hattinga-Verschure, J. C. M. (1977), *Het verschijnsel zorg. Een inleiding to de zorgkunde (The Phenomenon of Care. An Introduction to Care Knowledge)*, Lochem, De Tijdstroom.

Hattinga-Verschure, J. C. M. (1980), 'Kritisch onderzoek naar do zorgverlening rond do verpleeghuispatient (Critical Research on the Care of Nursing Home Patients)', in Hattinga-Vershure (ed.) *De identiteit van het verpleeghuis (The Identity of the Nursing Home)*, LOchem, De Tijdstroom: 129–51.

Heffernan, J. (2003), 'Care for Children and Older People in Japan: Laggard or Merely Different?', in A. Anttonen, J. Baldock and J. Sipila (eds) *The Young, the Old and the State: Social Care Systems in Five Industrial Nations*, Cheltenham, and Northampton, MA, Edward Elgar: 143–66.

Held, V. (1995), 'Feminist Moral Enquiry and the Feminist Future', in V. Held (ed.) *Justice and Care. Essential Readings in Feminist Ethics*. New York, Westview Press.

Heller, A. (1990), 'Hermeneutics of Social Science', in Heller (ed.) *Can Modernity Survive?*, Cambridge, Polity Press: 11–42.

Henderson, J. and L. Forbat (2002), 'Relationship-Based Social Policy: Personal and Policy Constructions of "Care" ', *Critical Social Policy* 22(4): 669–87.

Hernes, H. M. (1987), *Welfare State and Women Power: Essays in State Feminism*, Oslo, Norwegian University Press.

Hewitt, P. (1993), *About Time: The Revolution in Work and Family Life*, London, IPPR/Rivers Oram.

Hill, J., J. Waldfogel and J. Brooks-Gunn (2002), 'Differential Effects of High-Quality Child Care', *Journal of Policy Analysis and Management, Fall 2002*, 21(4): 601–27.

Hirschman, A. (1970), *Exit, Voice and Loyalty: Responses to Decline in Firms, Organizations and States*, Cambridge, MA, and London, Harvard University Press.

Hirst, M. (2001), 'Trends in Informal Care in Britain', *Health and Social Care in the Community*, 9 (6): 348–57.

Hoagland, S. L. (1991), 'Some Thoughts about Caring', in C. Card (ed.) *Feminist Ethics*, Lawrence, KS, University of Kansas Press.

Hobson, B. (1993), 'Feminist Strategies and Gendered Discourses in Welfare States: Married Women's Right to Work in the United States and Sweden', in S. Koven and S. Michel (eds) *Mothers of a New World: Maternalist Politics and the Origins of Welfare States*, New York, Routledge: 396–430.

Hochschild, A. R. (1983), *The Managed Heart. Commercialization of Human Feeling*, Berkley, CA, University of California Press.

Hochschild, A. R. (1997), *The Time Bind. When Work Becomes Home and Home Becomes Work*, New York, Metropolitan Books.

Hochschild, A. R. (2003), *The Commercialization of Intimate Life. Notes from Home and Work.*, Berkley, CA, University of California Press.

Hochschild, A. R. (2003), 'The Culture of Politics: Traditional, Postmodern, Cold-modern and Warm-modern Ideals of Care', in *The Commercialization of Intimate Life. Notes from Home and Work*, Berkley, CA, University of California Press: 213–23, (first pub. in 1995, *Social Politics*, 2 (3): 331–46).

Hochschild, A. R. and A. Machung (1989), *The Second Shift. Working Parents and the Revolution at Home*, New York, Viking.

Hoggett, P. (1990), *Modernisation, Political Strategy and the Welfare State. An Organisational Perspective*, Bristol, Studies in Decentralisation and Quasi-Markets No. 2, School for Advanced Urban Studies, University of Bristol.

Hoggett, P. (1994), 'A New Management in the Public Sector?', in R. Smith and J. Raistrick (eds) *Policy and Change*, Bristol, School for Advanced Urban Studies: 15–38.

Hoggett, P. (2001), 'Hatred of Dependency', in P. Hoggett (ed.) *Emotional Life and the Politics of Welfare*, Houndmills, MacMillan: 159–80.

Howe, A. and H. Schofield (1996), 'Will You Need One, or Will You Be One, in the Year 2004? – Trends in Carer Roles and Social Policy in Australia over the Last and Next 20 years', in *Towards a National Agenda for Carers: Workshop Papers*, Aged and Community Care Service Development and Evaluation Report No. 22, Canberra, AGPS.

HREOC (2005), *Striking the Balance: Women, Men, Work and Family*, Human Rights and Equal Opportunity Commission, Sydney, http://www.

humanrights.gov.au/sex_discrimination/strikingbalance/index.html downloaded August 2005.

Hu-Dehart, E. (2003), 'Globalization and its Discontents: Exposing the Underside. (Part 6: Globalizing)', *Frontiers – A Journal of Women's Studies*, 24 (2&3): 244–60.

Hugman, R. (1991), *Power in Caring Professions*, London, MacMillan.

Illich, I. (1975), *Medical Nemesis. The Expropriation of Health*, New York, Pantheon.

Inglis, J. and L. Rogan (eds) (1994), *Flexible Families. New Directions for Australian Communities*, Sydney, Pluto Press.

Ironmonger, D. (2004), 'Bringing up Bobby and Betty: The Inputs and Outputs of Childcare Time', in M. Bittman (ed.) *Family Time. The Social Organization of Care*, London, Routledge: 93–109.

Iversen, T. and A. Wren (1998), 'Equality, Employment, and Budgetary Restraint: The Trilemma of the Service Economy', *World Politics*, 50 (4): 507–46.

Jacobzone, S., E. Cambois, E. Chaplain and J-M. Robine (1998a), *Long-Term Care Services to Older People, A Perspective on Future Needs; The Impact of an Improving Health of Older Persons*, Ageing Working Papers AWP 4.2, Paris, OECD.

Jacobzone, S., E. Cambois, E. Chaplain and J-M. Robine (1998b), *The Health of Older Persons in OECD Countries: Is it Improving Fast Enough to Compensate for Population Ageing?*, Labor Market and Social Policy Occasional Papers, No. 37, Paris, OECD.

James, N. (1992), 'Care = Organisation + Physical Labour + Emotional Labour', *Sociology of Health and Illness*, 14 (4): 488–509.

Janssens, A. (ed.) (1998), *The Rise and Decline of the Male Breadwinner Family?*, Cambridge, Cambridge University Press.

Jenkins, A., F. Rowland, P. Angus and C. Hales (2003), *The Future Supply of Informal Care, 2003 to 2013. Alternative Scenarios*, AIHW Cat. No. AGE 32, Canberra, Australian Institute of Health and Welfare.

Jenkins, M. (2001), 'Ethics and Economics in Community Care', *Critical Social Policy* 21(1): 81–102.

Jenson, J. (2001), 'Family Policy, Child Care and Social Solidarity: The Case of Quebec', in S. Prentice (ed.) *Changing Child Care. Five Decades of Child Care Advocacy and Policy in Canada*, Halifax, Fernwood Publishing: 39–62.

Johansson, L. (1991), 'Informal Care of Dependent Elderly at Home – Some Swedish Experiences', *Ageing and Society*, 11 (1): 41–58.

Jones, K. and A. J. Fowles (1984), *Ideas on Institutions. Analysing the Literature on Long-Term Care and Custody*, London, Routledge and Kegan Paul.

Kamerman, S. B., M. Neuman, J. Waldfogel and J. Brooks-Gunn (2003), *Social Policies, Family Types and Child Outcomes in Selected OECD Countries*, OECD Social, Employment and Migration Working Papers No. 6 DELSA/ELSA/WD/SEM (2003) 6, Paris, OECD.

Kay, T. (2003), 'The Work–Life Balance in Social Practice', *Social Policy & Society*, 2 (3): 231–9.

Keith, Janice (1990). 'Aging in Social and Cultural Context: Anthropological Perspective', in R. H. Binstock and L. K. George (eds) *Handbook of Aging and the Social Sciences* (3rd edn), New York, Academic Press.

Keith, L. (1992). 'Who Cares Wins? Women, Caring and Disability.' *Disability and Society* 7(2): 167–75.

Keith, L. and J. Morris (1996). 'Easy Targets: A Disability Rights Perspective on the "Children as Carers" debate', in J. Morris (ed.) *Encounters with Strangers. Feminism and Disability*, London, Women's Press: 89–116.

Kemshall, H. (2002), *Risk, Social Policy and Welfare*, Buckingham, Open University Press.

Kemshall, H., N. Parton, M. Walsh and J. Waterson (1997), 'Concepts of Risk in Relation to Organisational Structure and Functioning within the Personal Social Services and Probation', *Social Policy and Administration*, 31 (3): 213–32.

Kendig, H. (1986). 'Towards Integrated Community Care for the Frail Aged', *Australian Journal of Social Issues* 21(2): 75–91.

Kittay, E. F. (1999). *Love's Labor. Essays on Women, Equality, and Dependency*, New York, Routledge.

Kittay, E. F. (2001), 'A Feminist Public Ethic of Care Meets the New Communitarian Family Policy', *Ethics*, 111 (April 2001): 523–47.

Kittay, E. F. (2002), 'When Caring is Just and Justice is Caring: Justice and Mental Retardation', in E. F. Kittay and E. K. Feder (eds) *The Subject of Care. Feminist Perspectives on Dependency*, Lanham, Rowman and Littlefield: 257–76.

Knijn, T. (1998), 'Social Care in the Netherlands', in J. Lewis (ed.) *Gender, Social Care and Welfare State Restructuring in Europe*, Aldershot, Ashgate: 85–110.

Knijn, T. (2001), 'Care Work: Innovations in the Netherlands', in M. Daly (ed.) *Care Work. The Quest for Security*, Geneva, International Labour Office: 159–74.

Knijn, T. (2004), 'Challenges and Risks of Individualisation in the Netherlands', *Social Policy and Society*, 3 (1): 57–65.

Knijn, T. and M. Kremer (1997), 'Gender and the Caring Dimension of Welfare States: Toward Inclusive Citizenship', *Social Politics*, 4 (Fall): 328–61.

Knijn, T. and C. Ungerson (1997), 'Introduction: Care Work and Gender in Welfare Regimes', *Social Politics*, 4 (Fall): 323–7.

Kohlberg, L. (1981), *The Philosophy of Moral Development: Moral Stages and the Idea of Justice*. San Francisco, Harper and Row.

Kohlberg, L. (1984), *The Psychology of Moral Development: The Nature and Validity of Moral Stages*, San Francisco, Harper and Row.

Kottow, M. H. (2001), 'Between Caring and Curing', *Nursing Philosophy* 2(1): 53–61.

Kramer, M. (1980), 'The Rising Pandemic of Mental Disorders and Associated Chronic Diseases and Disabilities', *Acta Psychiatrica Scandinavica*, 62 (Suppl. 285): 282–97.

Kroeger-Mappes (1994), 'The Ethic of Care vis-a vis the Ethic of Rights: A Problem for Contemporay Moral Theory.' *Hypatia* 9(3): 108–31.

Kurz, D. and A. Hirsch (2003), 'Welfare Reform and Child Support Policy in the United States', *Social Politics*, 10 (3): 397–412.

Lagergren, M. and I. Batljan (2000), *Will There Be a Helping Hand? Macroeconomic Scenarios of Future Needs and Costs of Health and Social Care for the Elderly in Sweden, 2000–30* (trans. by Clare James), Stockholm, Annex 8 to the Long-Term Survey 1999/2000.

Lagergren, M., L. Lundh, M. Okran and C. Sanne (1984), *Time to Care. A Report Prepared for the Swedish Secretariat for Future Studies* (trans. by Roger Tanner), Oxford, Pergamon.

Land, H. (1978), 'Who Cares for the Family?' *Journal of Social Policy*, 3 (7): 357–84.

Land, H. (1991), 'Time to Care', in M. Maclean and D. Groves (eds) *Womens Issues in Social Policy*, London, Routledge: 7–19.

Land, H. and J. Lewis (1998), 'Gender, Care and the Changing Role of the State in the UK', in J. Lewis (ed.) *Gender, Social Care and Welfare State Restructuring in Europe*, Aldershot, Ashgate: 51–84.

Laslett, P. (1995), 'Necessary Knowledge: Age and Aging in the Societies of the Past', in D. I. Kertzer and P. Laslett (eds) *Aging in the Past. Demography, Society, and Old Age*, Berkley, CA, University of California Press: 3–77.

Lawler, J. (1991), *Behind the Scenes: Nursing, Somology and the Problem of the Body*, Melbourne, Churchill Livingstone.

Layzell, S. and M. McCarthy (1992), 'Community-Based Health Services for People with HIV/AIDS: A Review from a Health Service Perspective', *AIDS Care*, 4 (2): 203–15.

Leininger, M. M. (ed.) (1988), *Care. The Essence of Nursing and Health*, Detroit, Wayne State University Press.

Leira, A. (1990), 'Coping with Care: Mothers in a Welfare State', in C. Ungerson (ed.) *Gender and Caring. Work and Welfare in Britain and Scandinavia*, Hemel Hemstead, Harvester: 133–59.

Lesthaeghe, R. (1995), 'The Second Demographic Transition in Western Countries: An Interpretation', in K. Oppenheim Mason and A-M. Jensen (eds) *Gender and Family Change in Industrialized Countries*, Oxford, Clarendon Press: 17–62.

Leutz, W. (1999), 'Five Laws for Integrating Medical and Social Services: Lessons from the United States and United Kingdom', *The Milbank Quarterly*, 77 (1): 77–110.

Levin, E., I. Sinclair and P. Gorbach (1989), *Families, Services and Confusion in Old Age*, Aldershot, Avebury.

Levy, D. U. and S. Michel (2002), 'More Can Be Less: Child Care and Welfare Reform in the United States', in S. Michel and R. Mahon (eds) *Child Care Policy at the Crossroads. Gender and Welfare State Restructuring*, New York, Routledge: 239–66.

Lewis, J. (1989), '"It All Really Starts in the Family . . .": Community Care in the 1980s', *Journal of Law and Society*, 16 (1): 83–96.

Lewis, J. (ed.) (1998), *Gender, Social Care and Welfare State Restructuring in Europe*, Aldershot, Ashgate.

Lewis, J. (2002), 'Individualisation, Assumptions about the Existence of an Adult Worker Model and the Shift towards Contractualism', in A. Carling, S. Duncan and R. Edwards (eds) *Analysing Families: Morality and Rationality in Policy and Practice*, London, Routledge: 51–6.

Lewis, J. (2003), 'Economic Citizenship: A Comment', *Social Politics*, 10 (2): 176–85.

Lewis, J. and B. Meredith (1988), *Daughters who Care: Daughters Caring for Mothers at Home*. London, Routledge.

Lewis, S. and J. Lewis (eds) (1996), *The Work–Family Challenge: Rethinking Employment*, London, Sage.

Lingsom, S. (1997), *The Substitution Issue. Care Policies and their Consequences for Family Care*, Rapport 6/97, Oslo, NOVA Norsk institutt for forskning om oppvekst, velferd og aldring.

Lister, R. (1994), ' "She Has Other Duties" – Women, Citizenship and Social Security', in S. Baldwin and J. Falkingham (eds) *Social Security and Social Change: New Challenges for the Beveridge Model*, Hemel Hempstead, Harvester Wheatsheaf.

Litwak, E. (1985), *Helping the Elderly: The Complementary Roles of Informal Networks and Formal Systems*, New York, London, Guilford Press.

Liu, W. T. and H. Kendig (eds) (2000), *Who Should Care for the Elderly? An East–West Value Divide*, Singapore, Singapore University Press and World Scientific Publishing.

Lloyd, L. (2000), 'Caring about Carers: Only Half the Picture?', *Critical Social Policy*, 20 (1): 136–50.

Lloyd, M. (2001), 'The Politics of Disability and Feminism: Discord or Synthesis?', *Sociology*, 35 (3): 715–28.

Luhmann, N. (1993), *Risk: A Sociological Approach*, New York, Walter de Gruyter.

Lukes, S. (1973), *Individualism*, Oxford, Blackwell.

Lupton, D. (1999), *Risk*, London, Routledge.

Mahon, R. (2002a), 'Child Care: Towards What Kind of "Social Europe"?', *Social Politics*, 9 (3): 344–79.

Mahon, R. (2002b), 'Gender and Welfare State Restructuring: Through the

Lens of Child Care', in S. Michel and R. Mahon (eds) *Child Care Policy at the Crossroads. Gender and Welfare State Restructuring*, New York, Routledge: 1–30.

Mahon, R. and S. Phillips (2002), 'Dual-Earner Families Caught in a Liberal Welfare Regime? The Politics of Child Care Policy in Canada', in S. Michel and R. Mahon (eds) *Child Care Policy at the Crossroads. Gender and Welfare State Restructuring*, New York, Routledge: 191–218.

Manton, K. G. and K. C. Land (2000), 'Active Life Expectancy Estimates for the US Elderly Population: A Multidimensional Continuous-Mixture Model of Functional Change Applied to Completed Cohorts, 1982–1996', *Demography*, 37 (3): 253–66.

Manton, K. G., E. Stallard and L. Corder (1995), 'Changes in Morbidity and Chronic Disability in the US Elderly Population: Evidence from the 1982, 1984 and 1989 National Long-Term Care Surveys', *Journal of Gerontology: Social Sciences*, 43 (1988): S194–204.

Marks, N. F. (1996), 'Caregiving across the Lifespan: National Prevalence and Predictors', *Family Relations*, 45 (1): 27–36.

Marriner-Tomey, A. (ed.) (1989), *Nursing Theorists and Their Work*, St Louis, Mosby.

Martin, J. (1989), 'Transforming Moral Education', in M. M. Brabeck (ed.) *Who Cares? Theory, Research and Educational Implications of the Ethic of Care*, New York, Praeger: 183–96

Martin, J. A. (2001), 'History, Lessons and a Case for Change in Child Care Advocacy', in S. Prentice (ed.) *Changing Child Care. Five Decades of Child Care Advocacy and Policy in Canada*, Halifax, Fernwood Publishing: 171–86.

Mathers, C. (1999), 'International Trends in Health Expectancies: Do They Provide Evidence for Expansion or Compression of Morbidity?', in *Compression of Morbidity Workshop Papers*, Department of Health and Aged Care Occasional Papers Series No. 4, Canberra, Department of Health and Aged Care.

Mathers, C., J. McCallum and J-M. Robine (1994), *Advances in Health Expectencies: Proceedings of the 7th Meeting of the International Network on Health Expectancy (REVES)*, Canberra, AIHW.

McDonald, P. (2002), 'Issues in Childcare Policy in Australia', *The Australian Economic Review*, 35 (2): 197–203.

McKechnie, R. and T. Kohn (1999), 'Introduction: Why Do We Care Who Cares?', in T. Kohn and R. McKechnie (eds) *Extending the Boundaries of Care. Medical Ethics and Caring Practices*. Oxford, Berg: 1–14.

McKeown, T. (1976), *The Modern Rise of Population*, New York, Academic Press.

McKnight, David (2005), *Beyond Right and Left: New Politics and the Culture Wars*. Allen and Unwin, St Leonards.

McLanahan, S. (2004), 'Diverging Destinies: How Children Are Faring Under the Second Demographic Transition', *Demography*, 41: 607–27.

McMichael, A. J. (1993), *Planetary Overload. Global Environmental Change and the Health of Human Species*, Cambridge, Cambridge University Press.

McMichael, T. (2001), *Human Frontiers, Environments and Disease. Past Patterns, Uncertain Futures*, Cambridge, Cambridge University Press.

McPherson, M. (1999), 'Extended Family Support, The State and Policy: Assumptions, Attitudes and Actualities', *Social Policy Journal of New Zealand*, (12): 139–54.

Meacher, M. (1972), *Taken for a Ride. Special Residential Homes for Confused Old People. A Study of Separatism in Social Policy*, London, Longman.

Meagher, G. (2003), *Friend or Flunkey? Paid Domestic Workers in the New Economy*, Sydney, University of New South Wales Press.

Means, R., S. Richards and R. Smith (2003), *Community Care. Policy and Practice* (3rd edn) Houndmills, Palgrave.

Merleau-Ponty, M. (1962), *Phenomenology of Perception*, trans. by Colin Smith, London; Routledge and Kegan Paul.

Merleau-Ponty, M. (1968), *The Visibile and the Invisible*, ed. by Claude Lefort, trans. by Alphonso Lingis, Evanston, IL, Northwestern University Press.

Michel, S. (1999), *Children's Interests/Mother's Rights: The Shaping of America's Child Care Policy*, New Haven, CT, Yale University Press.

Michel, S. and R. Mahon (eds) (2002), *Child Care Policy at the Crossroads. Gender and Welfare State Restructuring*, New York, Routledge.

Miller, E. and G. Gwynne (1972), *A Life Apart*, London, Tavistock.

Mills, C. W. (1959), *The Sociological Imagination*, London, Oxford University Press.

Moore, M. (1999), 'The Ethics of Care and Justice', *Women and Politics* 20(2): 1–16.

Moore, M. J., C. W. Zhu and E. C. Clipp (2001), 'Informal Costs of Dementia Care: Estimates from the National Longitudinal Caregiver Study', *The Journal of Gerontology*, 56B (4): 219–31.

Morgan, K. J. and K. Zippel (2003), 'Paid to Care: The Origins and Effects of Care Leave Policies in Western Europe', *Social Politics*, 10 (1): 49–85.

Morgan, M., M. Calnan and N. Manning (1985), *Sociological Approaches to Health and Medicine*, London, Croom Helm.

Morris, J. (1993a), *Independent Lives? Community Care and Disabled People*, London, Macmillan.

Morris, J. (1993b), ' "Us" and "Them"? Feminist Research and Community Care', in J. Bornat, C. Pereira, D. Pilgrim and F. Williams (eds) *Community Care: A Reader*, Houndmills, MacMillan: 156–66.

Morris, J. (1994), 'Community Care or Independent Living?', *Critical Social Policy* 40(1): 24–45.

Morris, J. (2001), 'Impairment and Disability: Constructing an Ethics of Care that Promotes Human Rights', *Hypatia*, 16 (4): 1–16.

Morris, J. (ed.) (1996), *Encounters with Strangers: Feminism and Disability*, London, Women's Press.

Mutschler, P. (1993), 'Bearing the Costs of our Eldercare Policies: Work Constraints among Employed Caregivers', *Journal of Aging and Social Policy*, 5 (4): 23–49.

Nelson, M. K. (1990), 'Family Day Care Providers and Their Work', in *The Experience of Family Day Care Providers: Negotiated Care*, Philadelphia, PA, Temple University Press: 19–46.

Nelson, S. (2000), *A Genealogy of Care of the Sick: Nursing, Holism and Pious Practice*. Southsea, Nursing Praxis Press.

Neysmith, S. (ed.) (1999), *Restructuring Caring Labour. Discourse, State Practice and Everyday Life*, Ontario, Oxford University Press.

Neysmith, S. (2000), 'Networking across Difference: Connecting Restructuring and Caring Labour', in S. Neysmith (ed.) *Restructuring Caring Labour: Discourse State Practice and Everyday Life*, Ontario, Oxford University Press: 1–28.

Neysmith, S. and M. Reitsma-Street (2000), 'Valuing Unpaid Work in the Third Sector: The Case of Community Resource Centres', *Canadian Public Policy*, 26 (3): 331–46.

Nissel, M. and L. Bonnerjea (1982), *Family Care of the Handicapped Elderly: Who Pays?*, London, Policy Studies Institute.

Noddings, N. (1984), *Caring. A Feminist Approach to Ethics and Moral Education*. Berkley, CA, University of California Press.

Noddings, N. (2002), *Starting at Home: Care as the Basis for Social Policy*, Berkley, CA, University of California Press.

Oakley, A. (1974), *The Sociology of Housework*, Oxford, Martin Robertson.

Oakley, A. (2002), *Gender on Planet Earth*, Cambridge, Polity.

O'Connor, J. S., A. S. Orloff and S. Shaver (1999), *States, Markets, Families. Gender, Liberalism and Social Policy in Australia, Canada, Great Britain and the United States*, Cambridge, Cambridge University Press.

OECD (1998), *Ageing and Care for Frail Elderly Persons: An Overview of International Perspectives*, DEELSA/ELSA/WP1(98)10, Paris, Organisation for Economic Co-operation and Development.

OECD (1999), *A Caring World. The New Social Policy Agenda*, Organisation for Economic Co-operation and Development, Paris.

OECD (2002), *Babies and Bosses – Reconciling Work and Family Life (Vol. 1: Australia, Denmark and the Netherlands)*, Paris, Organisation for Economic Co-operation and Development.

OED Online (http://dictionary.oed.com/cgi/entry/), accessed 23 June 2003.

OED (*Oxford English Dictionary*) (Online), Oxford, Oxford University Press, 2000–, http://www.oed.com, accessed June 2003.

Oliver, M. (1990), *The Politics of Disablement*, Basingstoke, Macmillan.

Oliver, M. and C. Barnes (1998), *Disabled People and Social Policy: From Exclusion to Inclusion*, London, Longman.

Olshansky, S. J. and J. B. Ault (1986), 'The Fourth Stage of the Epidemiological Transition: The Age of Delayed Degenerative Diseases', *Milbank Memorial Quarterly*, 64: 355–91.

Olshansky, S. J., M. A. Rudberg, B. A. Carnes, C. K. Cassel and J. A. Brody (1991), 'Trading off Longer Life for Worsening Health: The Expansion of Morbidity Hypothesis', *Journal of Aging and Health*, 3: 194–216.

Orem, D. E. (1991), *Nursing: Concepts of Practice* (4th edn), St Louis, Mosby.

Orem, D. E., M. J. Denyes and G. Bekel (2001), 'Self-Care: A Foundational Nursing Science', *Nursing Science Quarterly*, 14 (1): 48–54.

Orme, J. (2001), *Gender and Community Care: Social Work and Social Care Perspectives*, Houndmills, Palgrave.

Parker, G. (1990a), 'Whose Care? Whose Costs? Whose Benefit? A Critical Review of Research on Case Management and Informal Care', *Ageing & Society*, 10: 459–67.

Parker, G. (1990b), *With Due Care and Attention: A Review of Research on Informal Care*, London (2nd edn), Family Policy Studies Centre.

Parker, G. and H. Clarke (2002), 'Making the Ends Meet: Do Carers and Disabled People Have a Common Agenda?', *Policy & Politics*, 30 (3): 347–59.

Parker, R. (1981), 'Tending and Social Policy', in E. M. Goldberg and S. Hatch (eds) *A New Look at the Personal Social Services*, London, Discussion Paper 4, Policy Studies Institute.

Parrenas, R. S. (2001), *Servants of Globalisation. Women, Migration and Domestic Work*, Stanford, CA, Stanford University Press.

Parsons, T. (1951), *The Social System*, London, Routledge and Kegan Paul.

Parsons, T. (1957), 'Illness and the Role of the Physician: A Sociological Perspective', *American Journal of Orteropsychiatry*, 21 (4): 452–60.

Pateman, C. 91989), *The Disorder of Women: Democracy, Feminism and Political Theory*, Stanford, CA, Stanford University Press.

Peng, I. (2002), 'Gender and Generation: Japanese Child Care and the Demographic Crisis', in S. Michel and R. Mahon (eds) *Child Care Policy at the Crossroads. Gender and Welfare State Restructuring*, New York, Routledge: 31–58.

Penglase, J. (2005), *Orphans of the Living. Growing up in 'Care' in Twentieth-Century Australia*, Fremantle, Fremantle Arts Centre Press.

Penning, M. and N. Chappell (1990), 'Self-Care in Relation to Informal and Formal Care.' *Aging and Society* 10: 41–59.

Percival, R. and S. Kelly (2004), *Who's Going to Care? Informal Care and an Ageing Population*, NATSEM, report prepared for Carers Australia by the National Centre for Social and Economic Modelling, Canberra, http://www.natsem.canberra.edu.au/pubs/otherpubs/informal_care/care_report.pdf accessed July 2004.

Pickard, L., R. Wittenberg, A. Comas-Herrera, B. Davies and R. Darton

(2000), 'Relying on Informal Care in the New Century? Informal Care for Elderly People in England to 2031', *Ageing & Society*, 20 (6): 745–72.

Pijl, M. (1994), 'When Private Care Goes Public. An Analysis of Concepts and Principles concerning Payments for Care', in A. Evers, M. Pijl and C. Ungerson (eds) *Payments for Care: A Comparative Overview*, Aldershot, European Centre Vienna, Avebury: 3–18.

Pitkeathley, J. (1989), *It's My Duty Isn't It? The Plight of Carers in Our Society*, London, Souvenir Press.

Pocock, B. (2003), *The Work/Life Collision: What Work is Doing to Australians and What to Do about It*, Annandale, NSW, Federation Press.

Powles, J. (1992), 'Changes in Disease Patterns and Related Social Trends', *Social Science and Medicine*, 35 (4): 377–87.

Prentice, S. (2001), 'Changing Child Care: Looking Back, Moving Forward', in S. Prentice (ed.) *Changing Child Care. Five Decades of Child Care Advocacy and Policy in Canada*, Halifax, Fernwood Publishing: 15–26.

Press, F. and A. Hayes (2000), *OECD Thematic Review of Early Childhood Education and Care Policy: Australian Background Report*, Canberra, Commonwealth of Australia.

Price, J. and M. Shildrick (2002), 'Bodies Together: Touch, Ethics and Disability', in M. Corker and T. Shakespeare (eds) *Disability/Postmodernity. Embodying Disability Theory*. London, Continuum: 62–75.

Puka, B. (1993), 'The Liberation of Caring: A Different Voice for Gilligan's "Different Voice" ', in M. J. Larrabee (ed.) *An Ethic of Care. Feminist and Interdisciplinary Perspectives*, New York, Routledge: 215–39.

Putnam, R. (1993), *Making Democracy Work: Civic Traditions in Modern Italy*, Princeton, NJ, Princeton University Press.

Putnam, R. (2000), *Bowling Alone. The Collapse and Revival of American Community*, New York, Simon and Schuster.

Qureshi, H. (1990), 'Boundaries Between Formal and Informal Care-giving Work', in C. Ungerson (ed.) *Gender and Caring. Work and Welfare in Britain and Scandinavia*. Hemel Hemstead, Harvester: 59–79.

Qureshi, H. and A. Walker (1989), *The Caring Relationship. Elderly People and their Families*. Houndmills, MacMillan.

Randall, V. (2002), 'Child Care in Britain, or How Do You Restructure Nothing?', in S. Michel and R. Mahon (eds) *Child Care Policy at the Crossroads. Gender and Welfare State Restructuring*, New York, Routledge: 219–38.

Reich, W. T. (1995), 'History of the Notion of Care', in W. T. Reich (ed.) *Encylopedia of Bioethics* (revised edn), New York, Simon and Shuster Macmillan: 319–31.

Reinhardt, U. E. (2000), 'Health Care for the Sging Baby Boom: Lessons from Abroad', *Journal of Economic Perspectives*, 14 (2): 71–83.

Reinhardt, U. E. (2001), 'Commentary: On the Apocalypse of the Retiring Baby Boom', *Canadian Journal on Aging*, 20 (suppl. 1): 192–204.

Ritzer, G. (1993), *The McDonaldization of Society*, Thousand Oaks, CA, Pine Forge Press.

Ritzer, G. (1999), *Enchanting a Disenchanted World*, Thousand Oaks, CA, Pine Forge Press.

Rønning, R. (2002), 'In Defense Of Care: The Importance of Care as a Positive Concept', *Quality in Ageing – Policy, Practice and Research* 3(4): 34–43.

Rossiter, C., D. Kinnear and A. Graycar (1983), *Family Care of Elderly People: 1983 Survey Results*, Sydney, SWRC Reports and Proceedings No. 38, Social Welfare Research Centre, University of New South Wales.

Rostgaard, T. and T. Fridberg (1998), *Caring for Children and Older People – A Comparison of European Policies and Practices*, Copenhagen, Danish Institute of National Research.

Ruddick, S. (1989), *Maternal Thinking: Towards a Politics of Peace*, Boston, Beacon Press.

Sass, J. S. (2000), 'Emotional Labor as Cultural Performance: The Communication of Caregiving in a Nonprofit Nursing Home', *Western Journal of Communication*, 64 (3): 330–58.

Scarr, S. (1984), *Mother Care Other Care*, New York, Basic Books.

Schor, J. (1992), *The Overworked American: The Unexpected Decline of Leisure*, New York, Basic Books.

Sevenhuijsen, S. (1993), 'Paradoxes of Gender: Ethical and Epistemological Perspectives on Care in Feminist Political Theory', *Acta Politica* 28(2): 131–49.

Sevenhuijsen, S. (1998), *Citizenship and the Ethics of Care: Feminist Considerations on Justice, Morality and Politics*, London and New York, Routledge.

Sevenhuijsen, S. (2000), 'Caring in the Third Way: The Relation between Obligation, Responsibility and Care in Third Way Discourse', *Critical Social Policy*, 20 (1): 5–37.

Shaddock, A. J. and P. Bramston (1991), 'Individual Service Plans: The Policy–Practice Gap', *Australia & New Zealand Journal of Developmental Disabilities*, 17 (1): 73–80.

Shakespeare, T. (2000a), *Help*. Birmingham, Venture Press.

Shakespeare, T. (2000b), 'The Social Relations of Care', in G. Lewis, S. Gewiriz and J. Clarke (eds) *Rethinking Social Policy*, London, Open University/Sage: 52–65.

Shaver, S. (2002), 'Gender, Welfare, Regimes and Agency', *Social Politics*, 9 (2): 203–11.

Shaw, C. and J. Haskey (1999), 'New Estimates and Projections of the Population Cohabiting in England and Wales', *Population Trends*, 95 (1): 7–17.

Shelly, J. A. and A. B. Miller (1999), *Called to Care : A Christian Theology of Nursing*, Millers Downers Grove, IL, InterVarsity Press.

Shilling, C. (1995), *The Body and Social Theory*, Newbury Park, CA, Sage.

Sleebos, J. (2003), *Low Fertility rates in OECD Countries: Facts and Policy Responses* Paris, OECD Social, Employment and Migration Working Papers, No. 15.

Smith, C. (2002), 'The Sequestration of Experience: Rights Talk and Moral Thinking in "Late Modernity" ', *Sociology*, 36 (1): 43–66.

Smith, M. H. and C. F. Longino, jun. (1994), 'Demography of Caregiving', *Educational Gerontology*, 20 (7): 633–44.

Stacey, J. (1990), 'The Postmodern Family, For Better and Worse', in J. Stacey (ed.) *Brave New Families: Stories of Domestic Upheaval in Late Twentieth Century America*, New York, Basic Books: 251–72.

Standing, G. (2001), 'Care Work: Overcoming Insecurity and Neglect', in M. Daly (ed.) *Care Work. The Quest for Security*, Geneva, International Labour Office: 15–32.

Stark, A. (2005), 'Warm Hands in Cold Age – On the Need of a New World Order of Care', *Feminist Economics*, 11 (2): 7–36.

Stehr, N. (1994), *Knowledge Societies*, London, Sage.

Sundstrom, G., L. Johansson and L. B. Hassing (2002), 'The Shifting Balance of Long-Term Care in Sweden', *Gerontologist*, 42 (3): 350–5.

Super, N. (2002), *Who Will Be There to Care? The Growing Gap between Caregiver Supply and Demand*, NHPF Background Paper, 23 January 2002, Washington, National Health Policy Forum.

Sybylla, R. (2001), 'Hearing Whose Voice? The Ethics of Care and the Practices of Liberty: A Critique', *Economy & Society* 30 (1): 66–84.

Takahashi, M. (2003), 'Care for Children and Older People in Japan: Modernizing the Traditional', in A. Anttonen, J. Baldock and J. Sipila (eds) *The Young, the Old and the State: Social Care Systems in Five Industrial Nations*, Cheltenham, Northampton, MA, Edward Elgar: 81–108.

Taylor-Gooby, P. (ed.) (2000), *Risk, Trust and Welfare*, London, MacMillan.

Thomas, C. (1993). 'De-constructing Concepts of Care.' *Sociology* 27(4): 649–760.

Thomas, C. and M. Corker (2002), 'A Journey around the Social Model', in M. Corker and T. Shakespeare (eds) *Disability/Postmodernity. Embodying Disability Theory*. London, Continuum: 18–31.

Thomas, J. E. (2000), 'Incorporating Empowerment into Models of Care: Strategies from Feminist Women's Health Centers', *Research in the Sociology of Health Care*, 17: 139–52.

Thomson, D. (1983), 'Workhouse to Nursing Home: Residential Care of Elderly People in England since 1840', *Ageing and Society*, 3 (1): 43–69.

Titmuss, R. (1958), *Essays on the Welfare State*, London, Allen and Unwin.

Titmuss, R. (1979), 'Community Care: Fact or Fiction', in R. Titmuss (ed.) *Commitment to Welfare*, London, George Allen and Unwin.

Tong, R. (1998), *Feminist Thought: A More Comprehensive Introduction*, St Leonards, NSW, Allen and Unwin.

Torpey, J. (1988), 'A New "Slave Revolt in Morals?" The Meaning of the

Debate over a Feminist Ethics', *Berkeley Journal of Sociology* 9, 3–4 (July): 207–19.

Townsend, P. (1962), *The Last Refuge: A Survey of Residential Institutions and Homes for Old People in England and Wales*, London, Routledge and Kegan Paul.

Townsend, P. (1963), *The Family Life of Old People*, Harmondsworth, Penguin.

Tremlett, G. (2005), 'Blow to Machismo as Spain Forces Men to do Housework', *The Guardian*, 8 April 2005.

Tronto, J. (1993), *Moral Boundaries: A Political Argument for an Ethic of Care*, New York, Routledge.

Tronto, J. C. (1998), 'An Ethic of Care', *Generations San Francisco* 22(3): 15–20.

Turner, B. (1984, 2nd edn, 1996), *The Body and Society. Explorations in Social Theory*, Oxford, Blackwell.

Turner, B. and C. Rojek (2001), *Society and Culture. Principles of Scarcity and Solidarity*, London, Sage.

Twigg, J. (2000), *Bathing – The Body and Community Care*, London, Routledge.

Twigg, J. (2002), 'The Body in Social Policy: Mapping a Territory', *Journal of Social Policy*, 31 (3): 421–39.

Twigg, J. and K. Atkin (1994), *Carers Perceived: Policy and Practice in Informal Care*, Buckingham, Open University Press.

Twigg, J, K. Atkin and C. Perring (1990), *Carers and Services: A Review of Research*, London, Social Policy Research Unit, HMSO.

Ungerson, C. (1987), *Policy is Personal*, London, Tavistock.

Ungerson, C. (1990), 'The Language of Care. Crossing the Boundaries', in C. Ungerson (ed.) *Gender and Caring: Work and Welfare in Britain and Scandinavia*, Hemel Hempstad, Harvester Wheatsheaf: 8–33.

Ungerson, C. (1997), 'Payment for Caring – Mapping a Territory', in C. Ungerson and M. Kember (eds) *Women and Social Policy. A Reader* (2nd edn), Houndmills, MacMillan: 369–79.

Ungerson, C. (2000), 'Thinking about the Production and Consumption of Long-Term Care in Britain: Does Gender Still Matter?', *Journal of Social Policy*, 29 (4): 623–43.

Ungerson, C. (2003), 'Commodified Care Work in European Labour Markets', *European Societies*, 5 (4): 377–96.

Ungerson, C. (2004), 'Whose Empowerment and Independence? A Cross-National Perspective on 'Cash for Care' Schemes', *Ageing & Society*, 24 (2): 189–212.

van de Kaa, D. (1987), 'The Second Demographic Transition', *Population Bulletin*, 42 (1): 3–57.

Verbrugge, L. M. (1991), 'Survival Curves, Prevalence Rates and Dark Matter Therein', *Journal of Aging and Health*, 1991 (3): 217–36.

Waerness, K. (1984), 'Caring as Women's Work in the Welfare State', in H. Holter (ed.) *Patriarchy in a Welfare Society*, Oslo, Universitetsforlaget.

Waerness, K. (1989), 'Caring', in K. Boh, M. Bak, C. Clason, M. Pankratova, J. Qvortrup, G. Sgritta and K. Waerness (eds), *Changing Patterns of European Family Life: A Comparative Analysis of 14 European Countries.* London and New York, Routledge: 217–47.

Waidmann, T. and K. Manton (1998), *International Evidence on Disability Trends among the Elderly*, Washington DC, Department of Health and Human Services.

Waidmann, T. A. and K. G. Manton (2000), *Measuring Trends in Disability Among the Elderly: An International Review*, Washington, Urban Institute/Duke University (downloaded from http://nltcs.cds.duke.edu/publications/ 8 February 2004.

Walker, A. (1993), 'Under New Management: The Changing Role of the State in the Care of Older People in the United Kingdom', in S. A. Bass and R. Morris (eds) *International Perspectives on State and Family Support for the Elderly*, New York, Hawthorn Press: 127–54.

Walker, A. (1999), 'Ageing in Europe – Challenges and Consequences', *Zeitschrift für Gerontologie und Geriatrie*, 32 (6): 390–97.

Wallace, S. P. (1990), 'The No-Care Zone: Availability, Accessibility, and Acceptability in Community-Based Long-Term Care', *The Gerontologist*, 30 (2): 254–61.

Ward-Griffin, C. and V. W. Marshall (2003), 'Reconceptualizing the Relationship between "Public" and "Private" Eldercare', *Journal of Aging Studies*, 17 (2): 189–208.

Waters, K. R. and N. Easton (1999), 'Individualized Care: Is it Possible to Plan and Carry out?' *Journal of Advanced Nursing*, 29 (1): 79–87.

Watson, E. and J. Mears (1995), '*I Go to Work for a Holiday': Women, Work and Care of the Elderly*, MacArthur (Sydney), Department of Social Policy and Research Studies, Faculty of Arts and Social Science, University of Western Sydney.

Watson, E. and J. Mears (1999), *Women, Work and Care of the Elderly*, Aldershot, Ashgate.

Watson, J. (1979), *Nursing. The Philosophy and Science of Caring.* Boston, Little, Brown and Company.

Weber, M. (1976), *The Protestant Ethic and the Spirit of Capitalism* (orig. published 1905, trans. by Talcott Parsons), London, Allen and Unwin.

Weber, M. (1978), *Economy and Society*, (ed. and trans. by G. Roth and C. Wittich), Berkley, CA, University of California Press.

Wesorick, B. (1991), 'Creating an Environment in the Hospital Setting that Supports Caring via a Clinical Practice Model (CPM)', in D. A. Gaut and M. M. Leininger (eds), *Caring: The Compassionate Healer*, New York, National League for Nursing Press: 135–49.

Wheelock, J. and K. Jones (2002), 'Grandparents Are the Next Best Thing': Informal Childcare for Working Parents in Urban Britain', *Journal of Social Policy*, 31 (03): 441–63.

Whitaker, J. K. (1986), 'Integrating Formal and Informal Care: A Conceptual Framework', *British Journal of Social Work* 16 (Suppl.): 39–62.

Wilkinson, J. and M. Bittman (2003), *Relatives, Friends and Strangers: The Links between Voluntary Activity, Sociability and Care,* Social Policy Research Centre Discussion Paper No. 125, University of New South Wales, Sydney

Wilkinson, R. G. (1994), 'The Epidemiological Transition: From Material Scarcity to Social Disadvantage', *Daedalus,* 1994 (Fall): 61–77.

Williams, F. (2001), 'In and beyond New Labour: Towards a New Political Ethics of Care', *Critical Social Policy,* 21 (4): 467–93.

Williams, F. (2004), *Rethinking Families,* London, Calouste Gulbenkian Foundation.

Williams, R. (1976), *Keywords: A Vocabulary of Culture and Society,* Oxford, Oxford University Press.

Williams, S. J. and G. Bendelow (1998), *The Lived Body: Sociological Themes, Embodied Issues,* London and New York, Routledge.

Wilson, E. (1977), *Women and the Welfare State,* London, Tavistock.

Wilson, G. (1994), 'Co-production and Self-care: New Approaches to Managing Community Care Services for Older People', *Social Policy and Administration,* 28 (3): 236–50.

Wilson, J. Q. (2003), *The Marriage Problem,* New York, Harper Collins.

Wilson, R. (1997), *Bringing Them Home: Report of the National Inquiry into the Separation of Aboriginal and Torres Strait Islander Children from their Families,* (Ronald Wilson, Commissioner) National Inquiry into the Separation of Aboriginal and Torres Strait Islander Children from their Families (Australia), Human Rights and Equal Opportunity Commission, Sydney.

Wise, S. (2002), 'Parents' Expectations, Values and Choice of Child Care: Connections to Culture', *Family Matters,* 61: 48–55.

Wolfensberger, W. (1972), *Normalization. The Principle of Normalization in Human Services,* Toronto, National Institute on Mental Retardation.

Wright, F. (1986), *Left to Care Alone,* Aldershot, Gower.

Wrong, D. (1961), 'The Oversocialized Conception of Man in Modern Sociology', *American Sociological Review,* 26 (2): 183–93.

Wuthnow, R. (1993), *Acts of Compassion. Caring for Others and Helping Ourselves,* Princeton, NJ, Princeton University Press.

Zola, I. (1972), 'Medicine as an Institution of Social Control', *Sociological Review,* 20 (4): 487–504.

Index

Note: Page numbers in *italics* represent tables and page numbers in **bold** represent figures.

abortion counselling 53
Abrams, P. 77
accountability 219
age care: health care 117
age care: planning 120–40
ageing 102, 105–40; population 172; work force 117
ageing societies: demography 21; 105–20, 137–40
altruism 26; family life 7
Alzheimer's Disease 174
anti-professional spirit 77
apocalyptic demography 138
Australasia 106
Australia 9; disability survey 132; informal care 132–7; time-use 150
avian flu viruses 120

Baldock, J. 87, 163; and Evers, A. 19
Barnes, C.: and Oliver, M. 93
Barton, R. 76
Batljan, I.: and Lagergren, M. 138
Baulmol's Law 211
Bauman, Z. 206
Baumol, W. 211
Beaujot, R. 146, 149
Beck, U. 15, 180–1, 185, 215; and Beck-Gernsheim, E. 183, 184
Beck-Gernsheim, E. 183, 184; and Beck, U. 15, 180–1, 185, 215
Bellah, R. 63–4
Benhabib, S. 62
Benner, P. 44–7, 48; and Wrubel, J. 44–5

Bettio, F.: and Plantenga, J. 166
Beveridge, W. H. (1879–1963) 217
bio-technical developments 172
biophysical needs: lower order 43
birth rate 14, 107
Bittman, M. 150; and Wilkinson, J. 65
Blau, D. 162
bleeding hearts 23
blended family 185
body 171–98; sociology 171
body work: care work 173–5; dirty work 175–8
bounce-back: fertility levels 110
Bourdieu, P. 63
Bowden, P. 37, 47
Brennan, D. 162
Brody, E. 81
Bubeck, D. G. 62
burden of care 12, 81, 92
bureaucracy 203
bureaucratic iron cage 203–4

Cancian, F. 49
Cantor, M. 86
care: deficit 5, 103; definition 2, 4; definitions 30–1; ideals 222; individualization 188–90
care of children and elders (Europe) *167*
care ethic: moral element 59
care market: participation 88, 147–9
care model: traditional 10
care process 35; caring about/giving/receiving 35

care provision *200*; restructuring 219–21
care recipient: decision-making 17
care restructuring 201; contracting state 201; fragmentation 202
Care, Values and the Future of Welfare Programme (CAVA) 18
care work: body work 173–5
care/justice dichotomy 63
carers/care-givers 27, 30, 79–80, 82–7, 129–37, 190–1, 223
career development 15
caring: about/for 32–3; for dependents 84; meanings 27–9; for superiors 84; in symmetrical relationships 84
caring primacy 44–7
cash nexus (Simmel) 181
Castells, M. 204, 208, 221
Challis, D.: and Knapp, M. 90
Chamberlayne, P.: and King, A. 10, 224
child care 89, 103, 141–68, 211; continental Europe 163; employment 159–68; policy 142–6; private market 163; services 8; southern Europe 164
child care public support *144*
child-care corporations 162
children: moral reasoning 53
children/day care *160*
citizenship 95–101, 225; inclusive 223
clients: social recognition 192
Clinical Practice Model of Nursing (Wesorick) 49
co-resident partners 191
cold modern ideals 12
Commission for the Re-Division of Unpaid Work (Holland) 9
community: rebuilding 64
community care 16, 80, 82, 86; study (UK) 175
Compression of Morbidity hypothesis (Fries) 121
consumer service user 192
Corker, M.: and Shakespeare, T. 94
cost disease 211
costs: elderly 128

counselling: abortion 53
criminal responsibility 2
Crittenden, C. 60
cultural politics 30

Dalley, G. 50
Daly, M. 10; and Lewis, J. 19, 34
Davis, A.: and Ellis, K. 219
day-care centres (USA) 161
Deacon, A.: and Mann, K. 187
Dean, H. 213
decision-making: care recipient 17
defamilization 158
degenerative diseases 119
deinstitutionalisation: mental health 193
dementia 195–6
democratic family 185
demographic transition: second 107
demography 16, 102, 105–40; ageing societies 21; apocalyptic 138; projections 138
dependency work: definition 69; ethics 68–74
diet 121
dirty work: body work 175–8
disability 87, 92–5; social model 94; wheelchair access 94; epidemiological trends 120–6
disability adjusted life years (DALYs) 123
disability survey: Australia 132
disability-free life expectancy at birth *124–5*
diseases 195; of affluence 118, *see also* Alzheimer's; degenerative diseases
disposable labour force 209
divorce 147
domestic care workers 177
domestic violence 3
Douglas, M. 172
doulia 72, 74
dual-earner family 147
Duncan, S. 140
Dunlop, M.J. 29, 41, 43, 49

Early Childhood Education and Care (Press and Hayes) 144

Eastern European socialism 12
elderly: costs 128; residential care 76
elderly people in private households
      131
electronic surveillance 11
Elias, N. 175, 179
Ellis, K.: and Davis, A. 219
emotional labour 33
empathy 46; nursing theory 40
employment: child care 159–68;
      female (OECD) *148*; work/life
      conflict 146–9
empowerment 24
England 129–32
epidemiological transition 118–26
Esping-Andersen, G. 155, 156, 158,
      165, 224
ethic of care 52–74, 96–101, 223–4
ethics: dependency work 68–74
ethnic minority 209, 211
Europe 106
European Community Household
      Panel (ECHP) 165
Evers, A.: and Baldock, J. 19
exercise regimes 121
Expansion of Morbidity (Gruenberg)
      121

Fagermoen, M.S. 43
family: blended 185; dual earner 147;
      nuclear 185; single parent 185;
      social reproduction 157
family care: women 183–6
family life: altruism 7
family-friendly policy 151
female/male 5, 6, **31**, 53–5, 58–62,
      76, 79–81, 86–7, 116, 133–5, 147,
      176–8, 190
female employment (OECD) *148*
feminism 5, 7, 8, 57, 80; research 34;
      second-wave 172; theorizing 31–4
feminists 83
fertility: gendered issue 140
fertility levels: bounce-back 110
fertility rates 102, 107
fertility rates/life expectancy OECD
      (1970–2000) *108–9*
finance: health care 89

Finch, J. 32; and Groves, D. 80
Fineman, M. 69
five-dollar-a-day policy (Quebec) 145,
      161
Folbre, N. 169
Forbat, L.: and Henderson, J. 95
formal care 190–4; services 85
formal/informal care 77
Foucault, M. 77
Friedan, B. 17

gay community 191
gender 54; equality 143; social
      construction 19
General Household Survey (GHS)
      129
Giddens, A. 96, 177, 183, 185, 187,
      215
Gilligan, C. 20, 53–4, 55
global capitalism 199–225
Goffman, E. 77, 189, 204
Golini, A. 110
Goyder, J. 174
Graham, H. 32, 35, 79–81, 82
Groves, D. 32; and Finch, J. 80

Hakim, C. 153, 154
Hall, L. 41
Hamington, M. 196
Hattinga-Vershure, J. C. M. 78
Head Start (USA) 145
health: urban environmemts 119
health care: finance 89
health spending/demographic
      structure (1997) *139*
hegemony: professional care 78
Heinz dilemma (Kohlberg)
Henderson, J.: and Forbat, L. 95
Hirst, M. 82
HIV/AIDS 120
Hoagland, S. 67
Hochschild, A.R. 5, 10, 12, 33
Hoggett, P. 221
housework: sociology 80
Howe, A.: and Schofield, H. 120
Hugman, R. 32
human agency: social structure 178,
      182

human rights 223
human services 6, 13–18

ideals of care 222
identity and self 179–82
Illich, I. 77
illness 195
In a Different Voice (Gilligan) 55
Individualiserung (institutionalized individualism) 180
individualization 171–98; liberation 182; social theory 178–82
inequalities 117
infants 197
informal care 130, 190–4
informal care (*mantelzorg*) 78
informal care-givers 9, 82, 105
institutionalization 189; mental health 76–7
institutionalized individualism (*Individualiserung*) 180
International Journal of Human Caring 40
intimacy: life politics 182–3
Israeli kibbutz 12
Italy: vignette 110
Iversen, T.: and Wren, A. 213

Japan 106, 107
Jenkins, A. F. 136–7
Johnston, D. J. 8
justice and care 60–6, *61*, 72

Keith, L.: and Morris, J. 92
Kemshall, H. 217, 219
King, A.: and Chamberlayne, P. 10, 224
Kittay, E. F. 19, 65, 68–71, 194
Knapp, M.: and Challis, D. 90
Knijn, T.: and Kremer, M. 95, 223
Kohlberg, L. 53
Kohlberg's Heinz dilemma 53
Kohn, T.: and McKechnie, R. 26
Kremer, M.: and Knijn, T. 95, 223

labour: division of 29
labour force: disposable 209
labour market: segmented 208
Lagergren, M.: and Batljan, I. 138

Land, H.: and Lewis, J. 163
language of care 27–31
Laslett, P. 106
Lawler, J. 47–8, 177
legal judgment 3
Lewis, J.: and Daly, M. 19; and Land, H. 163
life politics: intimacy 182–3
lifestyle choices: women 153
Litwak, E. 85
Living for Others (Beck-Gernsheim) 183
Lloyd, M. 95
long-term care: workforce 105
low-paid occupations 176
Lupton, D. 216

McDonaldization 206, 209, 220
McKechnie, R.: and Kohn, T. 26
McMichael, A.J. 119
Mahon, R. 158
male: breadwinners 5, 36; care-givers 82; carers 191 (*see also* female/male)
management: risk 200
Mann, K.: and Deacon, A. 187
manufacturing 211
markets 15, 157
Marks, N. 103
marriage 14, 141; Spain 9
Marshall, V.: and Ward-Griffen, C. 86
Maslow's schema 43
mass individualization 180
maternity leave: northern Europe 164
Mathers, C. 123
men 4, 5, 9, 17, 20, 33, 36, 56–7, 65–6, 80, 82, 96, 121, 123, *124*, 132, 141, 147–9, 151–2, 154–5, 178, 191, 208–9, 217, 222–4
mental health: deinstitutionalisation 193; institutionalization 76–7
Michel, S. 161
mobile phones 11
modernization: risk 214–17
Moore, M. 63
Moral Boundaries (Tronto) 58
moral element: care ethic 59

moral reasoning: children 53
Morris, J. 98, 223; and Keith, L. 92

National Childcare Strategy (UK) 163
natural caring 55–7
Nelson, S. 39, 41
neo-liberal ideology 8
network logic 205
new economy 204–6
newly industrialized countries 111
Neysmith, S. 75
Noddings, N. 55–7
non-profit associations 15
normalization 78
North America 106, *see also* United States of America (USA)
novice student nurses 48
nuclear family 64–5, 185
nursery education 163
nursing: definition 39; professionalization 51
nursing practice 47–8
Nursing, The Philosophy and Science of Caring (Watson) 42
nursing theory 39–44; empathy 40; humanistic value system 42; self-car deficit (Orem) 40

Oakley, A. 80, 154
occupations: low-paid 176
old age ratios OECD countries (1980–2050) *114–15*
older carers 136
Oliver, M.: and Barnes, C. 93
ongoing care estimates 120–6
Orem, D. 40
organizational logic 205

Parker, R. 83
Pateman, C. 217–18
pension pressures 117
Personnel Social Services Research Unit (PSSRU) 90
Piaget, J. 54
Pickard, L.R. *et al.* 136
Plantenga, J.: and Bettio, F. 166
Pocock, B. 150, 151, 152

policy: child-care 142–6; family-friendly 151; good 10
policy-makers: UK 79
politics 102–68; third way 96
population ratios 110
post-Fordism 205
Postponement of Morbidity (Manton *et al.*) 122
power: social justice 66–8
preference theory (Hakim) 154
primacy of caring 44–7
primary carative functions (Watson) 42–3
primary carers 82, *134–5*
primary prevention 122
private care 199
private care *vs* public issues 6–10
private market: child care 163
private paid care-givers 82
professional care: hegemony 78
professional managerial core 208
professionalization: nursing 51
Protestant ethic 205, 206
provider: third party 71
public issues *vs* private care 6–10
Puka, B. 67

quasi-experimental design 91
Quebec: five-dollars-a-day 161
Quesheri, H. 77

Rawls, J. 63, 71
Reich, W. T. 28
remarriage 14,141
research: feminist 34
research (USA) 210
residential care: elderly 76
risk 199–225; management 200, 212, 219; modernization 214–17; welfare 217–19
risk society 215
Ritzer, G. 206
Rojek, C.: and Turner, B. 171, 173
Rønning, R. 24

SARS 120
Scandinavia 164
Schofield, H.: and Howe, A. 120

secondary labour market 214
secondary prevention 122
segmented labour market 208
self-actualization 183
sequestration of experience 183, 193
service economy 207–8
Sevenhuijsen, S. 96, 97, 98
Shakespeare, T.: and Corker, M. 94
shared care **201**
Shilling, C. 172
single-parent family 185
Smith, A. 151
Smith, C. 100
smoking 121
social capital 63–6
social care 13–18
social care mix 87
social citizenship 71
social divisions of care 81–7
social ideal 10–13
social inequality 186, 187
social isolation 81
social justice: power 66–8
social policy analysts 75–101
social recognition: clients 192
social reproduction: family 157
social response to bodily need 194–8
social science literature 18–20
social structure: human agency 178, 182
social theory 169–98; individualization 178–82
sociological perspective 1
sociology: body 171–3; housework 80
Spain: marriage 9
spouse carers/caregivers 82, 130, 136
Standing, G. 225
state dependency 7
Super, N. 106
supermum 11
Sweden 126–9
Sybylla, R. 60

targeting 202
Taylorism 205
tertiary prevention 122
The Last Refuge (Townsend) 77
third-party provider 71

third-way politics 96
Thomas, C. 76, 79
Thomson, D. 120
time for family care of children *151*
Time to Care (Lagergren *et al.*) 126
time-use studies 150
Titmuss, R. 156
Tong, R. 55
total institutions 189
Townsend, P. 77
Tronto, J. 20, 27, 32, 36, 50, 58, 62
Turner, B. 172; and Rojek, C. 171, 173, 197
Twigg, J. 5, 175–6, 177

Ungerson, C. 83, 88
United Kingdom (UK) 163, 175, 185, 212; policy makers 79, *see also* England
United States of America (USA): day-care centres 161; Head Start 145; research 210
University of Leeds 185
unpaid care 80
unpaid domestic care 18
urban environments: health 119

Verbrugge, L. 122
vignette: Italy 110
voucher payments 14

Waerness, K. 84, 85
Walker, A. 221
Ward-Griffen, C.: and Marshall, V. 86
warm modern ideal 12
Watson, J. 42
Weber, M. 203
welfare 87–92; risk 217–19; state 5; triad 157
welfare approach **90**
welfare regimes 157; post-industrial 155–9
widowed women 130
Wilkinson, J.: and Bittman, M. 65
Will There be a Helping Hand? (Lagergren and Batljan) 126
Williams, F. 99, 185, 186, 223

Williams, R. 26
Wolfensberger, W. 78
women 4, 14, 57, 209; family care
    183–6; home work 79–81; lifestyle
    choices 153; widowed 130
women's-career-preference scenario
    133
work/life conflict 141–68

workforce: long-term care 105
Wren, A.: and Iversen, T. 213
Wright Mills, C. 8
Wrubel, J.: and Brenner, P. 44–5
Wuthnow, R. 65

young age ratios in OECD countries
    (1980–2050) *112–13*